REA: THE TEST PREP AP® TEACHERS REC

# AP® MACROECONOMICS CRASH COURSE®

Jason Welker, M.Ed.

Research & Education Association
www.rea.com

***Research & Education Association***
1325 Franklin Ave., Suite 250
Garden City, NY 11530
Email: info@rea.com

**AP® MACROECONOMICS CRASH COURSE®, 2nd Edition**

**Published 2022**


Printed in the United States of America

Library of Congress Control Number 2019946640

ISBN-13: 978-0-7386-1259-1
ISBN-10: 0-7386-1259-6



Cover image: © iStockphoto.com/shapecharge

D22

# AP® Macroeconomics Crash Course TABLE OF CONTENTS

## ABOUT OUR BOOK

REA's *AP® Macroeconomics Crash Course* is designed for the last-minute studier or any student who wants a quick refresher on the AP® course. The *Crash Course* is based on the latest changes to the AP® Macroeconomics course and exam and focuses only on the topics tested, so you can make the most of your study time.

Written by a veteran AP® Macroeconomics test expert, our *Crash Course* gives you a concise review of the major concepts and important topics tested on the exam.

- **Part I** offers **Keys for Success**, so you can tackle the exam with confidence. It also gives you the **Key Formulas and Definitions** that you must know.
- **Part II** presents a **Content Review** that covers all the essential topics found on the exam, including basic economic concepts, the financial sector, economic growth, and international trade and finance, among others.
- **Part III** gives you specific **Test-Taking Strategies** to help you conquer the multiple-choice and free-response questions, along with AP®-style practice questions to prepare you for what you'll see on test day.
- Our handy **Glossary of Economics Terms** defines the most important economics terms and concepts you need to understand.

## ABOUT OUR ONLINE PRACTICE TEST

How ready are you for the AP® Macroeconomics exam? Find out by taking REA's online practice exam available at *www.rea.com/studycenter*. This test features automatic scoring, detailed explanations of all answers, and diagnostic score reporting that will help you identify your strengths and weaknesses so you'll be ready on exam day!

Whether you use this book throughout the school year or as a refresher in the final weeks before the exam, REA's *Crash Course* will show you how to study efficiently and strategically, so you can boost your score.

*Good luck on your AP® Macroeconomics exam!*

## ABOUT OUR AUTHOR

Since earning degrees in economics and education, **Jason Welker** has been an economics teacher, content creator, textbook author, and YouTube lecturer for 15 years. His classroom experience spans over a decade of teaching economics courses for the AP® and International Baccalaureate programs on three continents. After 13 years abroad, Mr. Welker returned to the United States in 2017 to join Khan Academy as its Economics Content Fellow—partnering with the College Board to create AP® Economics video courses. Mr. Welker currently teaches IB Economics for Pamoja Education, a UK-based educational technology company. In between lessons, he adds to his resource-rich website, *Econclassroom.com*, and his YouTube channel, *www.youtube.com/JasonWelker*. His pastimes include camping, skiing, and bicycle riding with his wife and young daughter.

## ABOUT REA

Founded in 1959, Research & Education Association (REA) is dedicated to publishing the finest and most effective educational materials—including study guides and test preps—for students of all ages.

Today, REA's wide-ranging catalog is a leading resource for students, teachers, and other professionals. Visit *www.rea.com* to see our complete catalog.

## ACKNOWLEDGMENTS

We would like to thank Larry B. Kling, Editorial Director, for his overall guidance; Pam Weston, Publisher, for setting the quality standards for production integrity; John Cording, Technology Director, for coordinating the development of the REA Study Center; Wayne Barr, Test Prep Project Manager, for editorial project management; Fiona Hallowell for proofreading; and Jennifer Calhoun for file prep.

We would also like to extend special thanks to Tyson Smith for technically reviewing the manuscript, Karen Lamoreux for copyediting, and Kathy Caratozzolo of Caragraphics for typesetting this edition.

# PART I

# INTRODUCTION

Chapter 1

# Keys for Success on the AP® Macroeconomics Exam

Macroeconomics is vast in content. In fact, at the university level it may be taught over the span of several years. Indeed, one could even major in a macroeconomics topic and pursue advanced degrees within the field. You, on the other hand, are probably taking AP® Macroeconomics as a one- or possibly two-semester high school course in the 11th or 12th grade.

So how can a high school student be expected to learn all the AP® course content and be sufficiently prepared to earn a credit-granting score on the AP® exam? Rest assured, with a few important pieces of information and some helpful hints and tips, you can focus your studies in and out of the classroom on the important concepts you are most likely to see on the exam.

This *Crash Course*, along with your course textbook, your teacher, and the College Board's online resources, is one of your greatest keys to success on the AP® Macro exam.

## AP® MACRO BIG IDEAS

The Big Ideas form the foundation of the course and allow students to make connections across the different units. These four foundational areas represent the "threads" that run throughout the course. More information on the Big Ideas and how they relate to the various units in AP® Macro can be found in the AP® Macroeconomics Course and Exam Description (CED) available at the College Board's AP® Central website.

These Big Ideas represent a boiled-down view of what you must know and be able to demonstrate on the exam.

### BIG IDEA 1: ECONOMIC MEASUREMENTS (MEA)

Economists construct measurements to monitor the state of an economy and evaluate its performance over time. Governments, firms, and citizens often use these measurements to help inform policy, business, and personal decisions.

### BIG IDEA 2: MARKETS (MKT)

Competitive markets bring together buyers and sellers to exchange goods and services for mutual gain. The simple model of supply–demand can be applied in different market contexts.

### BIG IDEA 3: MACROECONOMIC MODELS (MOD)

Macroeconomic models are simplified representations that depict basic economic relationships and can be used to predict and explain how those relationships are affected by economic shocks.

### BIG IDEA 4: MACROECONOMIC POLICIES (POL)

Government taxation and spending policies and central bank monetary policy can affect an economy's output, price level, and level of employment, both in the short run and in the long run.

## CONTENT AND STRUCTURE OF THE EXAM

AP® Macro students should understand the relative importance of each of the units in the course. There are two sections in the AP® Macro exam. The first is the multiple-choice section, which is comprised of 60 multiple-choice questions. The 60 questions come from the six units of the AP® Macro course. Thankfully, the College Board publishes the approximate percentage of multiple-choice questions that will come from each of the six units. The breakdown is as follows:

- Unit 1 | Basic Economic Concepts: 5%–10%
- Unit 2 | Economic Indicators and the Business Cycle: 12%–17%
- Unit 3 | National Income and Price Determination: 17%–27%
- Unit 4 | Financial Sector: 18%–23%
- Unit 5 | Long-run Consequences of Stabilization Policies: 20%–30%

- Unit 6 | Open Economy—International Trade and Finance: 10%–13%

Knowing the percentages of each unit's representation on the multiple-choice section will help you focus your studies appropriately. For example, the most commonly tested units are 3 through 5. These three units together could make up as much as 80% (that's 48) of the 60 questions on the multiple-choice section!

Note that the most heavily assessed units are given the most attention in this *Crash Course* book. Units 3, 4, and 5, for example, are covered at a level proportional to their importance in the AP® course and exam. Likewise, when you complete the practice questions in Chapter 10 or when you take REA's online practice exam, the number of questions provided is proportional to the weight given to each unit.

The free-response question (FRQ) section of the exam includes three questions.

- The first question is always a long FRQ, on which you are expected to spend about 25 minutes.
- The second and third questions are short FRQs, on which you are expected to spend about 12.5 minutes each.
- The topics the FRQs cover could come from any section of the syllabus, although there are certain topics that are more commonly tested than others, giving the FRQ section some degree of predictability. Chapters 9 and 11 of this *Crash Course* provide more information about how to best prepare for both the multiple-choice and free-response sections of the AP® Macro exam.

## AP® MACRO GRADE SCALE

You may think with all the units in this course and only one or two semesters to learn them all, you'll never be able to get a 5 on the AP® Macroeconomics exam. However, getting a 4 or 5 on the AP® Macro exam may not be as difficult as you think. The table below shows the approximate range of scores needed to earn each of the possible AP® scores, from the top mark of 5 to the lowest score of 1.

Remember that the exam includes a 60-question multiple-choice section (two-thirds of your grade) and a 3-question free-response section (one-third of your grade). The number of points on the free-response section usually varies between 20 and 24, so the total points in any given year's exam will be between 80 and 84. In addition, the exact range of each of the five possible grades will vary depending on how well the test-takers perform. But, a typical range of scores is as follows:

| AP® Grade | Minimum Percentage Correct on MC and FRQ Sections Combined |
|---|---|
| 5 | 81% |
| 4 | 62% |
| 3 | 48% |
| 2 | 33% |
| 1 | 0% |

The preceding score ranges are only an approximation. The precise score range is adjusted annually based on the yearly performance of students worldwide.

## WHEN TO GUESS IN THE MULTIPLE-CHOICE SECTION

There is no additional penalty for wrong answers. Therefore, guessing is always advised if, of course, you have no idea what the correct answer is. Before resorting to a blind guess, you should use all of your knowledge and understanding of economics to eliminate the possible incorrect answers, so that any guess you are forced to make is an *educated guess*.

## THE IMPORTANCE OF DIAGRAMS

To earn a score of 4 or 5 on the AP® Macro exam, you must have more than just a solid understanding of the course material. You also must be skilled at illustrating the concepts from the course in detailed, correctly drawn economic diagrams.

The good news is that all the graphs you need to know are drawn exactly as they should be drawn in the exam right here in this *Crash Course*. Study these diagrams closely as you progress through this book. Examine the labels, the shapes of the lines, the way arrows are used to indicate directions of shifts, and the way dotted lines are used to identify equilibrium points on the axes. Seek to understand the meaning of the various macroeconomic models in this book, not just memorize them.

Drawing graphs well in the free-response section (and interpreting their meaning in the MC section) is a crucial skill that will impress the test examiners.

## USING THE AP® MACROECONOMICS CRASH COURSE TO PREPARE FOR SUCCESS

This *Crash Course* is the result of a detailed analysis of the AP® Macroeconomics Course and Exam Description released in 2019. Chapter 2 contains all the key formulas and definitions that you should know prior to taking the exam. Chapters 3–8 provide a concise breakdown of each of the AP® Macro course topics and include precisely drawn diagrams. Study these diagrams closely, and as you prepare for the exam, practice drawing all the graphs you see in this book.

You are advised to review each chapter, focusing on the units or sections about which you feel less certain. Each chapter outlines the essential knowledge for each unit as determined by the College Board. Pay attention to the Test Tips that highlight difficult topics and help you make important distinctions.

Chapters 9–11 prepare you for test day with test-taking strategies for both the multiple-choice and free-response sections, along with AP®-style practice questions.

## SUPPLEMENT CRASH COURSE WITH COLLEGE BOARD MATERIALS

This *Crash Course* has everything you need to know to earn a 4 or a 5 on the exam. However, astute AP® Macro students will use this book as just one of the many resources available, supplementing it with material provided in class and the online resources available at the College Board's AP® Central website. Bookmark the site and use it frequently throughout the course and during your exam prep. The AP® Central website provides information about the test structure, question types, and most importantly, additional study materials and sample questions.

Chapter 2

# Key Formulas and Definitions
## for AP® Macroeconomics

### I. Key Formulas

1. **GDP = C + I + G + Xn:** The expenditure approach to measuring GDP correlates well with aggregate demand (AD).
2. **GDP = W + I + R + P:** The income approach to measuring GDP correlates well with aggregate supply (AS).
3. **Calculating Nominal GDP:** The quantity of various goods produced in a nation times their current prices, added together.
4. **GDP Deflator:** A price index used to adjust nominal GDP to arrive at real GDP. Called the "deflator" because nominal GDP will usually overstate the value of a nation's output if there has been inflation. The Consumer Price Index (CPI) is another commonly used price index.
5. **Real GDP:** $\frac{\text{Nominal GDP}}{\text{GDP deflator}} \times 100$.
6. **GDP Growth Rate:** $\frac{\text{Current year's GDP} - \text{Last year's GDP}}{\text{Last year's GDP}} \times 100$.

   The GDP growth rate is a percentage change in a nation's real output between one year and the next.
7. **The Inflation Rate via the CPI:**
   $\frac{\text{This year's CPI} - \text{Last year's CPI}}{\text{Last year's CPI}} \times 100$. The inflation rate is the percentage change in the CPI from one period to the next.
8. **Real Interest Rate** = nominal interest rate – inflation rate.

9. **Unemployment Rate** = $\frac{\text{Number of unemployed}}{\text{Number in the labor force}} \times 100$. The labor force includes all non-institutionalized people of working age who are employed or seeking employment.

10. **Money Multiplier** = $\frac{1}{\text{RRR}}$ where RRR equals the required reserve ratio. Application: An initial injection of $1,000 of new money into a banking system with a reserve ratio of 0.1 will generate up to $1,000 × (10) = $10,000 in total money.

11. **Quantity Theory of Money:** MV = PQ = Y. A monetarist's view that explains how changes in the money supply (M) will affect the price level (P) and/or real output assuming the velocity of money (V) is fixed in the short run.

12. **MPC + MPS = 1.** The fraction of an increase in disposable income that is spent (MPC) plus the fraction that is saved (MPS) must equal 1.

13. **Spending Multiplier** = $\frac{1}{1-\text{MPC}}$ or $\frac{1}{\text{MPS}}$. This tells you how much total spending an initial injection of spending in the economy will generate. For example, if the MPC = .8 and the government spends $100 million, then the total increase in spending in the economy = $100 million × 5 = $500 million.

14. **Tax Multiplier** = $\frac{-\text{MPC}}{\text{MPS}}$. This tells you how much total spending will result from an initial change in the level of taxation. It is negative because when taxes decrease, spending increases, and vice versa. The tax multiplier will always be smaller than the spending multiplier.

## II. Key Definitions

1. **Absolute Advantage:** A country or entity has an absolute advantage in the production of a good when the country can produce the good using fewer resources than another country or entity.

2. **Aggregate Demand (AD):** A schedule or curve that shows the total quantity demanded for all goods and services of a nation at various price levels at a given period of time.
3. **Aggregate Supply (AS):** The total amount of goods and services that all the firms in all the industries in a country will produce at various price levels in a given period of time.
4. **Appreciation:** An increase in the value of one currency relative to another, resulting from an increase in demand for or a decrease in supply of the currency on the foreign exchange market.
5. **Balance of Payments:** Measures all the monetary exchanges between one nation and all other nations. Includes the current account and the capital account.
6. **Bonds:** A certificate of debt issued by a company or a government to an investor.
7. **Budget Deficit:** When a government spends more than it collects in tax revenues in a given year.
8. **Business Cycle:** A model showing the short-run periods of contraction and expansion in output experienced by an economy over a period of time.
9. **Capital:** Human-made resources (machinery and equipment) used to produce goods and services; goods that do not directly satisfy human wants. Sometimes separated into human capital (education, know-how) and physical capital (tools you can touch and operate).
10. **Capital Account (also called the Financial Account):** Measures the flow of funds for investment in real assets (such as factories or office buildings) or financial assets (such as stocks and bonds) between a nation and the rest of the world.
11. ***Ceteris Paribus*:** "Other things being equal"; used as a reminder that all variables other than the ones being studied are assumed to be constant.
12. **Circular Flow Diagram:** A model of the macroeconomy that shows the interconnectedness of businesses, households, government, banks, and the foreign sectors. Money flows in a circular direction, and goods, services, and resources flow in the opposite direction.
13. **Classical Economic Theory:** The view that an economy will self-correct from periods of economic shock if left alone. Also known as "laissez-faire."

14. **Comparative Advantage:** When an individual, a firm, or a nation is able to produce a particular product at a lower opportunity cost than another individual, firm, or nation. Comparative advantage is the basis on which nations trade with one another.
15. **Consumer Price Index (CPI):** An index that measures the price of a fixed market basket of consumer goods bought by a typical consumer. The CPI is used to calculate the inflation rate in a nation.
16. **Consumption:** A component of a nation's aggregate demand; measures the total spending by domestic households on goods and services.
17. **Contractionary Fiscal Policy:** A demand-side policy whereby government increases taxes or decreases its expenditures in order to reduce aggregate demand. Could be used in a period of high inflation to bring down the inflation rate.
18. **Contractionary Monetary Policy:** A demand-side policy whereby the central bank reduces the supply of money, increasing interest rates and reducing aggregate demand. Could be used to bring down high inflation rates.
19. **Cost-Push Inflation:** Inflation resulting from a decrease in AS (from higher wage rates and raw material prices, such as the price of oil) and accompanied by a decrease in real output and employment. Also referred to as "stagflation" or "adverse aggregate supply shock."
20. **Crowding-Out Effect:** The rise in interest rates and the resulting decrease in investment spending in the economy caused by increased government borrowing in the loanable funds market. Seen as a disadvantageous side effect of expansionary fiscal policy.
21. **Current Account:** Measures the balance of trade in goods and services and the flow of income between one nation and all other nations. It also records monetary gifts or grants that flow into or out of a country. Equal to a country's *net* exports, or its exports minus its imports.
22. **Cyclical Unemployment:** Unemployment caused by a fall in aggregate demand in a nation. Not included in the natural rate of unemployment. When a nation is in a recession, there will be cyclical unemployment.
23. **Deflation:** A decrease in the average price level of a nation's output over time.

24. **Demand Deposit:** A deposit in a commercial bank against which checks may be written. Also known as a "checkable deposit."
25. **Demand-Pull Inflation:** Inflation resulting from an increase in AD without a corresponding increase in AS.
26. **Depreciation:** A decrease in the value of one currency relative to another, resulting from a decrease in demand for, or an increase in the supply of, the currency on the foreign exchange market.
27. **Devaluation:** When a government intervenes in the market for its own currency to weaken it relative to another currency. Usually achieved through direct intervention in the foreign exchange (forex) market or through the use of monetary policy that affects interest rates, and thereby affects international demand for the currency.
28. **Discount Rate:** One of the three tools of monetary policy, it is the interest rate that the federal government charges on the loans it makes to commercial banks.
29. **Economic Growth**: An increase in the potential output of goods and services in a nation over time.
30. **Economic Resources:** Land, labor, capital, and entrepreneurial ability that are used in the production of goods and services. They are "economic" resources because they are scarce (limited in supply and desired). Also known as "factors of production."
31. **Excess Reserves:** The amount by which a bank's actual reserves exceed its required reserves. Banks can lend excess reserves; when they do, they expand the money supply. The amount of excess reserves in the banking system determines equilibrium interest rate.
32. **Exchange Rate:** The price of one currency in terms of another currency, determined in the forex market.
33. **Exports:** The spending by foreigners on domestically produced goods and services. Counts as an injection into a nation's circular flow of income.
34. **Federal Funds Rate (FFR):** The interest rate banks charge one another on overnight loans made out of their excess reserves. The FFR is the interest rate targeted by the Fed through its open-market operations.
35. **Fiscal Policy:** Changes in government spending and tax collections implemented by government with the aim of either increasing or decreasing aggregate demand to achieve the macroeconomic objectives of full employment and price-level stability.

36. **Floating Exchange Rate System:** When a currency's exchange rate is determined by the free interaction of supply and demand in international forex markets.

37. **Forex Market (Foreign Exchange Market):** The market in which international buyers and sellers exchange foreign currencies for one another to buy and sell goods, services, and assets from various countries. It is where a currency's exchange rate relative to other currencies is determined.

38. **Fractional Reserve Banking:** A banking system in which banks hold only a fraction of deposits as required reserves and can lend some of the money deposited by their customers to other borrowers.

39. **Frictional Unemployment:** Unemployment of workers who have employable skills, such as those who are voluntarily moving between jobs or recent graduates who are looking for their first job.

40. **Full Employment:** When an economy is producing at a level of output at which almost all the nation's resources are employed. The unemployment rate when an economy is at full employment equals the natural rate, and includes only frictional and structural unemployment. Full-employment output is also referred to as "potential output."

41. **GDP (Gross Domestic Product):** The total market value of all final goods and services produced during a given time period within a country's borders. Equal to the total income of the nation's households or the total expenditures on the nation's output.

42. **GDP Deflator:** The price index for all final goods and services used to adjust the nominal GDP into real GDP.

43. **Human Capital:** The value skills integrated into labor through education, training, knowledge, and health. An important determinant of aggregate supply and the level of economic growth in a nation.

44. **Imports:** Spending on goods and services produced in foreign nations. Counts as a leakage from a nation's circular flow of income.

45. **Inflation:** A rise in the average level of prices in the economy over time (percentage change in the CPI).

46. **Inflationary Gap:** The difference between a nation's equilibrium level of output and its full employment level of output when the nation is overheating (producing beyond its full employment level).

47. **Inflationary Spiral:** The rapid increase in average price level resulting from demand-pull inflation leading to higher wages, causing cost-push inflation.

48. **Interest Rate:** The opportunity cost of money. Either the cost of borrowing money or the cost of spending money (e.g., the interest rate is what would be given up by not saving money). Conversely, this is the price a lender is paid for allowing someone else to use money for a time.

49. **Investment:** A component of aggregate demand, it includes all spending on capital equipment, inventories, and technology by firms. This does not include financial investment, which is the purchase of financial assets (stocks and bonds). Also includes household purchasing of newly constructed residences.

50. **Law of Increasing Opportunity Cost:** As more of a particular product is produced, the opportunity cost, in terms of what must be given up of other goods to produce each unit of the product, increases. Explains the convex shape of a nation's production possibilities curve.

51. **Loanable Funds Market:** The market in which the demand for private investment and the supply of household savings intersect to determine the equilibrium real interest rate.

52. **Long Run:** The period of time over which the wage rate and price level of inputs in a nation are flexible. In the long run, any changes in AD are cancelled out due to the flexibility of wages and prices and an economy will return to its full employment level of output. Sometimes referred to as the "flexible wage period."

53. **Long Run Aggregate Supply (LRAS):** The level of output to which an economy will always return in the long run. The LRAS curve intersects the horizontal axis at the full employment or potential level of output.

54. **M1:** A component of the money supply including currency and checkable deposits.

55. **M2:** A more broadly defined component of the money supply. Equal to M1 plus savings deposits, money-market deposits, mutual funds, and small-time deposits.

56. **M3:** The broadest component of the money supply. Equal to M2 plus large time deposits.

57. **Macroeconomics:** The study of entire nations' economies and the interactions between households, firms, government, and foreigners.

58. **Macroeconomic Equilibrium:** The level of output at which a nation is producing at any particular period of time. May be below its full employment level (if the economy is in recession) or beyond its full employment level (if the economy is overheating).

59. **Managed or Fixed Exchange Rate System:** When a government or central bank takes action to manage or fix the value of its currency relative to another currency on the forex market.

60. **Marginal Analysis:** Decision-making which involves a comparison of marginal (extra) benefits and marginal costs.

61. **Marginal Propensity to Consume (MPC):** The fraction of any change in income spent on domestically produced goods and services; equal to the change in consumption divided by the change in disposable income.

62. **Marginal Propensity to Save (MPS):** The fraction of any change in income that is saved; equal to the change in savings divided by the change in disposable income.

63. **Market Economic System:** A system of resource allocation in which buyers and sellers meet in markets to determine the price and quantity of goods, services, and productive resources.

64. **Microeconomics:** The study of the interactions between consumers and producers in markets for individual products.

65. **Monetarism:** The macroeconomic view that the main cause of changes in aggregate output and the price level are fluctuations in the money supply.

66. **Monetary Policy:** The central bank's manipulation of the supply of money aimed at raising or lowering interest rates to stimulate or contract the level of aggregate demand to promote the macroeconomic objectives of price-level stability and full employment.

67. **Money:** Any object that can be used to facilitate the exchange of goods and services in a market.

68. **Money Demand:** The sum of the transaction demand and the asset demand for money. Inversely related to the nominal interest rate.

69. **Money Market:** The market where the supply of money is set by the central bank; includes the downward-sloping money-demand curve and a vertical money-supply curve. The "price" of money is the nominal interest rate.

70. **Money Supply:** The vertical curve representing the total supply of excess reserves in a nation's banking system. Determined by the monetary policy actions of the central bank.
71. **Multiplier Effect:** The increase in total spending in an economy resulting from an initial injection of new spending. The size of the multiplier effect depends upon the spending multiplier.
72. **Natural Rate of Unemployment (NRU):** The level of unemployment that prevails in an economy that is producing at its full employment level of output. Includes structural and frictional unemployment. While countries' NRUs can vary, the NRU in the United States tends to be close to 5%.
73. **Net Exports (Xn):** A component of aggregate demand that equals the income earned from the sale of exports to the rest of the world minus expenditures by domestic consumers on imports.
74. **Official Reserves:** To balance the two accounts in the balance of payments (current and financial accounts), a country's official foreign exchange reserves measures the net effect of all the money flows from the other accounts.
75. **Open-Market Operations:** The central bank's buying and selling of government bonds on the open market from commercial banks and the public. This is aimed at increasing or decreasing the level of reserves in the banking system and thereby affects the interest rate and the level of aggregate demand.
76. **Opportunity Cost:** What must be given up to have something else. Opportunity costs are not necessarily monetary costs, but rather include what you could do with the resources you use to undertake any activity or exchange.
77. **Phillips Curve (long-run):** A model that demonstrates that after inflation expectations have been adjusted, there is no trade-off between inflation and unemployment, as it is vertical and equal to the NRU.
78. **Phillips Curve (short-run):** A model that demonstrates the inverse relationship between unemployment (horizontal) and inflation (vertical axis).
79. **Production Possibilities Curve (PPC):** A graph that shows the various combinations of output that the economy can produce given the available factors of production and the available production technology.
80. **Productivity:** The output per unit of input of a resource. An important determinant of the level of aggregate supply in a nation.

81. **Protectionism:** The use of tariffs, quotas, or subsidies to give domestic producers a competitive advantage over foreign producers. Meant to protect domestic production and employment from foreign competition.

82. **Rational Expectations Theory:** The hypothesis that business firms and households expect monetary and fiscal policies to have certain effects on the economy and take, in pursuit of their own self-interests, actions which make these policies ineffective at changing real output.

83. **Recession:** A contraction in total output of goods and services in a nation between two periods of time. Could be caused by a decrease in aggregate demand or in aggregate supply.

84. **Recessionary Gap:** The difference between an economy's equilibrium level of output and its full employment level of output when an economy is in recession.

85. **Required Reserves:** The proportion of a bank's total deposits it is required to keep in reserve with the central bank. Determined by the required reserve ratio.

86. **Scarcity:** Something is scarce when it is both desired and limited in supply. Scarcity is the basic economic problem.

87. **Self-Correction:** The idea that an economy producing at an equilibrium level of output that is below or above its full employment will return on its own to its full employment level if left to its own devices. Requires flexible wages and prices and is associated with classical economic views.

88. **Stagflation:** A macroeconomic situation in which both inflation and unemployment increase. Caused by a negative supply shock.

89. **Sticky Wage and Price Model:** The short-run Aggregate-Supply Curve is sometimes referred to as the "sticky wage and price model," because workers' wage demands take time to adjust to changes in the overall price level, and therefore, in the short run an economy may produce well below or beyond its full employment level of output.

90. **Structural Unemployment:** Unemployment caused by changes in the structure of demand for goods and in technology; workers who are unemployed because they do not match what is in demand by producers in the economy or whose skills have been left behind by economic advancement.

91. **Supply Shock:** Anything that leads to a sudden, unexpected change in aggregate supply. Can be negative (decreases AS) or

positive (increases AS). May include a change in energy prices, wages, or business taxes, or may result from a natural disaster or a new discovery of important resources.

92. **Trade Deficit:** When a country's total spending on imported goods and services exceeds its total revenues from the sale of exports to the rest of the world. Synonymous with a deficit in the current account of the balance of payments and with a negative net export component of GDP.

93. **Trade Surplus:** When a country's sale of exports exceeds its spending on imports. Synonymous with a surplus in the current account of the balance of payments.

94. **Wealth:** An important determinant of consumption. Wealth is the total value of a household's assets minus all its liabilities.

# PART II

# CONTENT REVIEW

Chapter 3

# UNIT 1 Basic Economic Concepts

## I. Scarcity

**A.** Economics Defined

1. Economics is the social science that studies scarcity and the choices society must make over the use of the world's limited resources.
2. Scarcity is the "basic problem of economics." Scarcity arises because the world's resources are limited, while humans' wants and needs are, for all intents and purposes, unlimited.
3. Due to scarcity, a conflict arises over how the world's resources (land, capital, labor, and entrepreneurship) should be allocated across various uses.

**B.** Basic Economic Questions

1. Economic systems are needed for allocating scarce resources across society's competing wants and needs.
2. Economic systems have been developed throughout history to answer three basic economic questions:
   - i. What should be produced?
   - ii. How should it be produced?
   - iii. How should society's output be distributed?

**C.** Economic Systems

1. A command and control economy (such as the communist economies of the Soviet Union in the 20th century and North Korea today) are those in which the government owns or directs the different factors of production toward different uses.

2. A free market economy is one in which there is limited or no government intervention in the allocation of the factors of production.
   i. Economic decisions are made entirely by private actors (buyers and sellers).
   ii. Prominent examples today are Hong Kong and Mexico.
3. A mixed economy (common in most major economies such as the U.S. and Germany) is one in which the government provides certain goods and services (such as roads, schools, defense, and so on), but most consumer goods are provided by private businesses.

**D.** Economist Defined

1. An economist studies how economic systems, especially in the preceding list, work.
2. Economists develop theories that inform economic policies to address economic questions.

**E.** Main Fields of Economics: Microeconomics ("Micro") and Macroeconomics ("Macro")

1. "Micro" examines how the producers and consumers of individual goods, services, and resources interact in markets to determine equilibrium prices and quantities.
   i. Micro also examines the role of government in the markets for particular goods, such as healthcare. This involves the extent to which governments can improve market efficiency by either encouraging or discouraging a good's production and consumption through subsidies, taxes, or price and quantity controls.
   ii. Micro studies the markets for factors of production, such as land, labor, and capital. This includes situations in which markets operate inefficiently, such as when there is pollution or other harmful effects of a good's production or consumption on society as a whole.
   iii. Microeconomists also study "utility-maximizing" choices of consumers and the "profit-maximizing" behaviors of firms.
2. "Macro" examines the outcomes of entire nations' economies, rather than outcomes in individual markets.

i. Macro concepts include the aggregate level of output and the average price level of goods in a country, the level of unemployment across all industries, the growth rate in a country's output, and the role of government in promoting certain macroeconomic objectives relating to these macroeconomic measurements.

ii. The three macroeconomic objectives that economic policy in nearly every economy intends to promote are:

- Full employment—nearly everyone who is willing and able to work has a job and the economy is using all of its available resources efficiently.
- Price level stability—the average price level of a country's output is neither increasing too fast ("inflation") nor falling ("deflation") over time.
- Economic growth—national output (known as gross domestic product) and employment opportunities increase over time.

A government's role in its national economy is to employ policies to promote these three objectives.

## II. Choice, Opportunity Cost, and the Production Possibilities Curve (PPC)

A. The conflict between humans' unlimited wants and the limited resources needed to satisfy those wants means that choices must be made in how to allocate the planet's scarce resources between various uses.

1. An economic decision weighs the costs and benefits about how to use a scarce resource, whether it is an individual's time, a parcel of land, a piece of capital equipment, or one's own labor.
2. Every decision comes with an opportunity cost, which is the next best alternative use of a resource.
3. For example, consider a farmer who has 100 acres of land that is equally suited for growing corn or soybeans.

i. The farmer must choose what combination of the two crops should be grown. The following table depicts the production possibilities (the possible output) of corn and soybeans the farmer is able to produce based on how much land is allocated toward each good's production.

| Thousands of kilograms of corn | Thousands of kilograms of soybeans |
|---|---|
| 100 | 0 |
| 80 | 20 |
| 60 | 40 |
| 40 | 60 |
| 20 | 80 |
| 0 | 100 |

i. The table shows that if the farmer grows just corn, 100,000 kg can be harvested, but there will be no resources left to grow soybeans.

ii. If nothing but soybeans are grown, 100,000 kg can be harvested but no corn.

iii. Every 20,000 kg increase in soybean production results in a fall in corn output of 20,000 kg.

iv. In other words, the opportunity cost of one kg of soybeans is one kg of corn.

**B.** The Production Possibilities Curve (PPC). The farmer's production possibilities can be depicted in a graph known as the production possibilities curve, or PPC.

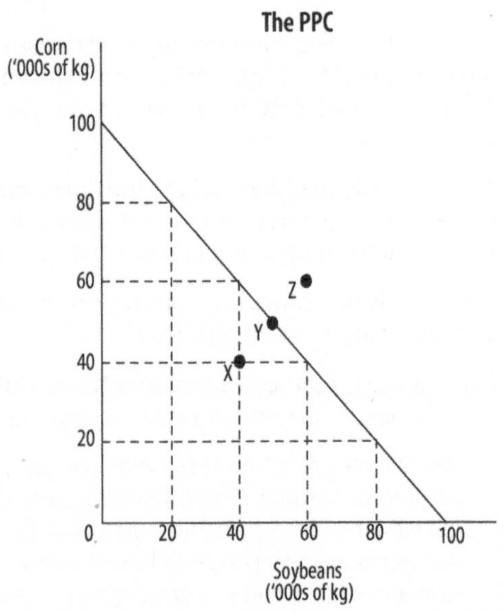

1. The farmer's PPC shows the potential output of two crops assuming all 100 acres are planted.
2. In this simple model we can also see what would happen if the farmer only used some of the land and produced less than the maximum potential output, as well as what would be possible if the farmer could increase the productivity of the land or acquire more acreage.
   - i. Point X represents a level of output of 40,000 kg of soybeans and 40,000 kg of corn. Since point X lies inside the PPC, it represents what the farmer would produce if he were underutilizing his resources or using his resources inefficiently.
   - ii. Point Y represents a level of output of 50,000 kg of soybeans and 50,000 kg of corn. Since point Y lies on the PPC, it represents a possible level of output assuming the farmer utilizes his resources to their full efficiency.
   - iii. Point Z represents a level of output of 60,000 kg of soybeans and 60,000 kg of corn. Since Point Z lies beyond the PPC, it represents a level of output that is impossible given the quantity and quality of resources (land, labor, and capital) available to the farmer. However, should the farmer experience an improvement or an increase in his resources, point Z could become possible in the future.

C. The Shape of the PPC. The shape of the PPC depends on whether opportunity costs are constant, increasing, or decreasing.

1. Increasing opportunity cost PPCs. A PPC that is bowed outward from the origin represents two goods for which the opportunity cost of producing more of one good increases as output increases.
   - i. For example, let's assume that the country of Westoverland can produce truck tires or driveshafts.
   - ii. The following PPC shows the potential output of these two goods assuming Westoverland fully employs its resources toward tires and driveshafts.

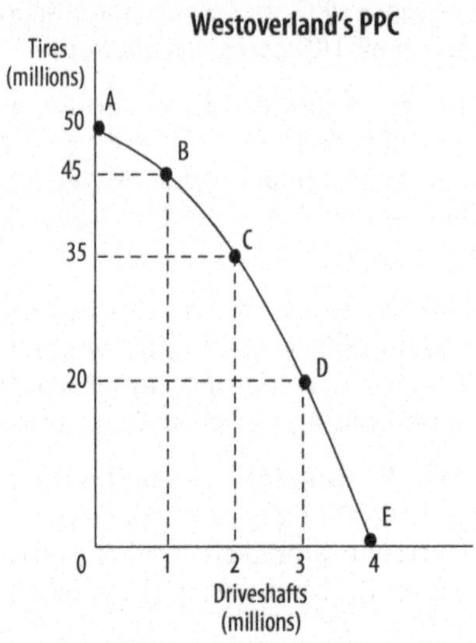


iii. Assume Westoverland is currently allocating all of its resources toward tire production (point A). As the country moves from point A to point B, it produces its first 1 million driveshafts and gives up 5 million tires.

iv. However, the next 1 million driveshafts (from point B to C) "cost" Westoverland 10 million tires.

v. As driveshaft production continues to increase, the opportunity cost of additional driveshafts increases.

vi. The next million driveshafts (from C to D) cost 15 million tires, and the last million driveshafts (D to E) cost Westoverland 20 million tires.

vii. The average opportunity costs of driveshafts ("d") in terms of tires ("t") along Westoverland's PPC can be calculated as in the following table:

| Movement along the PPC | Opportunity cost of driveshafts (d) in terms of tires (t) |
|---|---|
| From A to B | 1d = 5t |
| From B to C | 1d = 10t |
| From C to D | 1d = 15t |
| From D to E | 1d = 20t |

2. Constant opportunity cost PPCs. Goods that require similar resources to produce (such as truck tires and bike tires) are likely to have a constant opportunity cost. Consider the PPC shown in the following chart, which shows the number of truck tires and bike tires that the country could produce.

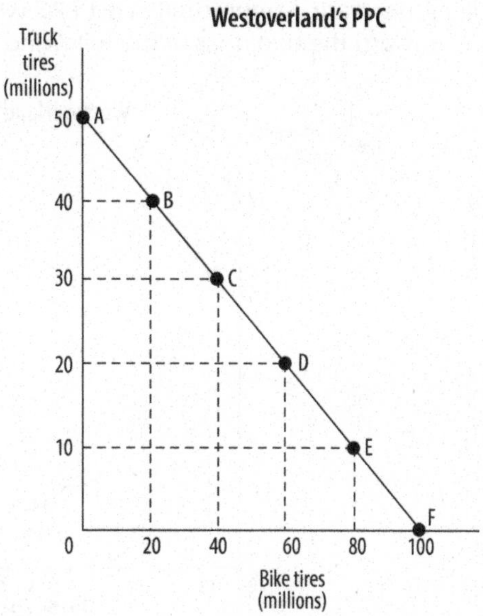


   i. Westoverland can produce either 100 million bike tires or 50 million truck tires.

   ii. Every bike tire comes with the opportunity cost of half a truck tire, an opportunity cost that is constant between all points on the PPC.

   iii. In contrast to the opportunity cost of driveshafts, which increases in terms of tires as driveshaft production increases, the opportunity cost of bike tires and truck tires is constant along Westoverland's PPC because the two goods require nearly identical resources to produce.

3. Decreasing opportunity cost PPCs. In theory, two goods can have decreasing opportunity costs, which would occur when producing additional units of one good results in fewer and fewer units of the other good being given up. Such a phenomenon could occur if the resources needed to produce a good become less scarce as more of the good is produced, such as might be the case with technology goods like smartphones and electric cars.

i. As more electric cars are produced, battery technology improves and it becomes less costly to produce electric cars.

ii. As the number of electric cars produced increases, fewer and fewer cell phones must be given up for each additional electric car due to better and cheaper battery technology.

iii. A decreasing opportunity cost PPC would be bowed inward toward the origin, as in the following graph.

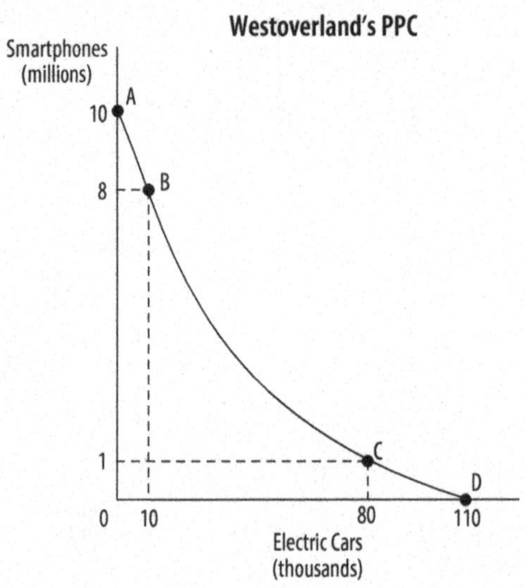


iv. The first 10,000 electric cars (from A to B) cost Westoverland 2 million smartphones, at an opportunity cost of 200 smartphones per electric car produced.

v. However, by the time the country is producing 80,000 electric cars the technology to produce more cars has become so abundant and cheap that the country can achieve 30,000 additional cars (from C to D) and give up only 1 million smartphones, at an opportunity cost of only 33.33 smartphones per car.

vi. As electric car production increases, the opportunity cost of additional cars decreases in Westoverland, explained by the fact that the resources needed to produce electric cars (expensive batteries) become more abundant and thus less costly as production increases.

**D.** Shifts of the PPC: Let's consider the PPC for truck tires and driveshafts again, and discuss the factors that can cause a shift outward or inward of the PPC itself.

1. Shifts along a single axis. Assume that Westoverland invests in technology that increases the productivity of workers in the tire industry.

   i. The country's potential output of tires will increase, while its potential output of driveshafts will remain unchanged.

   ii. As a result, the PPC will shift out along the tire axis. Improvements in tire production have increased the potential output of tires.

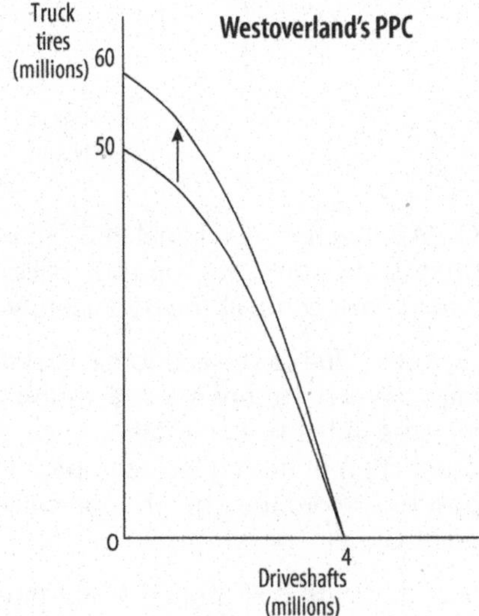


2. Shifts along both axes. Assume next that there is an increase in the size of the workforce in Westoverland, allowing the country to produce more of both goods. The entire PPC will now shift out, showing an increase in the potential output of both goods.

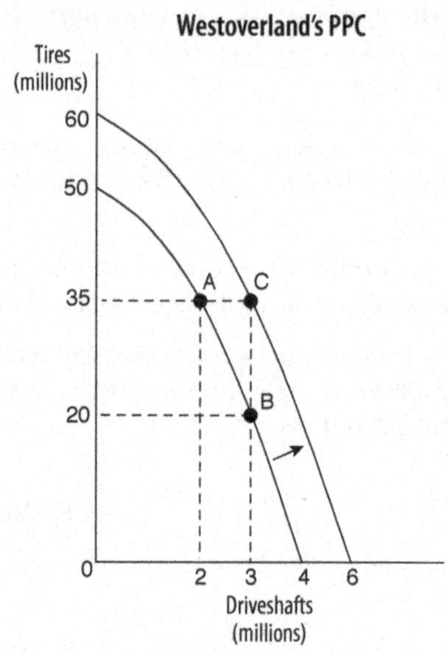


i. On Westoverland's original PPC, an increase of driveshaft production from 2 million to 3 million units (from A to B) would have come at the opportunity cost of 15 million tires.

ii. However, due to the economic growth resulting from improvements in tire manufacturing technology and an increase in the size of its labor force, the country can increase production of both goods compared to what would have been possible before the growth took place (from points A or B to point C).

3. Economic growth is illustrated as an outward shift of the PPC and is made possible by an increase in either the quantity or the quality of a country's resources (land, labor, and capital).

***Expect multiple-choice questions about production possibilities curves. For example, the AP® Macro exam often asks about the meaning of a nation producing inside its PPC, at a point on its PPC, and what would be necessary for a nation to produce beyond its current PPC. Questions about opportunity costs and trade-offs involving PPCs are also common.***

## III. Comparative Advantage, Specialization, and Trade

A. Absolute Advantage. So far we have looked at production possibilities curves for individuals (the farmer) and for a single country (Westoverland).

1. By examining the opportunity costs faced by two different individuals or countries, however, we can determine whether it may be beneficial for trade to take place.
2. In economics, trade refers to the voluntary exchange of goods and services between two or more individuals or countries.
3. Trade can be beneficial to those who participate in it if it allows an individual or country to acquire a good at a lower opportunity cost than it could be acquired without trade.
4. Let's look at the PPCs for two countries, Sandyland and Wetworld. The PPCs show the potential output of two goods, bicycles and skis, given a fixed allocation of resources.

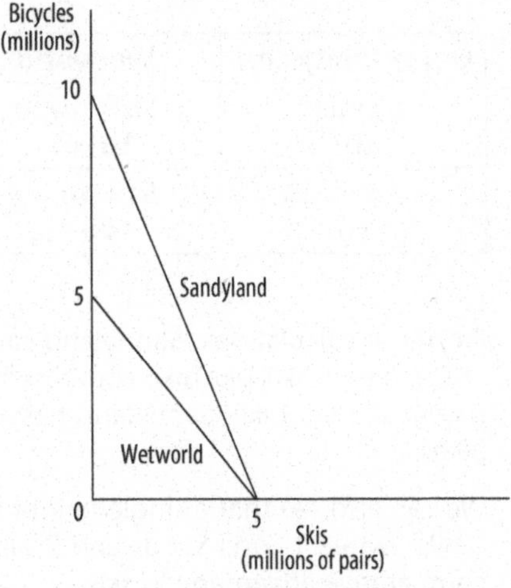


   i. From the PPCs we can determine that Sandyland has an absolute advantage in bicycles, since it is more efficient in their manufacture.
   ii. Given a certain allocation of resources, Sandyland can produce more bikes than Wetworld.

iii. Both countries are equally efficient in ski production, as with the same amount of resources both can produce up to 5 million pairs of skis.

iv. Neither country, therefore, has an absolute advantage in ski production.

**B.** Comparative Advantage. You may be inclined to assume that since Sandyland can produce bikes more efficiently than Wetworld and is equally efficient in ski production, it would not benefit from trading with Wetworld. However, whether a country can benefit from trade with other countries does not depend on whether it has an absolute advantage, rather whether it has a comparative advantage in a good's production.

1. An individual or a country has a comparative advantage in a good's production when it can produce it at a lower opportunity cost than another individual or country.
2. Consider again Sandyland and Wetworld. The opportunity costs of bikes (b) and skis (s) are calculated in the following table:

| Opportunity cost | Wetworld | Sandyland |
|---|---|---|
| Bicycles (b) | 5b = 5s, so **1b = 1s** | 10b = 5s, so **1b = 0.5s** |
| Skis (s) | 5s = 5b, so **1s = 1b** | 5s = 10b, so **1s = 2b** |

i. From our calculations, Sandyland can produce bikes at a cost of 0.5 pair of skis per bike compared to Wetworld's cost of 1 pair of skis per bike. Sandyland has a comparative advantage in bikes.

ii. We can also see that a single pair of skis costs Wetworld only 1 bike, while it costs Sandyland 2 bikes. Wetworld has a comparative advantage in skis.

**C.** Specialization and Trade. When a country specializes in the production of a good in which it has a comparative advantage and trades with other countries for goods in which they have comparative advantages, a level of consumption beyond what is achievable on its own becomes possible.

1. Trading price. Assume that Wetworld produces only skis and Sandyland only bikes. If the countries then trade with one another

at a trading price of 0.8 skis per bike (which equals 1.25 bikes per pair of skis), then both countries can experience an increase in potential consumption compared to what is possible domestically.

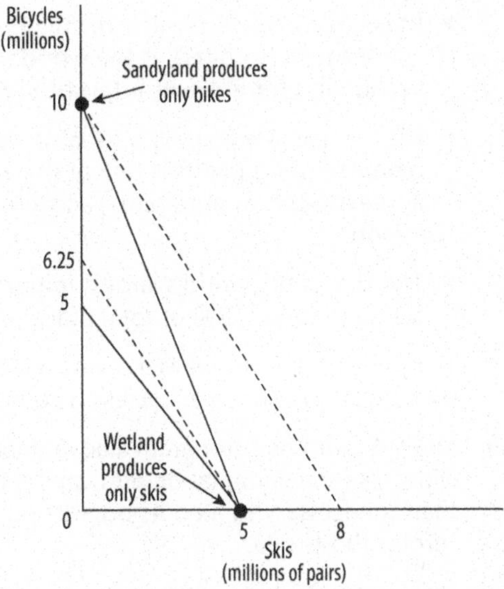


i. The dashed lines in the preceding graph indicate the trading possibilities both countries experience when trading at a rate of 1.25 bikes per pair of skis or 0.8 pair of skis per bike.

ii. Note that with trade, both countries are able to consume a combination of the two goods that would not have been possible before trade.

2. Terms of trade. Mutually beneficial trade can occur when two countries specializing in two different goods can agree upon a terms of trade that allows each country to import the good the other is producing at a cost lower than it could be produced for domestically.

   i. In the real world, specialization and trade underscore international relations and are demonstrated by some observations about how countries trade with one another. For example, consider the following example of the U.S. and Mexico[1]:

[1] Data source: The Observatory of Economic Complexity, *https://atlas.media.mit.edu*

- ➤ The U.S. is the world's largest producer and exporter of corn, a good for which it has a comparative advantage. 30% of the corn traded on the global marketplace is produced in the U.S.
- ➤ Mexico, where corn is the main ingredient in one of its staple foods (tortillas), is the world's largest importer, accounting for 9.4% of total corn imports.
- ➤ Meanwhile, Mexico, with its large labor force and its many manufacturing plants is one of the world's largest producers and exporters of auto parts, accounting for 7.7% of global exports.
- ➤ The U.S. is the world's largest importer of auto parts, accounting for 18% of total global imports.

ii. The preceding example is a real-world application of specialization and trade based on comparative advantage.

iii. The U.S. with its comparative advantage in corn production allocates more land, labor, and capital to corn production than is necessary to feed its population, exporting much of the surplus to Mexico.

iv. Meanwhile, Mexico with a comparative advantage in auto parts produces far more than it needs for its domestic auto industry. The surplus is exported to the U.S., where the demand for auto parts exceeds the domestic quantity supplied.

3. International trade based on comparative advantage allows both countries to consume goods that each is not particularly efficient at producing more cheaply than would be possible without trade.

## IV. Demand

A. The "Invisible Hand." Market economies are those in which the basic questions of what is produced, how it is produced, and for whom output is produced are answered not by the government, but by what 18th-century philosopher Adam Smith referred to as the invisible hand.

1. No central authority. Smith observed that the interactions of buyers and sellers in free markets appeared to achieve a more efficient and socially optimal allocation of resources than what could have been achieved by a central authority such as a king

or government that attempted to determine what, how, and for whom production should take place.

2. Basic model. Later, economists built on Smith's observations and constructed a basic model for understanding how the prices and quantities of output are determined in the markets for different goods and services.

**B.** Demand and Supply. The demand-and-supply model looks at how the quantities consumers demand and the quantities producers are willing to supply relate to market price, and together determine the equilibrium level of output and price in a market.

1. The following table represents weekly consumer demand for grapes in a small town.

| Price of grapes ($ per pound) | Quantity of grapes demanded (pounds) |
|---|---|
| $5 | 0 |
| $4 | 30 |
| $3 | 60 |
| $2 | 90 |
| $1 | 120 |

i. Observe that at high prices the quantity of grapes consumers demand is relatively low.

ii. However, as the price of grapes falls, consumers demand an increasing quantity (30 additional pounds for each $1 decrease in the price).

iii. The inverse relationship between price and quantity demanded demonstrated above reflects the law of demand, which is a basic economic principle that observes that as the price of a good decreases, the quantity consumers demand increases, and as the price increases, quantity demanded decreases.

iv. In other words, assuming all else is held constant, there is an inverse relationship between price and quantity demanded.

**C.** The Demand Curve. A good's demand can also be illustrated in a demand curve, which is a graph showing the quantity demanded on the horizontal axis and price on the vertical axis. The following graph represents a demand curve for grapes.

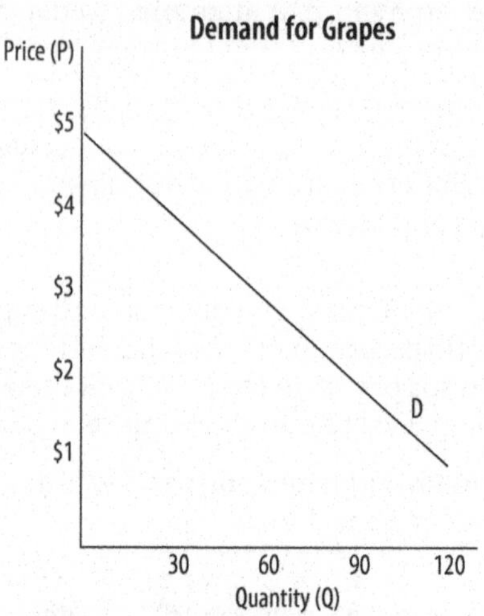


**D.** Movements Along a Demand Curve. A change in a good's price causes a movement along a demand curve and a change in quantity demanded.

1. Assume, for example, that grapes are currently selling at $3 per pound. At that price, 60 pounds per week are demanded by consumers, as seen in the following graph.

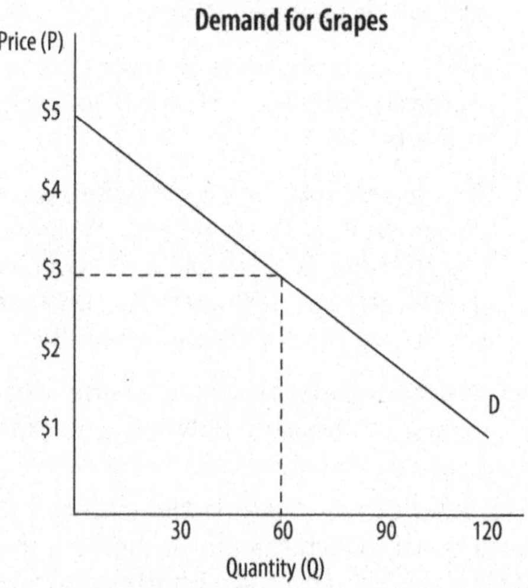


2. What happens if the price of grapes increases to $4 per pound? According to the law of demand, an increase in price should cause a decrease in quantity demanded.

3. This is shown as a movement along a demand curve upward and to the left, as seen in the following graph.

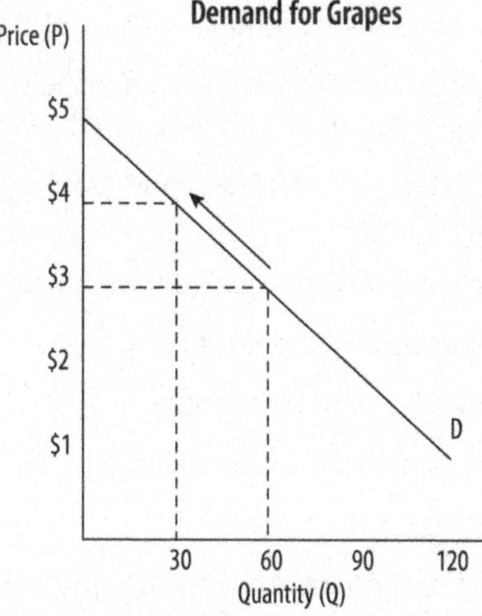


4. If the price falls, there is a movement down and to the right along the graph and an increase in the quantity of grapes demanded.

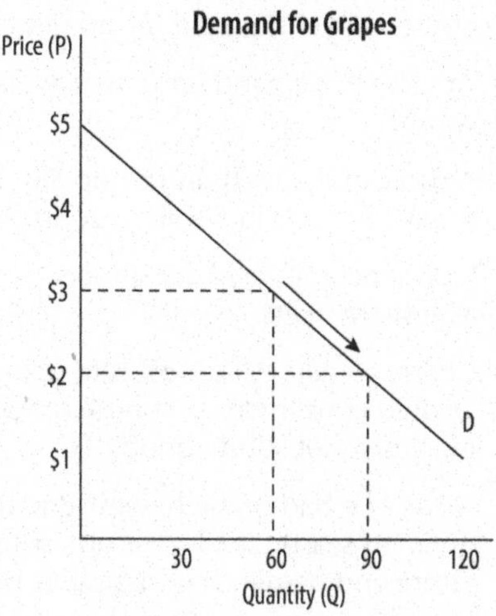


5. Note that following a price change, assuming all else remains constant, there is a change in the quantity of grapes demanded.

6. However, demand itself remains the same (e.g., there is still only one demand curve).

**E.** Determinants of Demand and Shifts of a Demand Curve

1. Factors that influence consumer demand cause the market demand curve for a good to shift.
2. The determinants of demand (sometimes called the demand shifters) include:

   i. consumers' tastes and preferences

   ii. consumers' incomes

   iii. prices of related goods

   iv. expectations of future prices

   v. size of the market

   If any of these factors change, there will be an increase or a decrease in a good's demand and a shift of the demand curve.

F. Increase in Demand

1. Let's consider the demand for grapes again looking at an example of how a change in each of the determinants of demand would affect the market demand for grapes.
2. An increase in demand for grapes would result from any of the following:

   i. A successful advertising campaign by the Grape Farmers of America results in a shift in consumers' tastes toward grapes.

   ii. Rising incomes lead consumers to demand more fresh grapes at supermarkets.

   iii. Cherry tomatoes, a substitute good for grapes, rise in price, leading consumers to choose grapes instead of the now more expensive substitute good.

   iv. News of a bad grape harvest due to an unseasonably dry growing season leads consumers to expect prices to rise in the future and demand more grapes now.

   v. An influx of new residents causes the number of consumers to increase, thus more grapes are demanded.

3. If any of the above changes occur, demand for grapes will increase and the demand curve will shift outward, as in the following graph.

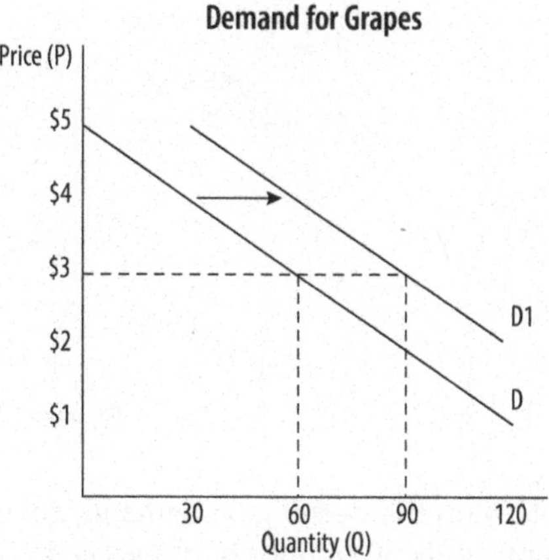


   i. As a result of the increase in demand from "D" to "D1," the quantity of grapes consumers are willing and able to buy at every price has increased.

   ii. At the initial price of $3, for example, consumers now demand 90 pounds of grapes compared to 60 pounds before the demand shift.

G. Decrease in Demand

1. A decrease in demand would result if any of the determinants changed in such a way that consumers would wish to buy fewer grapes at each price.
2. If tastes shifted to other fruits, if consumers' incomes fell, if the price of cherry tomatoes decreased, if consumers expect lower prices in the future, or if the number of consumers decreased, then demand would shift to the left, as in the following graph.

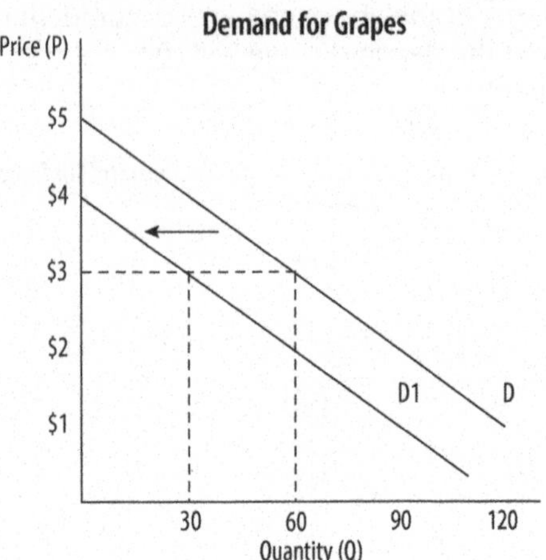


3. Following the decrease in demand, consumers are willing and able to buy only 30 pounds of grapes at $3.

H. Normal vs. Inferior Goods

1. Whether an increase in income causes a good's demand to increase or decrease depends on whether the good is a "normal" or an "inferior" good.

   i. A normal good is any good that consumers demand more of when their incomes rise and less of when their incomes fall. For example, new cars are normal goods. When the average income of a country's consumers rises, demand for new cars increases.

   ii. An inferior good is a good for which an inverse relationship exists between income and demand. Used cars, for example, tend to sell better when average incomes are falling, and sell less when incomes are rising. Demand for an inferior good will increase when consumers' incomes decrease, and decrease when incomes rise.

I. Substitutes vs. Complements

1. Goods can be related to one another in two ways. They can be *substitutes*, which is when two goods can be used or consumed instead of one another, or they can be *complements*, which is when two goods are used or consumed in combination with one another.

i. Substitutes. There is a direct relationship between a good's demand and the price of its substitutes. For example, when taco prices rise, demand for hamburgers should increase as consumers switch from tacos to burgers. If taco prices fall, demand for hamburgers decreases as consumers switch from burgers to tacos.

➤ Other examples of substitutes are air travel and rail travel, apples and pears, beef and chicken, Nike and Adidas.

ii. Complements. There is an inverse relationship between a good's demand and the price of its complements. When gas prices rise, demand for large pickup trucks (which require large amounts of gas to operate) decreases. If gas prices fall, demand for trucks should increase, as consumers are more willing to buy gas-guzzling vehicles when gas is cheap.

➤ Examples are pickup trucks and gasoline, ice cream and ice cream cones, ski lift tickets and skis, hamburgers and hamburger buns.

***A typical question about the determinants of demand might read: "Which of the following will cause the demand for _________ to increase/decrease?" Based on your knowledge of the good in question, you must choose which of the five possible answers is most likely a determinant of demand.***

## V. Supply

A. Law of Supply. The old joke is that the answer to any question asked of an economist is "demand and supply." We've learned about demand, so let's now look at the other side of the market, supply.

1. Supply is the quantity of a good or service producers are willing and able to provide at a range of prices in a period of time.
2. A good's supply can be represented by either a supply schedule (or table) or a supply curve.
3. Consider the following table, which shows how many pounds of grapes would be supplied weekly in a small town at a range of prices.

| Price of grapes ($ per pound) | Quantity of grapes supplied (pounds) |
|---|---|
| $5 | 100 |
| $4 | 80 |
| $3 | 60 |
| $2 | 40 |
| $1 | 20 |

i. Notice that as grape prices fall, the quantity supplied decreases.

ii. The direct relationship between a good's price and the quantity sellers are willing to supply is known as the law of supply.

iii. Assuming all else is held constant, as a good's price increases the quantity supplied increases, and as the price falls, quantity supplied falls.

iv. Sellers see a higher price as an opportunity to earn more profit; therefore, they are willing to bring more of a good to market as its price rises.

v. At lower prices, the potential profits of providing a good to the market decrease so sellers shift their resources toward other, more profitable goods.

**B.** The Supply Curve. The direct relationship between price and quantity supplied leads to an upward-sloping supply curve, such as that for grapes.

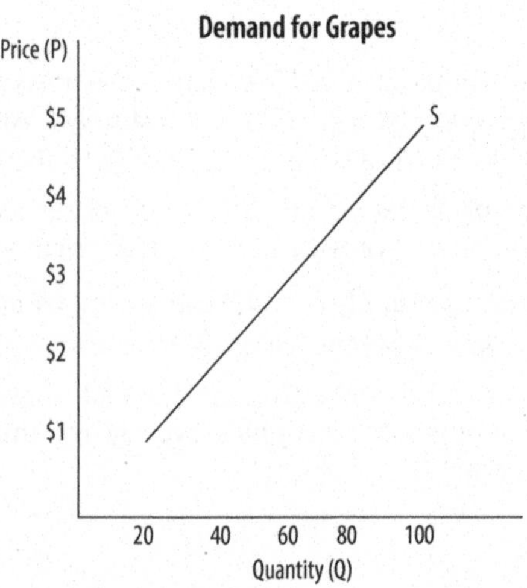

1. Movements along the supply curve.
   i. Assume the price of grapes increases from $2 to $3.
   ii. Sellers see the higher price as an opportunity to make more profits from selling grapes, thus they bring more grapes to the market.
   iii. A change in a good's price leads to a movement along the supply curve, as in the following graph.

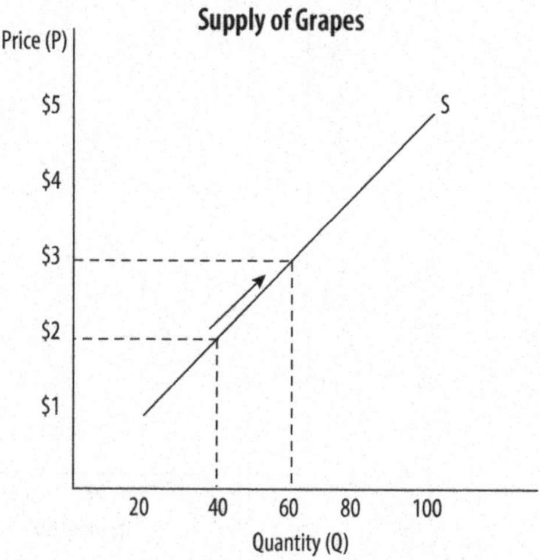


2. Determinants of supply and shifts in a supply curve. While a change in price causes a change in quantity supplied and a movement along a supply curve, a change in factors that influence producer supply, such as changes in input prices, cause the market supply curve to shift. The determinants of supply (or supply shifters) include:
   i. The prices of inputs, such as raw materials, labor, energy costs, transportation costs, etc.
   ii. Government intervention, such as subsidies (payments to producers) and taxes (payments from producers to the government) and the level of government regulation.
   iii. The prices of other goods that could be produced using the same resources.
   iv. Changes in technology used in the production of a good.
   v. The size of the market.
   vi. Producers' expectations of future prices.

3. Price of inputs. Assume the wages paid to fruit pickers increase, causing the cost of harvesting grapes to increase.
   i. At every price, suppliers would then be willing and able to supply fewer grapes to the market.
   ii. The resulting decrease in supply would cause the supply curve to shift inward, or to the left, as in the graph below.

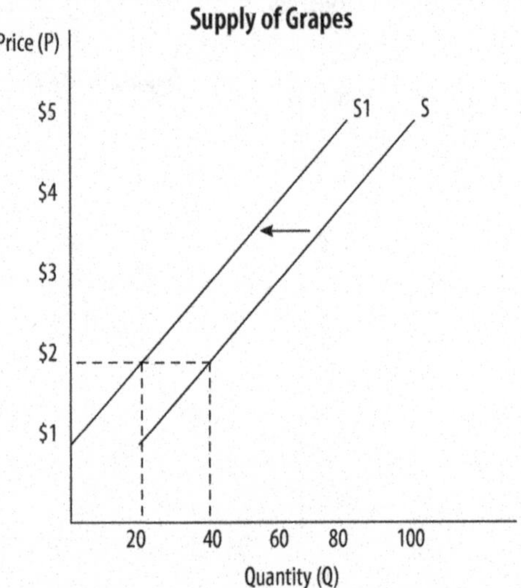


   iii. A decrease in wages or a change in any other factor that leads to an increase in supply would cause the supply curve to shift to the right, as in the following graph.

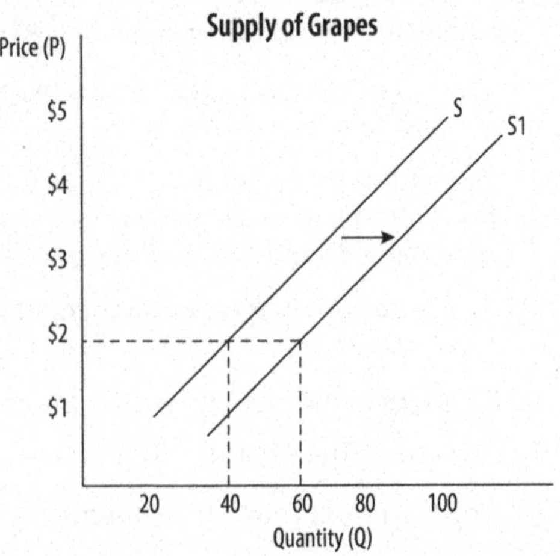

iv. Government intervention. Assume that the government decides to offer subsidies to grape growers, reducing their per unit cost of production. Such an intervention would lead to an increase in the supply of grapes.

v. Technology. Assume that instead of picking grapes by hand, growers install a new grape-harvesting machine that can be operated at a fraction of the cost of the wage-labor previously employed. New technology has lowered production costs and would result in an increase in supply. Due to government subsidies or a new technology, producers can now supply 60 pounds of grapes at $2 instead of just 40 pounds.

vi. Change in the price of other goods. If the price of almonds, which grow in similar conditions as grapes, increases, then over time grape farmers will allocate more land, capital, and labor to almond production, causing the supply of grapes to decrease.

vii. Change in expected future prices. If the price of grapes is expected to be higher in the future, sellers may reduce supply today in order to sell at the higher price down the road.

viii. Change in the number of producers. If the number of grape producers in the market changes, the supply will shift correspondingly. More producers mean supply increases, shifting the curve to the right; fewer producers mean a lower supply, and the curve shifts to the left.

***Although supply and demand is a microeconomic concept, questions might appear on the AP® Macro exam. Since a nation's economy is made up of individual markets, understanding how supply and demand interact in markets is fundamental to understanding how a national economy functions.***

## VI. Market Equilibrium, Disequilibrium, and Changes in Equilibrium

**A.** Market Equilibrium. A market is in equilibrium when the good's price is at the level at which the quantities demanded and supplied are equal.

1. Let's turn to the grape market again. If both the demand and the supply curves are plotted on a graph, we can determine the equilibrium price and the equilibrium quantity.

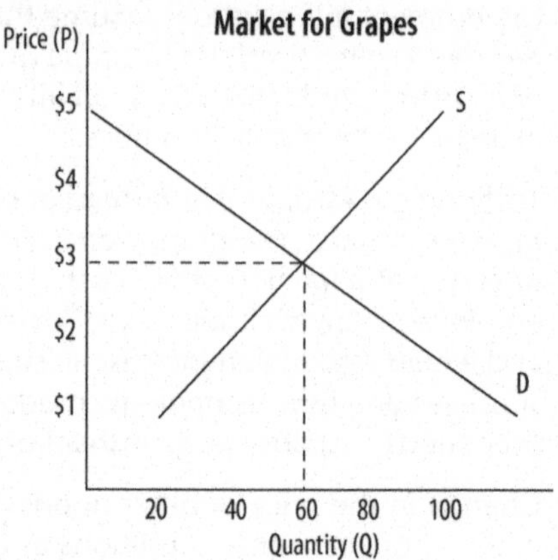


i. The grape market is in equilibrium at $3, at which 60 pounds of grapes are supplied and demanded.

ii. At $3, consumers are willing to buy the same amount of grapes that sellers are willing to provide to the market.

**B.** Disequilibrium. What would happen if sellers charged a price higher or lower than $3? Market imbalances occur when there is a disequilibrium, which result in either shortages or surpluses.

1. Surpluses. Assume, for example, grape sellers tried to charge $4 per pound of grapes. The following graph shows the effect this would have on the market.

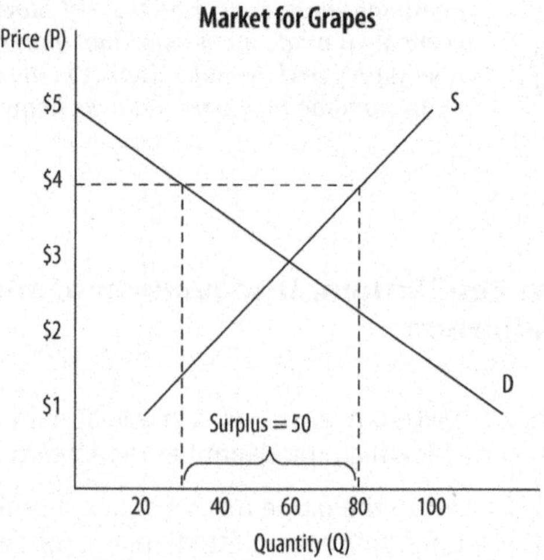

i. At $4, the market experiences a disequilibrium. The quantity supplied is greater than the quantity demanded, resulting in a surplus (or an excess supply) of grapes. Sellers wish to sell more than consumers are willing to buy.

ii. When a surplus exists, market forces tend to drive the price toward equilibrium. For example, sellers with 50 pounds of unsold produce might lower the price to incentivize consumers to buy grapes.

iii. If the price is lowered, the quantity demanded will increase, and producers will wish to sell fewer grapes. Over time, equilibrium should be restored where the quantities demanded and supplied are once again equal.

2. Shortages. If price is below equilibrium, the quantity demanded exceeds the quantity supplied, and there is a shortage in the market. The following graph shows the grape market in a disequilibrium where the price is too low.

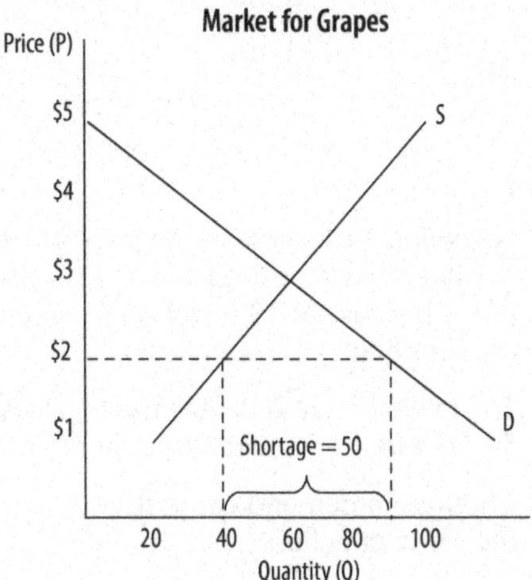


3. When a shortage exists, market forces will drive up the price toward equilibrium, leading sellers to supply more of the commodity. Buyers will demand less until the quantities demanded and supplied are equal.

C. Changes in Equilibrium. Changes in the determinants of demand and/or the determinants of supply result in a new market equilibrium price and quantity.

1. Changes in demand. Assume the prices of other available fruits fall, causing a decrease in the demand for grapes. The following graph shows how a fall in the price of substitute products would affect the market.

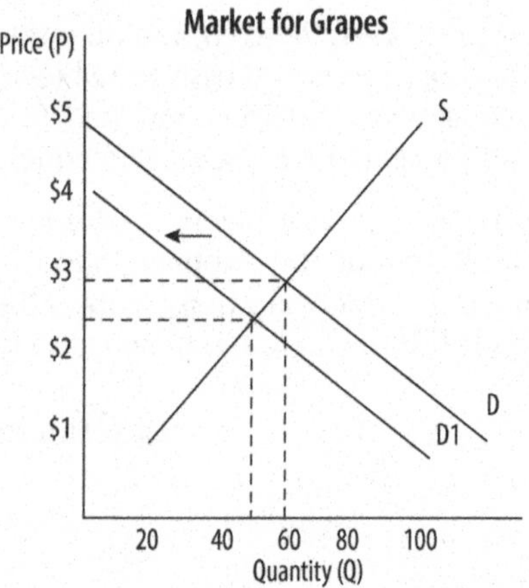


i. Following a decrease in the price of substitute goods, the demand for grapes has fallen. $3 is no longer the equilibrium price, because at $3 fewer grapes are demanded at D1 than are supplied.

ii. The fall in demand causes the equilibrium price to decrease to $2.50 and the equilibrium quantity to fall to 50 pounds.

iii. Changes in demand cause the price and quantity to change in the same direction.

- As seen above, a decrease in demand causes the equilibrium price to decrease and the equilibrium quantity to decrease.

- If demand increases, equilibrium price and equilibrium quantity both increase. Assume, for example, the health benefits of grapes become highly publicized, increasing demand. As seen below, greater demand for grapes causes both the equilibrium price and quantity to increase.

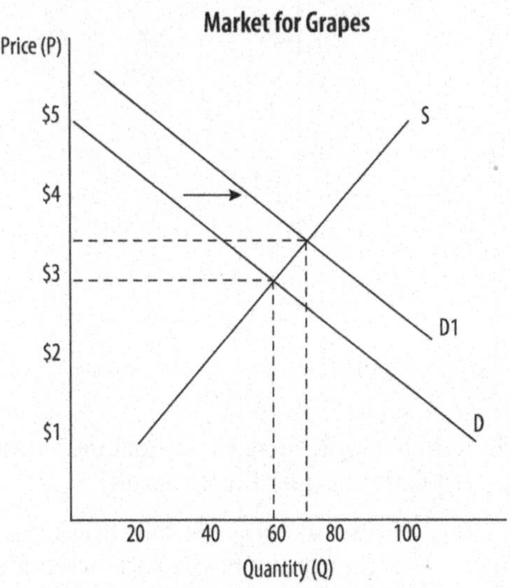


2. Changes in supply. A change in a determinant of supply will cause the supply curve to shift.
   i. When supply shifts, price and quantity change in the opposite direction.
      - For example, assume there is an increase in the wages of grape pickers, causing supply to decrease.
      - The resulting inward shift of supply causes equilibrium price to increase and equilibrium quantity to decrease.

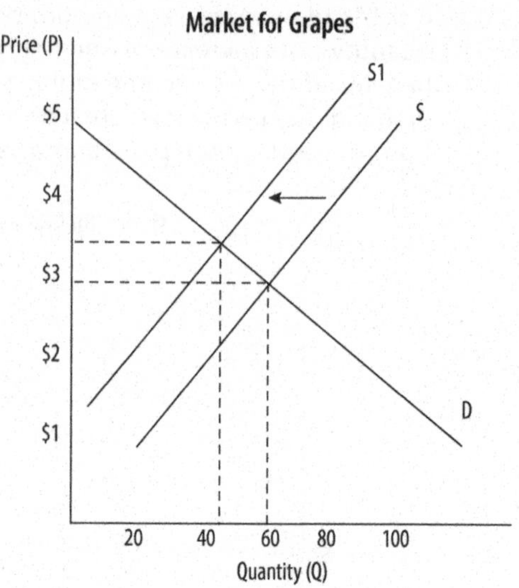


ii. When supply increases, equilibrium price decreases while equilibrium quantity increases.

➤ New technology will shift the supply curve rightward, lowering grape prices and increasing the quantity of grapes demanded.

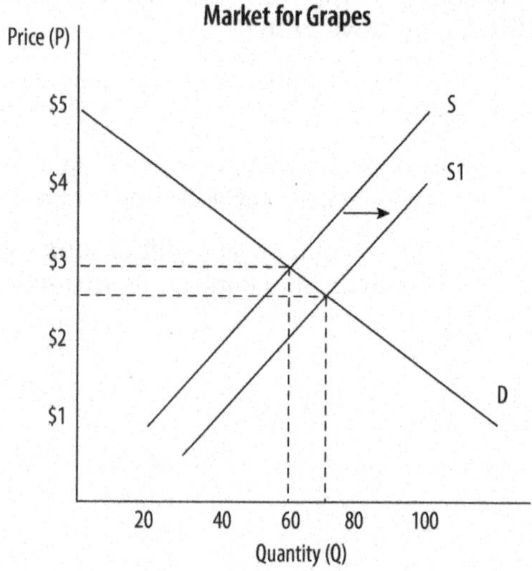

3. Changes in demand and supply. When demand and supply both shift, the change in the price and quantity will depend on the relative magnitude of each curve's shift.

    i. The impact of simultaneous shifts in demand and supply on equilibrium price and equilibrium quantity may, therefore, be indeterminate.

    ii. The following table shows the various possible effects of shifts in demand and supply on market equilibrium quantity and price.

| | **No change in supply** | **Supply increases** | **Supply decreases** |
|---|---|---|---|
| **No change in demand** | No change in quantity or price | Quantity increases, price decreases | Quantity decreases, price increases |
| **Demand increases** | Quantity increases, price increases | Quantity increases, change in price is indeterminate | Price increases, change in quantity is indeterminate |
| **Demand decreases** | Quantity decreases, price decreases | Price decreases, change in quantity is indeterminate | Quantity decreases, change in price is indeterminate |

***An AP® Macro question may not ask about demand or supply directly, but about changes in equilibrium price or quantity, and what could have caused particular changes. This would require you to combine your knowledge of the determinants of both demand and supply and apply that knowledge to find the effect of shifts in both curves. For example, "Which of the following shifts in supply and demand would definitely cause the equilibrium price to decrease and the quantity to increase?" To help you respond, you may sketch graphs on scratch paper which would help you to conclude that an increase in supply and no change in demand would result in the described outcome.***

Chapter 4

# UNIT 2 Economic Indicators and the Business Cycle

## I. The Circular Flow and GDP

**A.** Gross domestic product (GDP) is a measure of the value of a country's total final output of goods and services during a period, usually a year.

1. GDP is the most commonly referred to measure of national income.
2. Just as a household's income refers to how much a family earns in a year, and a firm's income refers to its total revenues, national income, or GDP, is the value of the total income earned by all of the nation's households.
3. GDP can also be considered a measure of the final output of the economy; the value of a nation's output is equal to its income, a concept that will be explained further below.

**B.** The circular flow of income model demonstrates how an entire country's economy operates at the most basic level.

1. In the model two agents interact in two markets: the factor market and the product market.
   - i. Households are the owners of all the factors of production in an economy, including the land, labor, capital, and entrepreneurial ability.
   - ii. Firms are formed by entrepreneurs to sell goods and services at a profit to households.
     - ➤ In a factor market, companies buy the factors of production or the resources needed to produce their goods and services.
     - ➤ These business entities combine the factors of production they obtain in the factor market to produce finished products, which are then sold in the product market.

2. The circular flow model shows how money, resources, and goods and services flow between households and firms in a hypothetical free market economy.

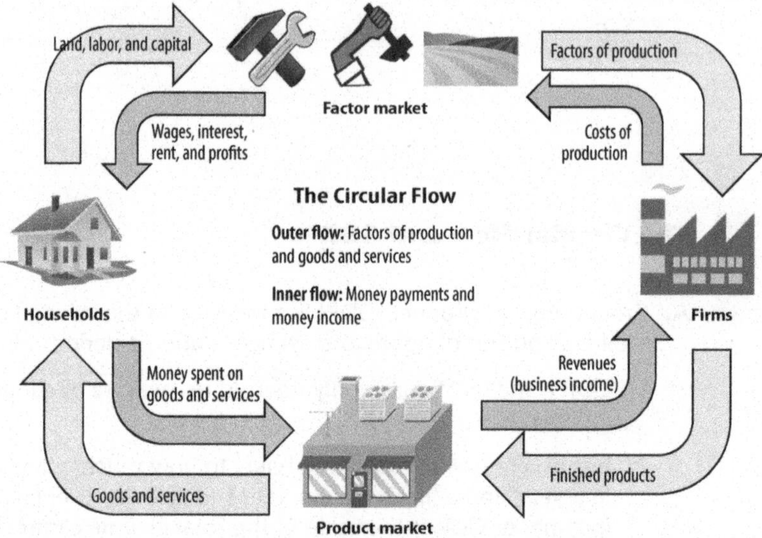


i. The outer flow in the model depicts the exchange of factors of production and goods and services between households and firms.

   ➤ Households provide land, labor, capital, and entrepreneurship to firms in the factor market for which they receive money incomes in return.

   ➤ Firms use these factors to produce finished goods and services, which are then supplied to households in the marketplace.

ii. The inner flow illustrates the flow of money between households and firms.

   ➤ Money earned by households from providing their factors of production to firms comes in the form of wages for labor, interest for capital, rent for land, and profits for entrepreneurs.

   ➤ Money firms spend on the factors of production represents their costs of production.

- Money spent by households on goods and services in the product market is earned as revenues by firms. If revenues exceed costs, firms earn a profit.

iii. Each agent in a market economy has its own reasons for engaging in exchanges with other agents.

- Households are motivated to provide their factors of production to firms by the incomes they can earn to buy desired goods and services in the marketplace.
- Firms are motivated by earning an economic profit, which is when the revenues in the product market exceed the costs in the factor market.

iv. The circular flow of money, factors of production, and goods and services represents the mutually beneficial trade that supports the market economic system.

v. The value of the goods and services sold in the marketplace in a particular period of time indicates the country's GDP.

***The circular flow model is not one you will commonly see or be asked to draw on the AP® Macro exam. So why know it? Understanding the concepts illustrated in this model, specifically the interdependence of households and firms in a market economy and the exchanges that take place in product and resource markets, is foundational to your knowledge of the other topics that will be tested on the exam. One example is why the income and expenditure approaches to GDP should be equal.***

C. Three Ways to Measure GDP. As seen in the circular flow, the money earned by households is spent on goods and services; therefore, the total value of national income equals the total value of national output.

1. The income approach to measuring GDP involves totaling all the money income households earn in a year. Total wages (W) plus total interest income (I) plus total rental income (R) plus all the profits earned by households (P) will equal the country's GDP.

   i. For instance, assume a country produces cars using only domestically sourced raw materials.

$$GDP = W + I + R + P$$

   ii. In the income approach, the auto industry's contribution to GDP would be measured by adding up all the income earned by the workers (wages), landlords (rent), shareholders (profit), and financiers (interest) involved in providing labor, land, entrepreneurship, and capital to the automobile industry.

iii. The incomes of those involved in all other domestic industries would then be added to the auto industry's income to determine the country's total GDP.

2. The expenditures approach combines the four components of a country's aggregate expenditures.

   i. Total consumer spending (C) plus total government spending (G) plus total business investment (I) plus export revenues (X) minus import spending (M) will equal the country's GDP.

$$GDP = C + I + G + (X - M)$$

   ii. To illustrate, the auto industry's contribution to GDP would be measured by adding the amount spent on cars by the country's households (consumption), businesses (investment), the government (government spending), and foreigners (exports), then subtracting the amount spent by domestic consumers on foreign cars (imports).

3. The value-added approach measures the amount spent during each stage of the production of an economy's final output, adding up the value added at each stage of production.

   i. For example, the auto industry's contribution to GDP is measured by adding the amount spent on steel, rubber, glass, and other raw materials plus labor by auto makers, the amount spent on distribution, marketing, and sales by their dealers, and all other intermediate spending needed to bring the finished cars to market.

   ii. However, the amount spent by consumers would not be included in the value-added approach, as that would result in double counting, since most of the value of the car has already been measured at the time of sale.

**D.** Importance of Expenditures Approach. The AP® Macroeconomics course focuses on the expenditures approach in measuring GDP. So, it is important to understand what each component of a country's expenditures actually measures and the factors that can cause each type of expenditure to change.

1. Consumption includes all household spending on finished goods and services. Consumer goods generally fall into one of two

categories: consumer durables and non-durable (or consumable) goods.

i. Durables are generally goods bought and used on an ongoing basis over months or years. Examples are cars, home appliances, consumer electronics, furniture, and tools.

ii. Nondurables, or consumable goods are bought and consumed over a short time. Groceries, fuel, medications, office supplies, clothing, and footwear are examples of nondurable goods.

iii. Nearly all household spending is recorded in the consumption component of GDP. The only exception is household investments in a real asset such as housing. A household purchase of real estate or a new home is considered an investment.

iv. The purchase of financial assets like stocks, bonds, and other financial instruments is excluded in the measurement of a country's GDP. These are purely financial transactions for which no goods or services were produced or changed hands.

v. Factors that influence the level of consumer spending on durable and nondurable goods and services include:

- Taxes. Increased taxation (either on income or on consumption) generally will reduce the level of household consumption, while lower taxes will result in more consumption.
- Consumer confidence. The sentiment among consumers around future income levels will affect current consumption. If households expect their income to rise, they tend to consume more durable goods (such as new cars) today. On the other hand, if there is uncertainty about future income, households tend to reduce current consumption.
- Expected inflation or deflation. When higher prices are anticipated (inflation), households tend to consume more today. If prices are expected to fall (deflation), households tend to postpone consumption today, causing GDP to fall.
- Interest rates. The interest rate is the opportunity cost of spending money. Higher interest rates make consumption less attractive because households can earn more income by putting money in the bank. Lower interest rates lead to more consumption because there is less income to be earned by saving money.

Usually, a change in any of the determinants of consumption just described will impact household consumption, resulting in an increase or a decrease in GDP.

2. Investment is the component of GDP that includes all business spending on capital equipment and technology and household spending on new housing or real estate.

   i. Some business investments might look like the durable goods that households consume. The difference is that when a firm buys a car, for example, it is intended for use in the production of or provision of a good or service.

   ii. If an individual buys a new Toyota Prius, it is considered consumption; but if a taxi company buys a new Prius, it is considered an investment.

      - A taxi company intends to use the new car as a factor of production in its business of providing transportation services (as a producer).
      - On the other hand, the individual will use the car to carry her kids to and from soccer practice and for family road trips (as a consumer).

   iii. Other examples of investment spending by businesses include:

      - An apparel company purchases new sewing machines.
      - An airline buys four new passenger jets.
      - A school invests in new laptop computers for its teachers.
      - A retail chain puts solar panels on the roofs of all of its outlets.
      - A young couple buys a new home.

   In the preceding examples, each decision to spend money comes with the expectation that income will be generated through the investment, either through the increased ability to provide goods or services or to earn rental income or capital gains.

   iv. Factors influencing the level of investment in an economy include:

      - Interest rates. As with consumption, there is an inverse relationship between the interest rate and the level of investment in a country.
         - When interest rates decrease, the opportunity cost of investing in new capital equipment or buying a new home

decreases, and households and firms are likely to invest more.

– At higher interest rates, the cost of borrowing money to finance investments is higher and the amount of investment is likely to fall.

➤ Business confidence.

– If businesses feel optimistic about the future, they are likely to invest more now in order to increase their capacity to produce more output.

– Conversely, if prospects for future sales are bleak, businesses will reduce current investment to prepare for less demand for their output later on.

➤ Expected inflation or deflation.

– Much like consumers, businesses will increase investment if higher prices are expected in the future (inflation). Expected inflation means businesses can expect higher profits tomorrow, so it is in their best interest to invest in production capacity today.

– The expectation of lower prices (deflation) will lead businesses to cut back on current investment and reduce output as prices fall.

➤ Business taxes and government regulation. The level of government intervention in the form of taxation and regulation can influence the level of investment in a country.

– Generally, lower business taxes and less government regulation will lead to more investment.

– Higher taxes and more burdensome regulations will reduce investment in the economy.

Changes in any of the preceding factors can lead to a change in the level of investment in a country and either an increase or a decrease in its GDP.

3. Government spending includes all public sector (local, state, and federal) spending on final goods and services in the economy.

   i. Government spending includes defense, police, fire, education, healthcare, infrastructure, the criminal justice system, and other public services and goods.

   ii. The level of spending relative to total GDP varies widely by country.

- In the U.S., total government spending (local, state, and federal) makes up roughly a third of the U.S. GDP.
- Put another way, one out of every three dollars spent and earned in the U.S. was spent by the government.

iii. A dollar spent by government must be either printed, earned, or borrowed by the government.

- Revenues come primarily from taxes on income and consumption.
  - Income taxes are usually progressive, meaning they increase in percentage as households' incomes increase.
  - Consumption taxes, such as the sales tax, are regressive, meaning they place a smaller burden on higher-income earners (who save a larger percentage of their income) than they do on lower-income earners (who spend a larger percentage of their income).

iv. When a government spends more than it earns in tax revenues, it experiences a budget deficit. On the rare occasion that governments earn more from taxes than they spend, they experience a budget surplus.

v. Government debt is the sum of all past budget deficits and surpluses.

- Every year that the government runs a deficit, its debt increases.
- When the budget is in surplus, its debt decreases.

vi. Changes in government spending and taxation will affect GDP. Fiscal policy refers to the government's use of taxation and government spending to either stimulate or contract the level of economic activity in a country.

- All else equal, an increase in government spending and/or a decrease in taxation causes GDP to increase.
- A decrease in government spending and/or an increase in taxation causes GDP to decrease.

4. Exports are the goods and services a country sells to the rest of the world. Imports are the goods and services that a country buys from the rest of the world.

   i. An increase in foreign spending on a country's exports, all else equal, causes the country's GDP to increase, while falling exports causes GDP to decrease.

ii. Import spending, on the other hand, damages a country's economy since the money spent on imports is earned by producers in another country.

   - When domestic consumers buy imports, there is no contribution to the country's GDP, since the domestic expenditure is offset by the leakage (M).
   - While the purchase of domestic goods and services increases GDP because it increases domestic production, the purchase of imported goods and services has no direct impact on GDP.

iii. Export revenues minus import expenditures (X – M) determine net exports.

iv. Factors that can cause a change in a country's net exports include:

   - Exchange rate. All else equal, a decrease in the exchange rate of a country's currency (the price of the currency against other countries' currencies) will cause net exports to increase, as the country's goods get cheaper to foreigners and they buy more of them while imports become more expensive to domestic consumers and they buy less of them. An increase in the exchange rate causes net exports to fall.
   - Incomes abroad. When foreign incomes rise, a country can expect its net exports to increase as foreigners are likely to demand more of the country's exports. If incomes abroad fall, net exports tend to fall as the demand for a country's exports decrease.
   - Relative price levels.
     - When a country's goods appear relatively cheap to potential trading partners, demand for its exports tends to increase. For example, if prices in Canada rise more rapidly than prices in the U.S., over time Canadians will demand more American goods, boosting U.S. net exports and U.S. GDP.
     - On the other hand, if U.S. prices rise more rapidly than Canadian prices, then over time American consumers will demand more Canadian goods, and U.S. net exports will fall.

A change in any of the factors above will cause net exports to change and lead to either an increase or a decrease in gross domestic product.

***The terms "national output" and "national income" are used interchangeably on the AP® Macro exam. The most commonly one referenced to measure a nation's output and income, however, is the expenditures approach: C+ I + G + Xn.***

## II. Limitations of GDP

**A.** GDP is a useful indicator of a nation's economic performance. It is widely relied on by economists, politicians, policymakers, and the media. GDP allows for a comparison of the relative sizes of different economies. For example, in the United States:

1. GDP is roughly twice the size of China's, despite China's much larger population.
2. Dividing GDP by the population results in GDP per capita. This figure tells us how many goods and services the average person consumes in a country. Per capita GDP is a strong indicator of relative income. Because U.S. GDP is larger and its population smaller, the average U.S. household earns a higher income than the average household in China.
3. When GDP grows faster than the population, living standards tend to increase since average incomes rise.

**B.** Limitations of GDP. As we can see, GDP is a useful measure for means of international comparisons of average incomes. However, GDP does have limitations:

1. GDP ignores all social aspects of human life. These include income distribution, access to healthcare and education, life expectancy, gender equality, religious freedom, and human rights.
2. Non-market transactions are not included in GDP. If money is not exchanged during a transaction, then its value is not part of GDP, including the following:

    i. Labor of homemakers, as well as work done by owners on their own property.

    ii. Value added to an asset by volunteer work in the community and elsewhere.

3. Black market transactions are not included in GDP. Some economies have large informal sectors in which transactions are not reported in order to evade taxes.
   i. If the government is unaware of these transactions, then they are not part of the GDP.
   ii. Actual economies are much larger than what their official GDP figures show because so much economic activity goes unnoticed by the government.
4. GDP does not reflect improved product quality.
   i. While a country's GDP increases, the living standards of its households could increase by even more if the quality of the country's output is improving faster than its GDP increases.
   ii. For example, the technology in the pocket of a typical American in the form of a smartphone far exceeds that on most people's desktops in the 1990s.
      - However, a smartphone today may cost less than a mid-range desktop computer in 1999, meaning its contribution to GDP is no greater than that clunky old computer.
      - Thus, GDP figures may underestimate public well-being since they do not account for technological improvements.
5. GDP does not put a market value/cost on the environment. Higher GDP may be accompanied by environmental degradation, which may diminish the quality of life while increasing incomes.
6. GDP does not indicate the best combination of goods and services to be produced.
   i. If the economy is producing more guns, then its GDP increases just as it would if more textbooks were printed.
   ii. However, more textbooks would likely lead to an improvement in human capital and the potential for higher incomes among the country's households, while more guns may lead to more violence and a diminished standard of living.
   iii. The GDP figure will not distinguish between "good" output and "bad" output, limiting its effectiveness for communicating information about social welfare.

## III. Unemployment

**A.** Unemployment is the state of a person who is not working but is actively seeking a job. Being "unemployed" is a technical term. "Not having a job" does not mean someone is unemployed; one must be of working age (usually 15 years old or above) and actively seeking work to be considered unemployed.

1. The unemployment rate is the percentage of the total labor force (TLF) that is unemployed.

   i. The rate is measured by dividing the number of workers who are unemployed by the number of workers that are either employed or unemployed (which together make up the total labor force) and multiplying the result by 100.

   $$\text{Unemployment rate} = \frac{\text{\# of workers unemployed}}{\text{total labor force (\# unemployed + \# employed)}} \times 100$$

   ii. The labor force includes the non-institutionalized (not in prison or hospitalized), civilian (not in the military) adult population (at least 15 years old in most countries) who are working part time or full time or that are unemployed.

   iii. Adults who are not seeking jobs or who are engaged in other activities such as pursuing education, volunteering, traveling, or voluntarily taking time off from work are not part of the labor force.

   iv. The following table shows the employment figures for the fictional country, Amazonia.

| Year | Non-institutionalized, civilian, adult population (millions) | Number of people employed (millions) | Number of people unemployed (millions) |
|---|---|---|---|
| 2019 | 200 | 100 | 20 |

   ➤ Amazonia's unemployment rate can be calculated with these numbers. The total labor force (TLF) in Amazonia includes the employed and the unemployed population.

   $$TLF = 100\text{m} + 20\text{m} = 120 \text{ million}$$

- To calculate the unemployment rate, find the percentage of the labor force that is unemployed.

$$\text{Unemployment rate} = \frac{20 \text{ m}}{200 \text{ m}} \times 100 = 16.7\%$$

- Unemployment in Amazonia is 16.7%. This means that out of every one hundred adults who are active in the labor force, nearly 17 are looking for work, but unable to find it.

2. Importance of the unemployment rate. A country's unemployment rate is a barometer of the economy's health.

   i. A high unemployment rate could be the result of either a negative macroeconomic shock, such as a fall in total demand for the country's output or a spike in production costs, or it could be evidence that the economy is simply underutilizing its resources (producing inside its PPC).

   ii. A low unemployment rate is evidence that the economy is utilizing its resources more efficiently or has experienced a positive economic shock such as an increase in total demand or an increase in productivity. Low unemployment indicates an economy is producing close to or on its PPC.

      - Rising unemployment usually accompanies falling GDP and indicates that an economy is in a recession.
      - Falling unemployment usually accompanies rising GDP and either a recovery from a past economic downturn or economic growth (an increase in long-run potential output of the economy).

3. Labor force participation rate. Another indicator of a country's labor market performance is the *labor force participation rate* (LFPR), which measures the percentage of the eligible population that is participating in the labor force.

   i. The LFPR is found by dividing the number of employed and unemployed by the eligible adult population and multiplying the result by 100.

$$\text{LFPR} = \frac{\text{\# of people employed} + \text{\# of people unemployed}}{\text{eligible adult population}} \times 100$$

   ii. Using data for Amazonia from the preceding table, we can calculate the country's LFPR:

$$\text{LFPR} = \frac{100 \text{ million} + 20 \text{ million}}{200 \text{ million}} \times 100 = 60\%$$

60% of the adults eligible to work (non-institutionalized civilians) are either employed or are actively seeking employment in Amazonia.

iii. The LFPR is an indicator of economic performance that is less often discussed than the more popular unemployment rate.

- When an economy is performing well (has strong demand, high productivity, rising incomes and output) persons who might otherwise have chosen not to participate (either stay at home, pursue higher education, or retire early) are drawn to the labor market by rising wages.
- However, during recessions, labor force participation tends to decline as unemployed workers become discouraged and give up on the job search, or those who might have joined the labor force choose to stay in school or retire early.
- An increase in the LFPR may also result from more opportunities for groups that were historically discriminated against by employers, such as women or minorities.
- The graph below shows U.S. labor force participation from 1950 to present.

- From 1950–2000, labor force participation generally increased as women became more active in the U.S. labor market.
- From the recession of 2001 and continuing during the "Great Recession" of 2009, the U.S. LFPR declined from its peak near 68% to around 63% by 2015.
- The fall in output and high unemployment in the years that followed the 2009 recession resulted in millions of Americans first losing their jobs and becoming unemployed, and then, after a prolonged job search, becoming discouraged and dropping out of the labor force.

– As of mid-2019, the country's LFPR had remained at around 62.8% for over four years.

4. Limitations of the unemployment rate. The unemployment rate, like GDP, is a valuable indicator of a country's economic performance. Generally, a falling unemployment rate indicates improved economic performance while a rising unemployment rate indicates economic decline. However, there are limitations to the simple measure of unemployment that may result in its understating or overstating the level of joblessness in the economy.
   i. For example, a part-time worker is considered by the government to be employed, regardless of whether that worker is employed to the level she desires. Even if a part-time worker is actively seeking full-time employment, she is not considered unemployed.
   ii. Additionally, workers who are overqualified for their work and cannot find jobs for which their qualifications are commensurate are considered "employed" by the government.
      - For example, a recent immigrant with a law degree and years of experience as a lawyer may be unable to find work in a law firm, so he may work at a bookstore instead.
      - Although he is searching for a job at a law firm, the official employment statistics consider the individual fully employed.
      - The preceding example illustrates underemployment, a condition not considered in official unemployment figures.
   iii. Another limitation of the unemployment rate is that as output increases in a country coming out of a recession, it is possible that the unemployment rate can actually rise.
      - Consider the example of discouraged workers following the U.S. 2009 recession. By 2019 the unemployment rate in the U.S. reached 3.7% while LFPR had declined to 62.8%.
      - If eligible adults who dropped out of the labor force after 2009 were to become encouraged and re-enter the labor market, they would go from being "not included" in the unemployment measurement to "unemployed," increasing the official unemployment rate.
      - In other words, economic growth and a booming labor market can actually lead to an increase in the unemployment rate as discouraged workers begin looking for jobs again. In this case, the unemployment rate would overstate the problem of joblessness in the economy.

5. Types of unemployment. There are several types of unemployment that economists measure, some of which are considered less desirable than others.

   i. Frictional unemployment describes workers who are in between jobs or are entering the labor market for the first time.

      - For example, a worker who quits his job and relocates his family to a new geographic area must then look for a new job once he's settled in their new home.
        - Such a worker is considered frictionally unemployed during the period in which he seeks a new job.
        - Another example is a college graduate who sends out résumés and interviews for jobs in her field of study.
        - While the graduate pursues her first "real" job, she is considered frictionally unemployed.
      - Frictional unemployment is typically short-term and often voluntary, meaning that a worker may have quit her job to pursue a better paying one or a job in a new locale.
      - Importantly, frictionally unemployed workers have skills that are in demand; therefore, their period of unemployment is likely to be short.

   ii. Structural unemployment occurs when a worker whose skills are no longer in demand by employers because of the changing structure of the economy, becomes unemployed.

      - Notably, structural unemployment arises when new technologies lead to a fall in the demand for certain types of labor.
        - As factories adopted high-tech robots throughout the 1990s and 2000s, demand for manufacturing workers fell, and millions became structurally unemployed across the developed world.
        - As globalization has opened most of Asia to the world's supply chains, lower-wage workers (and often more skilled workers) in many emerging market economies from China to India to Thailand and Vietnam have enjoyed rising employment. Conversely, their counterparts in the U.S. and Europe have become structurally unemployed.

- The two main causes of structural unemployment are improvements in production technologies and globalization of supply chains.
  - In the era of fiber optic internet and almost universal connectivity, structural unemployment is increasingly affecting workers not just in manufacturing, but in the service sectors of the economy as well.
  - Artificial intelligence and machine learning are allowing not just desktop computers, but also smartphones, to perform the tasks that until recently may have required a knowledgeable worker to perform.
  - High speed internet has allowed consumers in more developed countries to hire the services of skilled workers in developing countries for tasks ranging from graphic design to computer coding to paralegal work and diagnostic image analysis in the healthcare field.
  - As these service sector jobs have become increasingly outsourced to places like India, the Philippines, and other lower-wage countries, well-educated workers in the West have begun to experience rising levels of structural unemployment.
- The existence of structural unemployment is not necessarily a sign of a weak or struggling economy.
  - It is natural for a country to see structural unemployment in various sectors as technology and globalization impact the social and economic lives of citizens.
  - Overall the trend has been one of progress, and while there are those who lose jobs overall, improvements in technology and globalization tend to create more winners than losers.
- It is up to institutions in a country experiencing structural unemployment to adapt and retrain or better prepare workers with the skills that are in demand by employers not just today, but in the future.

iii. Cyclical unemployment arises when workers whose skills would normally be in demand in a healthy economy lose their jobs because of a downturn in the business cycle (a recession). Never desirable, it happens from a fall in total demand in the economy resulting from falling consumption, investment, government spending, or net exports.

- Assuming labor markets were perfectly flexible, a fall in demand for labor would cause the wage rate workers are paid to fall, leading some workers to leave the labor market and mitigating the decline in labor demand.
- However, for various reasons wages tend to stabilize in the short run, and as a result a fall in labor demand does not always cause a fall in the wage rate, causing a disequilibrium in the labor market in which more workers are looking for jobs than there are available openings.
- Cyclical unemployment can be remedied when one of two things happen:
  - The wage rate must decrease and adjust to the level of total demand in the economy, *or* demand must increase and restore the level of employment at the country's full employment level.
  - In Chapter 5, aggregate demand and aggregate supply analysis will be used to further examine the causes and solutions to cyclical unemployment, including the use of fiscal policy and monetary policy by a country's government and central bank.

6. Natural rate of unemployment. Some forms of unemployment are considered a "natural" part of a healthy economy.
   i. Economists consider every country to have a natural rate of unemployment (NRU), which is the unemployment rate that should prevail when the country is producing at its full employment level of output.
      - Even in a robust economy, a country will experience some unemployment.
      - It is normal for workers to come and go from their jobs as they seek better jobs or enter the labor force for the first time, both of which cause frictional unemployment.
      - It is natural for a country to experience changes in technology and expand its trading relationships with other countries, both of which cause structural unemployment.
      - The NRU, therefore, includes structurally and frictionally unemployed workers.

$$NRU = \frac{\#\text{ of structurally unemployed} + \#\text{ of frictionally unemployed}}{TLF} \times 100$$

***Be able to determine what type of unemployment someone is experiencing based on a description. The AP® Macro exam may state, "James has just finished school and is looking for his first job. James is . . ." and then asks you to choose from the different types of unemployment. You must be able to conclude that James is frictionally unemployed. Other examples of cyclical and structural unemployment may be given to test whether you can distinguish between types of unemployment.***

ii. Not considered natural, on the other hand, is cyclical unemployment.

- When workers lose their jobs because of a fall in aggregate demand and a recession, it is a sign that a country's economy is producing below its full employment level.
- The country suffers from a lack of demand and inflexible wages, meaning that there is a disequilibrium in the labor market.

iii. The "ideal" level of unemployment for a country to target is its NRU. That percentage varies from country to country.

- In the past 30+ years, U.S. economists estimated the NRU to be between 4% and 6%.
- During the "Great Recession" of 2009, unemployment in the U.S. climbed to 10%, evidence that around 5% of the country's labor force became cyclically unemployed because of the recession.
- In mid-2019, unemployment in the U.S. dipped as low as 3.7%.
- Economists have debated whether the country's NRU was actually decreasing in 2019 or whether the economy was overheating (e.g., temporarily producing beyond its full employment level).

*The NRU exists when an economy is at its full-employment level of output. This is a major point of confusion for students who often mistakenly assume that full employment corresponds with zero percent unemployment. This is incorrect; in fact, the NRU is the desired level of unemployment in an economy, since having some unemployed workers leaves the economy room to grow in the short run.*

iv. The natural rate of unemployment can gradually change over time from things such as changes in labor force characteristics.

- Factors that cause the level of frictional or structural unemployment to change will cause the natural rate of unemployment to change.
- For example, if a country's labor force becomes more highly skilled, then the level of structural unemployment will decrease, the NRU will decrease, and the country's potential output will increase as a result.

*Be prepared to calculate the unemployment rate from a set of data. For example, a question may read "Assume in a hypothetical economy the following: 800 people are employed full time, 150 are employed part time, 50 are unemployed, and 50 are discouraged workers and have quit the job search. What is the unemployment rate?" This problem requires not only a simple calculation, but also the definition of unemployment, discouraged workers, and knowledge of who is considered employed. If you know all of this, the unemployment rate would be* $\frac{50}{1{,}000} = 0.05 \times 100$ *or 5%.*

## IV. Price Indices and Inflation

**A.** Price Index Defined. The price index measures changes in the general price level over time. Economists use different price indices to measure how the prices of different categories of a country's output change over time.

1. The consumer price index, or CPI, measures the change in income a consumer would need in order to maintain the same standard of

living over time under a new set of prices as under the original set of prices.

i. This is done by measuring the cost of a fixed basket of goods and services in a given year relative to a base year.

ii. The CPI is used to calculate the inflation rate or the rate of change in the average price level of consumer goods and services between two periods of time.

iii. The CPI for a particular year is the price of a basket of goods in that year divided by the price of the same basket in a base year. Inflation is the rate of change in the CPI between the two years.

iv. Let's imagine a country where the typical consumer only buys three goods: pizza, haircuts, and wine. The following table shows the prices of the three goods over three years.

| Good or service | Price in 2019 | Price in 2020 | Price in 2021 |
|---|---|---|---|
| Pizza | $10 | $10.50 | $12 |
| Haircuts | $20 | $19 | $22 |
| Wine | $8 | $10 | $9 |
| **Total basket price** | $38 | $39.50 | $43 |

v. Assume 2019 is the base year in calculating the CPIs for 2019, 2020, and 2021:

$$\text{CPI for 2019} = \frac{\text{Price of the basket of goods in 2019}}{\text{Price of the basket in base year}} \times 100$$

$$= \frac{38}{38} \times 100 = 100$$

$$\text{CPI for 2020} = \frac{\text{Price of the basket of goods in 2020}}{\text{Price of the basket in base year}} \times 100$$

$$= \frac{39.5}{38} \times 100 = 103.9$$

$$\text{CPI for 2021} = \frac{\text{Price of the basket of goods in 2021}}{\text{Price of the basket in base year}}$$

$$= \frac{43}{38} \times 100 = 113.2$$

vi. The CPI for 2019 is 100 because 2019 is our base year. The price of the same basket in 2020 is $39.50, which when divided by the base year price and multiplied by 100 results in a CPI of 103.9. For 2021, the price index has once again increased to 113.2.

***Practice calculating inflation using a price index. This may be required for both the multiple-choice and free-response sections of the AP® Macro exam.***

**B.** Inflation Measurement. The inflation rate is measured as the rate of change in the CPI between two periods of time.

1. While inflation can be measured quarterly or even monthly, it is standard to report inflation annually.

2. To do so, we must divide the change in the CPI between two years (year 1 and 2) by the original CPI (year 1) and multiply the result by 100.

$$\text{Inflation rate} = \frac{\text{CPI in year 2} - \text{CPI in year 1}}{\text{CPI in year 1}} \times 100$$

3. Using the preceding CPI data we can calculate inflation between 2019 and 2020 and between 2020 and 2021:

   i. Inflation between 2019 and 2020 = $\frac{103.9 - 100}{100} \times 100 = 3.9\%$

   ii. Inflation between 2020 and 2021 = $\frac{113.2 - 103.9}{103.9} \times 100 = 8.95\%$

4. This country experienced inflation between all three years, first a moderate rate of 3.9% and then an accelerated rate of 8.95%.

   i. The price of a typical good purchased by consumers rose by almost 9% between 2020 and 2021.

   ii. Another way to say this is that a typical consumer would need to experience a 9% increase in nominal income in order to maintain the same standard of living in 2021 as she enjoyed in 2020.

C. Nominal vs. Real Variables. Through our preceding analysis, we can see the problem with high inflation.

1. Real income. An inflation rate higher than that at which nominal incomes increase leads to a decreased standard of living.

    i. In other words, real wages and other variables (such as interest rates) are nominal variables deflated by the price level.

    ii. For example, assume Julia is a retired school teacher who receives a retirement pension from the state.

    - Her pension grows at a fixed rate of 2% per year, regardless of the rate of inflation.
    - If inflation is below 2%, then Julia's *real income* would grow year to year.
    - But if inflation is greater than 2%, then her real income will fall as prices rise faster than her income, making her unable to maintain the same standard of living over time.

    iii. The percentage change in a worker's real income is the percentage change in her nominal income minus the inflation rate. Assume inflation is just 0.5%. The change in Julia's real income can be calculated:

    Change in real income = change in nominal income – inflation rate = 2% – 0.5% = 1.5%

    - Julia is 1.5% "richer" in real terms when inflation is just 0.5%. But what if inflation accelerates to 4%? Julia's real income will now be affected as follows:

    Change in real income = 2% – 4% = –2%

    - Julia would feel 2% poorer in real terms in the face of 4% inflation.

2. Real interest rates. A similar calculation can be applied to interest rates. The interest rate is the "price of money."

    i. For a saver, interest is the proportion of the total amount saved that is earned in income each year.

    ii. For a borrower, interest is the proportion of the total amount borrowed paid to the lender each year.

    iii. The real interest rate in an economy is the nominal interest rate minus the inflation rate. (The nominal interest rate is the actual interest rate before taking inflation into account.)

    Real interest rate = nominal interest rate – inflation rate

- Consider an individual who has just put a $1,000 inheritance into a savings account offering her a 2.5% annual interest rate.
  - After a year, our saver will have $1,025 in her bank account.
  - Whether or not her savings will be *worth* 2.5% more, however, depends on the inflation rate.
  - Much like the worker who earns a 2% annual pay increase, the nominal interest rate must be adjusted for inflation to determine the real interest rate.
  - As long as the inflation rate is lower than the nominal interest rate, the real interest rate will be positive.
  - But if inflation is higher than the nominal interest rate, then the real return on savings will actually be negative. Assume inflation is 4.5%. Our saver now faces a real interest rate of:

$$\text{Real interest rate} = 2.5\% - 4.5\% = -2\%$$

  - Our saver would actually see the real value of her savings *decrease* by 2% a year if inflation were 4.5% and she earns an interest rate of only 2.5%.

iv. Savers are made worse off by inflation. Borrowers, however, are actually better off.

- An individual who borrows in an economy where the inflation rate is higher than the nominal interest rate benefits because the money borrowed is essentially worth more than the money repaid.
- Assuming an individual borrows at a 2.5% interest rate when inflation is 4.5%, this borrower can expect to pay a real interest rate of –2%.

**D.** Shortcomings of the Consumer Price Index. The CPI has flaws as a macroeconomic indicator, such as substitution bias, which observes that consumers may switch to cheaper goods when goods included in the CPI increase in price.

1. For example, assume that the price of digital single-lens reflex cameras (DSLRs), which are measured and included in the "recreation" category of the U.S. CPI, for some reason doubles

in a particular year, pulling up the overall CPI ("photographic equipment" makes up 0.039% of the U.S. CPI[1]).

i. While the CPI and the inflation rate increase, the actual impact on consumers may be overstated as most people would simply avoid buying new DSLRs and instead use the cameras on their smartphones.

2. But consider what would happen if pork prices rose because of the spread of swine flu. Pork makes up 0.38% of the U.S. CPI.

i. As pork prices rise, the overall CPI and inflation increase, but consumers may simply switch from pork to chicken, causing the CPI to overstate the true inflation rate as experienced by consumers.

## V. Costs of Inflation

A. Effects of Inflation on Different Stakeholders.

1. Inflation reduces real wages and reduces the real interest rate, making those on fixed incomes and savers with fixed interest rates worse off.

2. Another effect inflation has on society is the redistribution of wealth from one group to another.

i. Businesses typically like inflation, as it means the prices of the goods they sell increase over time, allowing them to enjoy higher profits.

ii. Consumers, on the other hand, find their wallets squeezed in an inflationary environment and must face tough choices on how to spend their shrinking dollar.

iii. Another redistributive effect of inflation is the transfer of wealth from lenders to borrowers.

➤ An individual or a country with large debt benefits from inflation, especially when the interest rate owed on that debt is fixed or rises more slowly than the inflation rate.

---

[1] Source: "Relative importance of Components in the Consumer Price Index—U.S. city average," The Bureau of Labor Statistics, *https://www.bls.gov/cpi/tables/relative-importance/2016.pdf.*

   iv. Rising prices mean the value of money decreases, including the value of the money a debtor owes his or her lenders. Money borrowed is worth more than money repaid.

3. On a macro level, inflation erodes a country's international competitiveness as domestic prices rise making the country's exports less attractive to foreign consumers.
   i. Over time, falling demand for its exports will reduce the value of a country's currency (its exchange rate), making it harder for domestic consumers to afford imports, further contributing to higher prices at home.

4. Inflation can create a self-perpetuating cycle in which the expectation of higher prices in the future drives consumers and producers to spend more money now, realizing that its value will only decrease tomorrow.
   i. The result could be an inflationary spiral where expected inflation leads to an increase in consumption and investment, causing inflation.
   ii. In turn, this leads workers to demand higher nominal wages and suppliers to charge more for raw materials and other inputs, causing even more inflation.

5. Due to the many costs inflation imposes on different stakeholders in society, nearly every country's central bank aims for a target inflation rate, usually between 1.5% and 3%.
   i. When inflation dips below or rises above this target range, central bankers will pursue either contractionary or expansionary monetary policies to restore inflation within the target range.
   ii. The role of central banks in controlling inflation through monetary policy is explored in Chapter 6.

***Knowing who benefits and who suffers from inflation is important. The AP® Macro exam often asks questions about the effects of unanticipated inflation on savers, borrowers, creditors, and so on, to see if you understand how rising prices affect real interest rates.***

## VI. Real vs. Nominal GDP

**A.** Nominal GDP measures how much is spent on a country's output in a year.

1. It is the value of output produced in the prices for that year.
   - i. For example, if the fictional country Dairyland produces only butter, then the country's nominal GDP will be the total quantity of butter produced in a year multiplied by the price of butter.
   - ii. Let's assume one million pounds of butter is produced at a price of $5 per pound. Dairyland's nominal GDP is $5 million.
2. Nominal GDP increases when either the quantity of output increases or when prices increase.
   - i. For example, if Dairyland were more efficient and produced 1.1 million pounds of butter next year, even if the price remained $5 its nominal GDP would increase to 1.1 million pounds multiplied by $5 per pound, or $5.5 million.
   - ii. But what if its output remained the same and the price of butter increased to $5.50 per pound? This would also cause nominal GDP to increase, from $5 million to $5.50 × 1 million pounds, or $5.5 million.
3. Because nominal GDP can change when prices change, it is not a very good indicator of how much a country's real output of goods and services changes from year to year.

**B.** Real GDP measures the value of a nation's output in prices from a base year. By doing so, changes in the price level are ignored and the GDP figure reflects only whether actual output has increased or decreased over time.

1. If the price level increases (inflation), real GDP will be lower than the nominal GDP.
2. If the price level decreases (deflation), real GDP will be higher than the nominal GDP.

C. Measurement of Nominal and Real GDP. To calculate GDP, consider the level of output and the prices of all the output in a country in a period of time.

1. Measuring nominal GDP. Study the output and price data for Dairyland in 2019 and 2020 in the following table:

| Output in 2019 | Quantity produced in 2019 | Price in 2019 | Total value of output 2019 |
|---|---|---|---|
| Butter | 10 | $2 | $20 |
| Cheese | 20 | $2 | $40 |
| Yogurt | 5 | $10 | $50 |
| Nominal GDP in 2019 | | | $110 |

| Output in 2020 | Quantity produced in 2020 | Price in 2020 | Total value of output 2020 |
|---|---|---|---|
| Butter | 12 | $2.50 | $30 |
| Cheese | 25 | $3 | $75 |
| Yogurt | 5 | $11 | $55 |
| Nominal GDP in 2020 | | | $160 |

i. Dairyland's nominal GDP increased between 2019 and 2020 from $110 to $160. This increase is accounted for by both an increase in output and an increase in prices.

ii. Notice that both butter and cheese production increased, while yogurt output remained the same. However, the prices of all three goods increased between 2019 and 2020.

2. Nominal GDP growth rate. The GDP growth rate (the rate of increase in nominal GDP) is the percentage change between the two years being measured.

$$\text{Nominal GDP growth rate} = \frac{\text{2020 nominal GDP} - \text{2019 nominal GDP}}{\text{2019 nominal GDP}} \times 100$$

$$= \frac{\$160 - \$110}{\$110} \times 100 = 45.45\%$$

i. Dairyland's nominal GDP increased by 45.45%.

ii. However, this overstates the amount by which the country's real output of dairy products increased because all prices increased between 2019 and 2020.

3. Measuring real GDP. Using the same data, Dairyland's real GDP can be found by multiplying the output in one year by the prices in a base year. To determine the country's real GDP, calculate the value of 2020's output using the prices from a base year, which in this example is 2019.

| Output in 2020 | Quantity produced in 2020 | Price in 2019 | Total value of output 2020 |
|---|---|---|---|
| Butter | 12 | $2 | $24 |
| Cheese | 25 | $2 | $50 |
| Yogurt | 5 | $10 | $50 |
| **Real GDP in 2020** | | | **$124** |

i. Dairyland's real GDP in 2020 is only $124, significantly lower than its nominal GDP of $160.

ii. The nominal GDP was inflated because the prices of all three goods rose in 2020.

iii. In adjusting nominal GDP to real GDP, we multiplied 2020's output by 2019's prices, thus "deflating" the figure to its "real" level.

4. Real GDP growth rate. The rate of growth in real GDP can now be calculated between the two years.

$$\text{Real GDP growth rate} = \frac{\text{2020 real GDP} - \text{2019 real GDP}}{\text{2019 real GDP}} \times 100$$

$$= \frac{\$124 - \$110}{\$110} \times 100 = 12.72\%$$

i. By multiplying 2020's quantities by 2019's prices, we ignore the change in the price level. We can see that Dairyland's real GDP growth rate was far less impressive than its nominal GDP growth rate, at 12.72% versus 45.45%.

**D.** The GDP deflator price index is a measure of inflation indicating how much the average price level has changed since the base year.

1. Calculating the GDP deflator price index.

   i. By dividing a country's nominal GDP by its real GDP in a particular year, we can determine the value of the GDP deflator:

$$\text{GDP deflator price index} = \frac{\text{nominal GDP}}{\text{real GDP}} \times 100$$

   ii. The 2020 GDP deflator price index can be calculated:

$$\frac{\$160}{\$124} \times 100 = 129$$

   iii. The GDP deflator price index shows that prices in 2020 were 129% of 2019's prices. In other words, the average price of the country's output rose by 29% between the two years.

2. The GDP deflator price index can be used to adjust a nation's nominal GDP for changes in the price level.

   i. The deflator is an indicator of how much prices have changed between two years.

   ii. For a base year, the deflator always equals 100, since the real GDP is the nominal GDP in the base year.

   iii. If, in a later year, the index is 110, this means that prices have risen by 10% between those years.

   iv. If it is 120, prices have risen by 20%. If it is 95, then prices fell by 5%, and so on.

3. To calculate real GDP, the nominal GDP must be "deflated" by dividing it by the deflator price index, then multiplying the result by 100.

$$\text{Real GDP} = \frac{\text{Nominal GDP}}{\text{GDP deflator price index}} \times 100$$

   i. Consider the table below, showing nominal and real GDP data for the U.S.:

| Year | Nominal GDP (billions of $) | GDP Deflator | Real GDP (billions of 2005 $) |
|---|---|---|---|
| 2005 | 12,638.4 | 100 | $\frac{12,638.4}{100} \times 100 =$ **12,638.4** |
| 2006 | 13,398.9 | 103.25 | $\frac{13,398.9}{103.25} \times 100 =$ **12,977.14** |
| 2007 | 14,061.8 | 106.29 | $\frac{14,061.8}{106.29} \times 100 =$ **13,229.65** |
| 2008 | 14,369.1 | 108.61 | $\frac{14,391.1}{108.61} \times 100 =$ **13,250.25** |
| 2009 | 14,119.0 | 109.61 | $\frac{14,119}{109.61} \times 100 =$ **12,881.12** |

ii. Note that from 2006 on, real GDP was lower than nominal because the deflator increased each year, indicating that there was inflation; therefore, nominal GDP would have overstated the changes in real output from year to year.

***Understanding the relationship between real and nominal GDP will help you answer multiple-choice questions correctly. Two ways you might be asked about this relationship: 1) If in a specified year nominal gross domestic product grew by 11% and real gross domestic product grew by 4%, how much is inflation? And, 2) Last year the GDP deflator rose from 150 to 156 and nominal GDP increased by 2%. By how much did real GDP change?***

## VII. Business Cycles

A. Background. Fluctuations in an economy's aggregate output and employment can be illustrated in an economic model known as the *business cycle.* The business cycle shows how a country's real GDP fluctuates over time because of changes in aggregate supply and/or aggregate demand (concepts that will be explained further in Chapter 5).

1. Phases of the business cycle. The following graph tracks hypothetical business cycles over almost 30 years in the fictional country of Snowlandia.

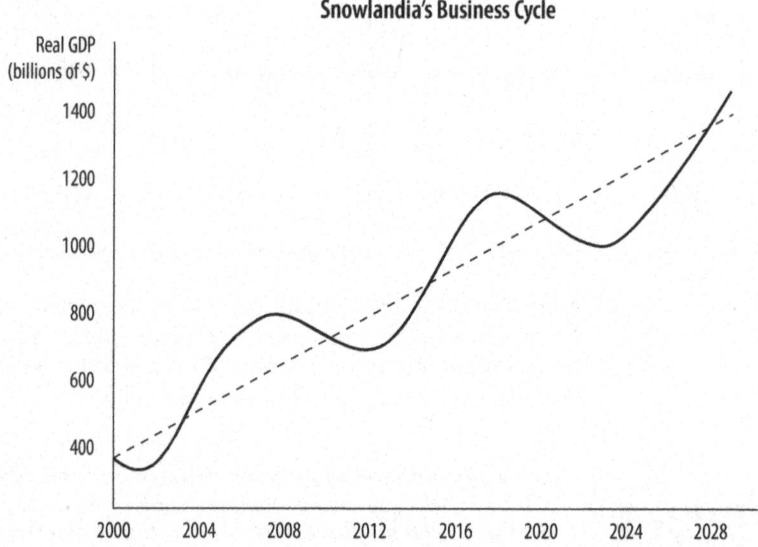


i. Snowlandia's business cycle over the first three decades of the 21st century shows the fluctuations in the country's output from a low of around $400 billion to a high of around $1,400 billion.

ii. The dashed line represents the growth trend line in the economy's output. While overall GDP increased, there were periods of both expansion and recession, with peaks and troughs in between.

iii. An expansion is a phase of the business cycle during which GDP increases.

iv. A peak is the turning point at which GDP stops increasing and begins decreasing.

v. A recession is the phase of the business cycle during which GDP decreases.

vi. A trough is the turning point at which GDP stops decreasing and begins increasing.

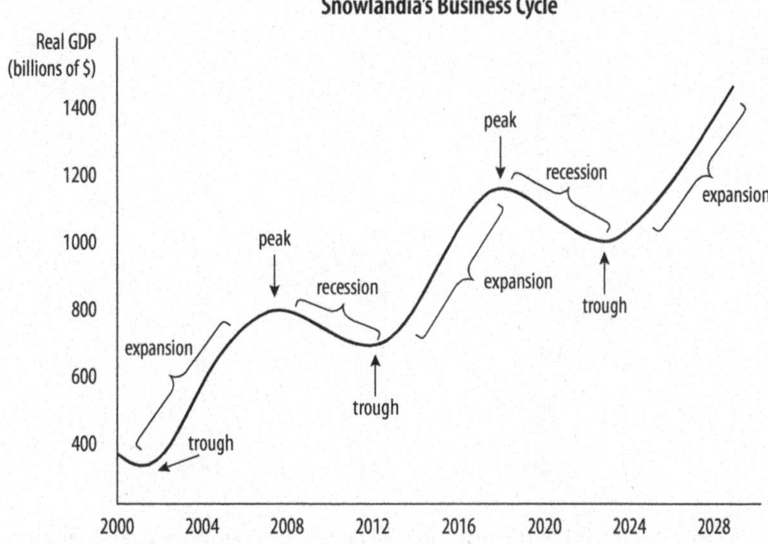


vii. Snowlandia experienced two recessions between 2004 and 2028, each lasting for a few years.

2. Recessions can be caused by either a fall in total demand for an economy's output (aggregate demand) or a fall in the total supply of output (aggregate supply), and are accompanied by rising unemployment and either deflation (in the case of a demand-deficient recession) or inflation (in the case of a recession caused by a negative aggregate supply shock).

3. Expansion occurred for much of the three decades depicted in Snowlandia's business cycle.

   i. Expansions result from increases in aggregate demand and/or aggregate supply and generally mean more employment, more output, higher incomes, and increases in people's standards of living.

4. Output gaps in the business cycle. Expansions and recessions can lead to positive and negative output gaps, which occur when an economy is producing at a level of output that is above or below what it would be achieving if it produced on its long-run growth trend line.

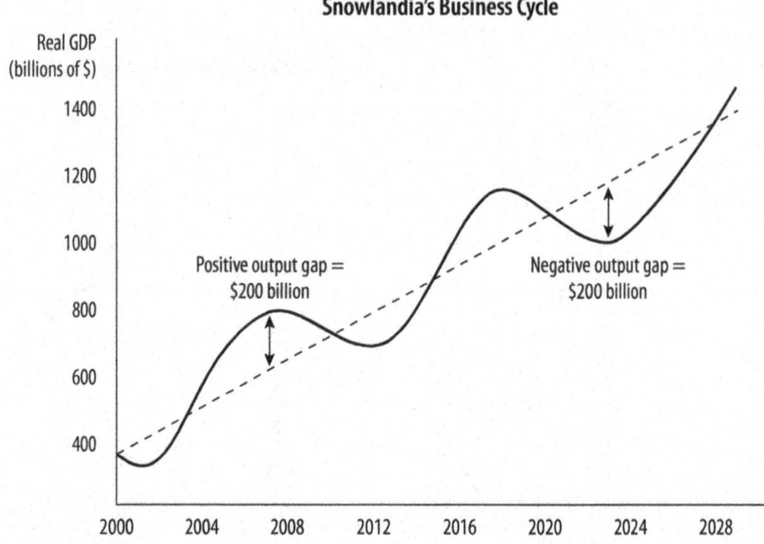


5. Positive output gaps occur in an economy that is overheating and are resolved when the business cycle reaches a peak and enters a recession.

   i. In a country with an overheated economy, unemployment is below its natural rate. This means labor markets are tight and nominal wages are set to increase.

   ii. As wages and other input costs rise, businesses are forced to reduce output and lay off workers, leading to a recession and a fall in aggregate output.

6. Negative output gaps occur in an economy that is producing below its full employment level of output because of a recession.

   i. Unemployment is higher than its natural rate, and in the case of a recession caused by a fall in aggregate demand, there is likely to be deflation (falling prices).

   ii. Assuming there is no recovery in demand or intervention by policymakers in the form of a fiscal or monetary stimulus, a negative output gap will be resolved in the long run as high unemployment leads to falling nominal wages and reductions in other input costs, at which point the economy will enter a recovery.

7. Potential output is also called full-employment output. It is the level of GDP where unemployment is equal to the natural rate of unemployment.
   i. In the business cycle, the economy's potential output is depicted by the long-run growth trend line.
   ii. Potential output increases as the economy's factors of production increase: either more workers or more productive workers, more or better land, technology, and entrepreneurial talent, or other improvements in or increases in the quantity of land, labor, or capital.
   iii. The upward slope of the growth trend line shows that the economy's production possibilities increase over time; in other words, the country experiences long-run economic growth.

***The business cycle diagram, like the circular flow, is one that you will rarely be asked to draw. But you will often be asked questions about which phase of its business cycle a country is likely in, given the existence of certain macroeconomic conditions, such as positive growth and low unemployment (expansion), or rising unemployment and deflation (contraction).***

Chapter 5

# UNIT 3 National Income and Price Determination

## I. Aggregate Demand

**A.** The AD curve. Aggregate demand is the amount of a country's output of goods and services demanded by households, firms, the government, and foreigners at a range of price levels in a specific time period.

1. The macroeconomic concept of AD is analogous to the microeconomic concept of "demand" introduced in Chapter 3.
2. The difference between micro "demand" and macro "aggregate demand" is that AD considers:
   i. all consumers domestic and foreign, of a nation's output of all goods and services.
   ii. the general, or average price level (not just the price of a particular good).
   iii. the quantity of output produced by all firms in all industries in a nation, not just the quantity produced of a particular good.
3. The AD curve describes the relationship between the price level and the quantity of goods and services demanded in a country. Consider the following graph, showing the AD of the fictional country, Snowlandia.

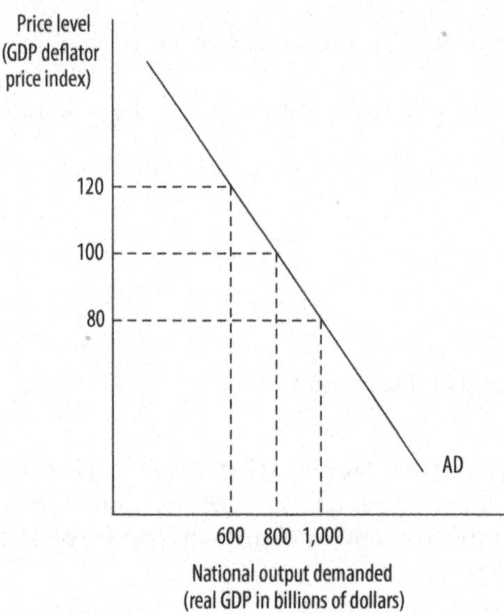


i. Recall from Chapter 4 that the GDP deflator price index measures the average price level of all the goods and services in a country. The vertical axis in our AD model depicts the average price level as measured by the deflator.

ii. Along the horizontal axis we see the quantity of national output (in billions of dollars) demanded by households, firms, the government, and foreigners at every possible price level.

iii. The negative slope of the AD curve shows that at lower price levels more of a nation's output is demanded, while at higher price levels less output is demanded, assuming all else is held constant.

4. Households, firms, the government, and foreigners will demand more of a country's goods and services as their average prices fall, and less as their prices rise. This relationship can be better understood by what economists call the wealth effect, the real interest rate effect, and the net export effect (also called the exchange rate effect).

   i. According to the wealth effect, higher price levels reduce the purchasing power or the real value of households' wealth and savings.

- The public feels poorer at higher price levels, thus demands a lower quantity of the country's output when price levels are high.
- At lower price levels, people feel wealthier and thus demand more of a nation's goods and services.

ii. The real interest rate effect observes that in response to a rise in the price level, banks will raise the interest rates on loans to households and firms who wish to consume or invest. They do this to assure that the money they are repaid by borrowers is worth at least as much as the money they loaned.

- At higher interest rates, the quantity demanded of products and capital for which households and firms must borrow money decreases, as buyers face higher borrowing costs.
- The opposite results from a fall in the price level and a decline in interest rates; that is, buyers' demand for products and capital that require borrowing increases. Lower interest rates and lower prices make borrowing more attractive and thus increase the quantity of output demanded.

iii. The net export effect (also called the exchange rate effect), looks at how a change in a country's average price level affects the flow of exports and imports.

- As the price level falls, all else being equal, goods and services produced in that country become more attractive to foreign consumers.
- Likewise, domestic consumers find imports less attractive as they now appear relatively more expensive. As a result, the net expenditures on the nation's goods rise as price level falls.
- The opposite results from an increase in the price level, which makes domestic output less attractive to foreigners and foreign products more attractive to domestic consumers.

iv. These three "effects" (the wealth effect, the interest rate effect, and the net export effect) explain the negative slope of the AD curve and why a change in the average price level in one direction causes the quantity of output demanded to change in the opposite direction.

***Understanding how changes in various factors will affect aggregate demand is very important. For example, you must know how lower interest rates will affect each of the components of AD, and how expectations of higher inflation will affect consumer and business behavior. Expect several questions in the multiple-choice section on changes to such variables.***

## II. Components of AD

**A.** Any change in the components of AD (consumption, investment, government spending, or net exports) that is not from changes in the price level leads to a shift of the AD curve. These include changes in any of the following:

1. For consumption: disposable income, wealth, consumer confidence, expected inflation or deflation, or interest rates.
2. For investment: interest rates, business confidence, expected inflation or deflation, business taxes, or government regulations.
3. For government spending: the government's fiscal policy, budget surpluses or deficits.
4. For net exports: the exchange rate, incomes abroad, or relative price levels between trading partners.

**B.** Shifts of the AD Curve

1. When a determinant of one or more of the components of AD changes, the entire AD curve will shift in or out, and the quantity of output demanded at every price level will change.
2. Assume, for example, the government of Snowlandia lowers income tax rates on all workers.
    i. This increases Snowlandians' disposable income and leads them to demand a greater quantity of goods and services at every price level.

ii. This increased demand shifts the AD curve outward, as in the following graph.

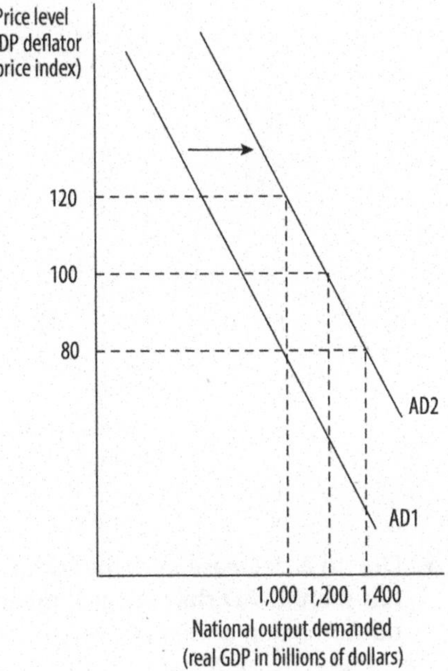


- Due to an increase in disposable income, households are now willing to buy more output in Snowlandia, and as a result, AD has shifted outward to AD2.
- At each of the price levels from the original AD curve (AD1), more output is now demanded.

iii. Any change in the level of business investment, government spending, or net exports will likewise cause the AD curve to shift. Consider the impact of a recession in Sandyland, a major trading partner of Snowlandia.

- Falling incomes abroad will result in a decrease in demand for Snowlandia's exports, causing the net export component of AD to decrease.
- As a result, the AD curve shifts to the left, meaning there will be less output demanded at every price level in Snowlandia.

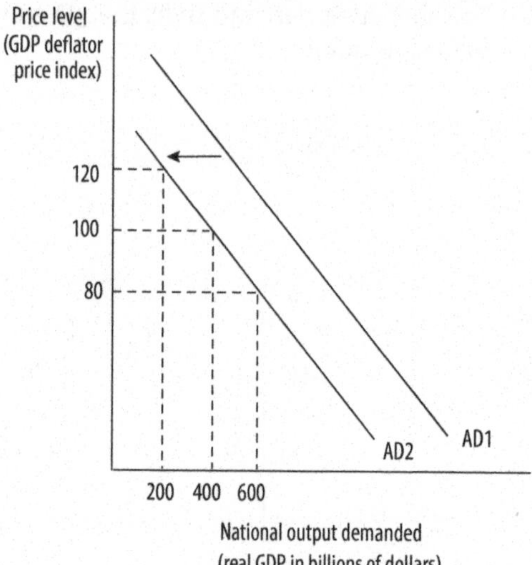


➤ Due to a decrease in demand for its exports, Snowlandia has seen its AD shift inward, meaning less of the country's output is demanded at every price level.

## III. Multipliers

A. The expenditure (or spending) multiplier. A $1 change to one of the components of AD leads to a further change in total expenditures and total output.

1. The expenditure multiplier quantifies the size of the change in AD as a result of a change in any one of the components of AD.
2. Consider how a change in government spending will impact total spending and total output in Snowlandia.

    i. Assume the government increases spending on infrastructure by $1 billion.

    ➤ The $1 billion of new spending in the economy will lead to an increase in household incomes of $1 billion. (Remember the circular flow discussion? Expenditures = output = income.)

- As their incomes rise, households will increase their spending on goods and services. (Remember, incomes are a determinant of consumption.)
- Due to increasing consumption, the economy's AD is stimulated by more than the initial $1 billion increase in government spending.

ii. The process continues: More spending leads to more income which leads to more spending.

- Ultimately, the initial change in expenditures is "multiplied" throughout the economy by a factor determined by the amount by which households increase their consumption in response to a particular increase in income. (This is called *marginal propensity to consume* and will be explained further, below.)

3. The expenditure multiplier quantifies the size of the change in AD as a result of a change in any of the components of AD.

**B.** The Tax Multiplier

1. Assume that instead of increasing spending on infrastructure by $1 billion, Snowlandia's government instead lowers taxes by $1 billion.
2. Snowlandians now see an immediate increase in disposable income, which in turn will lead to increased consumption by some amount less than $1 billion (assuming they choose to save some of their newly disposable income).

i. The initial tax cut will result in increased consumption, which leads to an increase in incomes and a further increase in consumption. The process continues:

- Lower taxes mean more income which leads to more consumption and more income.
- Ultimately, the initial change in taxes is "multiplied" throughout the economy by a factor determined by the amount by which households increase their consumption in response to a particular increase in disposable income.

ii. The tax multiplier quantifies the size of the change in AD as a result of a change in taxes.

C. Marginal Propensities to Consume and Save. To estimate the size of the expenditure and tax multipliers, we must know how much of any change in income the typical household will use to buy goods and services.

1. The marginal propensity to consume (MPC) is the change in consumer spending divided by the change in disposable income experienced by a country's households.

$$\text{Marginal propensity to consume (MPC)} = \frac{\text{change in consumption spending } (\Delta C)}{\text{change in income } (\Delta Y)}$$

2. Assuming that households can do only a few things with new income earned or received (consume or save), the marginal propensity to save (MPS) can be calculated by dividing the change in household savings by the change in disposable income experienced by a country's households.

$$\text{Marginal propensity to save (MPS)} = \frac{\text{change in savings } (\Delta S)}{\text{change in income } (\Delta Y)}$$

3. The sum of the marginal propensity to consume and the marginal propensity to save equals one. Any income not spent is considered saved.

$$MPC + MPS = 1$$

   i. Assume that the typical Snowlandian household spends $0.90 of every $1 increase in income and saves $0.10. The MPC and MPS can be calculated:

$$MPC = \frac{0.9}{1} = 0.9$$

$$MPS = \frac{0.1}{1} = 0.1$$

4. The sizes of the expenditure multiplier and tax multiplier depend on the marginal propensity to consume. To estimate the magnitude by which a particular change in expenditures will affect AD, we can determine the expenditure multiplier as a function of the MPC:

$$\text{Expenditure multiplier} = \frac{1}{1 - MPC}$$

i. With an MPC of 0.9, Snowlandia's expenditure multiplier can be determined:

$$\frac{1}{1-0.9}=\frac{1}{0.1}=10$$

ii. The multiplier indicates the amount by which any initial change in expenditures (C, I, G, or Xn) must be multiplied to determine the final change in total spending in the economy.

iii. We can calculate how much the government's $1 billion increase in infrastructure spending contributes to Snowlandia's GDP using the multiplier:

$$\Delta \text{ in AD} = \text{initial } \Delta \text{ spending} \times \text{spending multiplier}$$

$$\Delta \text{ in AD} = \$1 \text{ billion} \times 10 = \$10 \text{ billion}$$

iv. Given an MPC of 0.9, an initial increase in spending of $1 billion will ultimately increase Snowlandia's GDP by $10 billion.

5. The lower the MPC, the smaller the spending multiplier, because consumers will not spend as much of any increase in income, choosing to save instead. The following table shows the multiplier calculations for different marginal propensities to consume.

| MPC | Spending multiplier | Effect on GDP of $1 billion rise in AD |
|---|---|---|
| 0.9 | $\frac{1}{0.1}=10$ | $1b × 10 = $10b |
| 0.6 | $\frac{1}{0.4}=2.5$ | $1b × 2.5 = $2.5b |
| 0.5 | $\frac{1}{0.5}=2$ | $1b × 2 = $2b |
| 0.4 | $\frac{1}{0.6}=1.67$ | $1b × 1.67 = $1.67b |
| 0.2 | $\frac{1}{0.8}=1.25$ | $1b × 1.25 = $1.25b |

6. The tax multiplier is also a function of the marginal propensities to consume and save. The magnitude by which a particular change in taxes will impact AD is found in the formula:

$$\text{Tax multiplier} = \frac{-\text{MPC}}{\text{MPS}}$$

i. With its MPC of 0.9 and its MPS of 0.1, Snowlandia's tax multiplier can be calculated:

$$\frac{-0.9}{0.1} = -9$$

ii. Every $1 decrease in taxes will *increase* AD in Snowlandia by $9.

iii. We can estimate the impact of a $1 billion tax cut given to Snowlandian citizens using the tax multiplier.

$$\Delta \text{ in AD} = \text{initial } \Delta \text{ taxes} \times \text{tax multiplier}$$
$$= -\$1 \text{ billion} \times -9 = \$9 \text{ billion}$$

iv. Note that the tax multiplier is negative, because there is an inverse relationship between taxes and spending.

➤ Tax cuts (a negative change in taxes, like that experienced in Snowlandia) cause disposable incomes and consumer spending to increase while tax increases cause spending to fall.

v. Note also that the tax multiplier effect is smaller than the expenditure multiplier effect. Consider Snowlandia's two government policies: a $1 billion increase in infrastructure spending versus a $1 billion tax cut.

➤ The first option would result in a $10 billion increase in total spending, while the second would only result in $9 billion of new spending.

➤ The difference is explained by the fact that government spending is a direct injection into the circular flow of income, while a tax cut is an indirect injection.

➤ Before Snowlandians saw their incomes rise, AD had already been boosted by $1 billion in the case of new infrastructure spending.

- On the other hand, no jobs are directly created or output actually produced by a tax cut; the stimulus only occurs after households who receive it have set 10% aside as savings and begun to consume with the other 90%.

7. The impact of the expenditure and tax multipliers can be shown in an AD model.

   i. Assume, for example, the MPC is 0.5 and the multiplier is 2.

   - An increase in private investment of $20 billion will initially shift the AD curve out by $20 billion, as in the following graph.

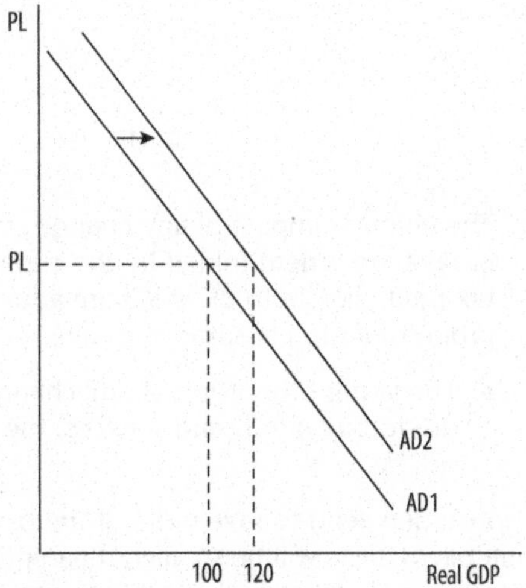


   - With the new income created by the $20 billion of new investments, further increases in spending will multiply the initial amount by an amount determined by the multiplier, which in this example is 2.
   - Ultimately, the AD curve will shift out by $20 billion × 2 or $40 billion, as in the following graph.

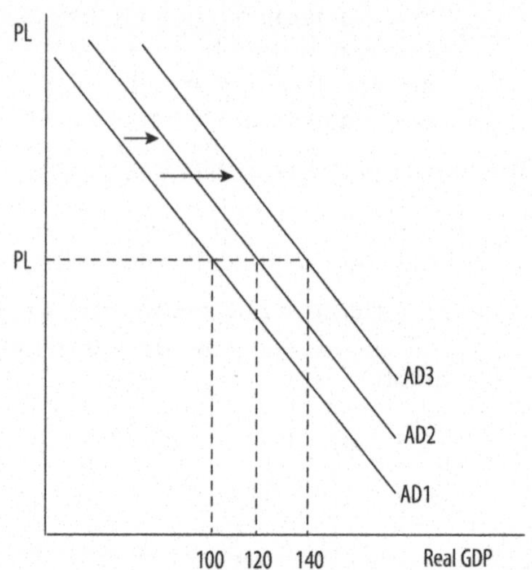


ii. The ultimate impact of any change in aggregate expenditures or taxation is determined by the expenditure multiplier or the tax multiplier, both of which are a function of the marginal propensities to consume and save.

  - The larger proportion of any change in income households use to buy goods and services, the larger the multipliers will be.

8. If consumers tend to save more of the new income they earn, the multiplier effects will be smaller, meaning a particular change in spending or taxation will result in a smaller change in total output.

***Be sure to know the difference between the spending multiplier and the tax multiplier. A common question on the AP® Macro exam is the relative impact of a particular change in taxes or government spending on GDP.***

## Short-Run Aggregate Supply (SRAS)

**A.** Sticky Wages. With our definition and graphical analysis of AD complete, let's consider the "supply side" of the economy.

1. Aggregate supply (AS) is the quantity of goods and services that a country's producers are willing and able to produce at a range of price levels in a period of time.
2. The short-run aggregate supply (SRAS) curve describes the relationship between the price level and the quantity of goods and services supplied in an economy in the period during which wages (the price of labor) and other input prices are fixed or inflexible.
   i. When the prices for which producers can sell their output rise, while the wages paid to their workers and the prices of other inputs remain fixed, producers will want to supply a greater quantity of goods and services. This is due to the opportunity for higher profits resulting from an increase in the price level.
   ii. At lower price levels, producers will reduce the quantity of output supplied, especially when their input prices remain fixed, as the prospect of losses forces suppliers to reduce output and employment.
3. The direct relationship described above is reflected in an upward-sloping SRAS curve, as seen in the following graph.

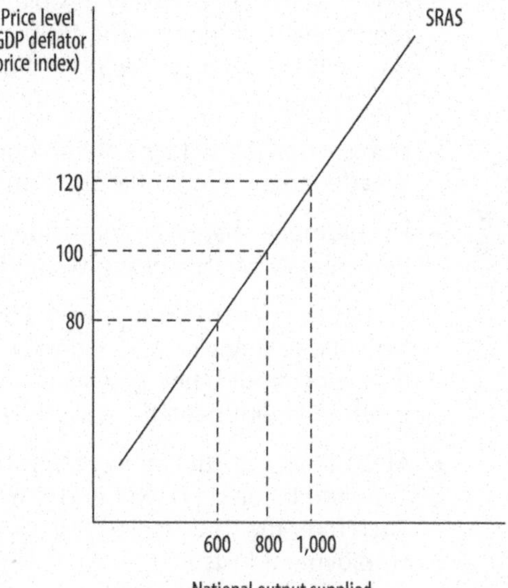


   i. The SRAS curve is upward-sloping because of sticky wages and prices. The "short run" is defined as the "sticky wage period." This is a time after a macroeconomic shock, such as a change in AD, during which firms cannot raise or lower wages quickly in response to the shock.

ii. Due to factors including labor contracts, minimum wage laws, the ability for workers to collect unemployment benefits after losing their jobs, and the power of labor unions, firms are unable to raise and lower wages quickly in response to a macroeconomic shock such as an increase or decrease in AD.

iii. As a result of sticky wages, workers are more likely to be hired and fired in the period following such a shock, rather than their wages simply adjusting to the level of demand in the economy.

iv. The following example focuses on how a single producer might respond to a sudden decrease in demand for its goods.

- Assume that following a sudden decrease in household wealth (due to a collapse in stock prices), demand for luxury SUVs suddenly decreases. ACC (American Car Company) is faced with a collapse in demand for its popular vehicle, the Unibog.
- The CEO must cut costs or face bankruptcy. In a world in which wages are perfectly flexible, the CEO would simply reduce every worker on the Unibog assembly line's wage by, say, 30%, in order to "weather the storm" of falling demand for Unibogs.
- However, ACC's workers are unionized, and the union has threatened a strike should the firm try to reduce wages.
- Furthermore, there is a state-wide minimum wage that prevents ACC from cutting wages by 30%.
- Finally, the government provides generous unemployment benefits, so many of ACC's workers may choose to leave their jobs should their pay fall by 30% and simply collect unemployment benefits while they search for a new job.
- ACC's ability to cut Unibog assembly line workers' wages is limited by union power and government regulations. Therefore, the CEO, facing "sticky wages," must reduce employment instead.
- Rather than lowering everyone's pay by 30%, the employer must lay off 30% of his workers and reduce production numbers in order to cut costs in the face of falling demand.

v. Now consider how sticky wages affect the national economy.

➤ In a country in which all employers face the same constraints as ACC, falling output prices will be met by falling employment and reduced output.

➤ In other words, in the short run, when wages are sticky, there is a direct relationship between the price level and the level of output and employment.

➤ Falling prices mean less output and less employment, while rising prices lead to more output and more employment.

**B.** Shifts of SRAS

1. Any factor that causes production costs to change will cause the SRAS curve to shift.

2. When any of the following factors change, AS will either decrease and shift inward or increase and shift outward.

i. Wage rates: Higher wages cause SRAS to decrease; lower wages cause SRAS to increase.

ii. Resource costs: When rents for land, interest rates, or raw material prices increase, SRAS will decrease. Lower resource costs cause SRAS to increase.

iii. Energy and transportation costs: Higher oil or energy prices will cause SRAS to decrease. Cheaper energy and transportation cause SRAS to increase.

iv. Government regulation: Regulations impose costs on firms that can cause SRAS to decrease. Reduced regulation makes it cheaper to produce output, increasing SRAS.

v. Business taxes/subsidies: Taxes are a monetary cost imposed on firms by the government; so higher taxes will cause SRAS to decrease. A tax cut or increased subsidies to producers reduce firms' costs and cause SRAS to increase.

vi. Exchange rates: If producers use imported raw materials, a weaker currency will cause these to become more expensive, reducing SRAS. A stronger currency makes imported raw materials cheaper and increases SRAS.

3. A shift in SRAS results in a larger or smaller amount of output being produced at every price level.

    i. Assume, for example, the government has reduced environmental regulations, making it cheaper for firms to produce their output as they are not required to pay for costly waste-reduction and air purification technologies.

        - As a result of reduced regulation, the countries' producers are willing to produce a greater quantity of output at every price level.
        - The impact is an outward shift of the SRAS curve, as seen in the following graph.

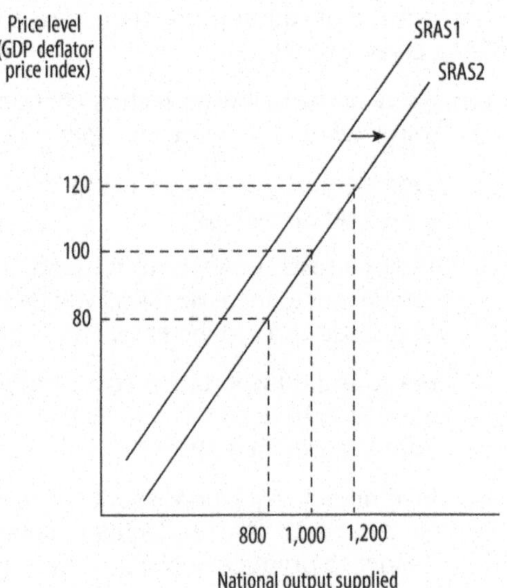


    ii. The shift from SRAS1 to SRAS2 reflects an increase in AS resulting from reduced government regulation.

        - Falling wages, lower energy prices, reduced business tax rates, and a stronger currency would cause a similar increase in SRAS.

➤ Higher wages, rising energy prices, increased regulation or taxation, or a weaker currency would cause SRAS to decrease, as in the graph below.

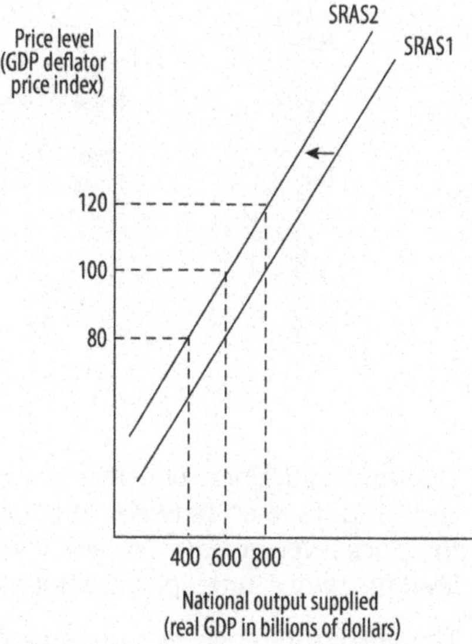


iii. Due to higher production costs, SRAS has shifted inward, resulting in a smaller quantity of national output produced at each price level.

C. Inflation and Unemployment. The SRAS curve demonstrates an indirect relationship between inflation and unemployment:

1. When the aggregate price level increases, output increases in the short run. At higher levels of output, firms employ more workers; therefore, unemployment decreases as the price level increases.
2. When the aggregate price level decreases, output decreases in the short run. At lower levels of output, firms employ fewer workers; therefore, unemployment increases as the price level decreases.

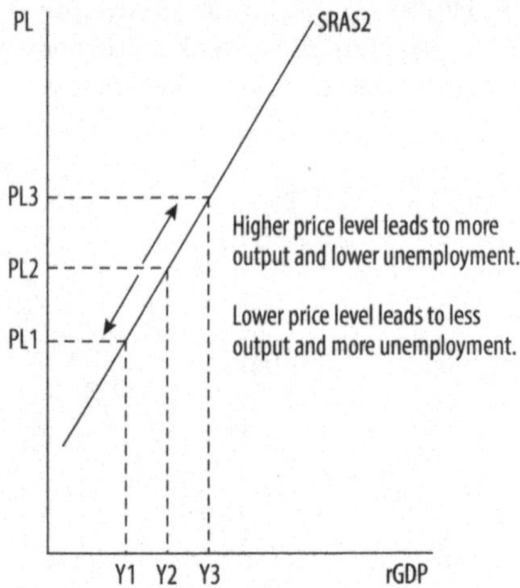


i. Due to the stickiness of wages and other input costs, there is a short-run trade-off between inflation and unemployment. As the price level increases, unemployment decreases; as the price level decreases, unemployment increases.

ii. The relationship between unemployment and inflation will be revisited in Chapter 7, when we learn about the Phillips curve.

## V. Long-Run Aggregate Supply

A. Flexible Wages. What if wages were perfectly flexible and adjusted to a change in the price level? According to classical economic theory, wages and prices are fully flexible in the long run, and therefore there is no trade-off between inflation and unemployment.

1. The long-run aggregate supply (LRAS) curve shows the level of output achieved in an economy when wages and prices are fully flexible and adjust to the economy's price level.

   i. In a world of flexible wages, an automaker like ACC (introduced earlier in this chapter) could maintain its level of output and employment even as the prices of its vehicles fall.

      ➤ In such a scenario, falling output prices would simply be offset by a decrease in wages and other input prices.

- ➤ Sellers would maintain their full employment level of production, and consumers would simply pay lower prices for their output.
- ➤ Workers would earn lower nominal wages, but since prices fall across the economy as a whole, real wages and real output would not be affected.

ii. In the case of a rising price level, firms would face higher wages and thus would not be willing or able to increase their output as the price level rose.

- ➤ While workers' nominal wages would increase, their real wages and the level of real output would remain constant as all prices increased across the economy.

iii. In the long run, all prices and wages are fully flexible, while in the short run, some input prices are fixed.

2. A consequence of flexible long-run prices and wages is the lack of a long-run trade-off between inflation and unemployment.

   i. The LRAS curve is vertical at a country's full employment level of output, or the real GDP that would be produced when all resources are fully utilized and wages have fully adjusted to the price level in the economy.

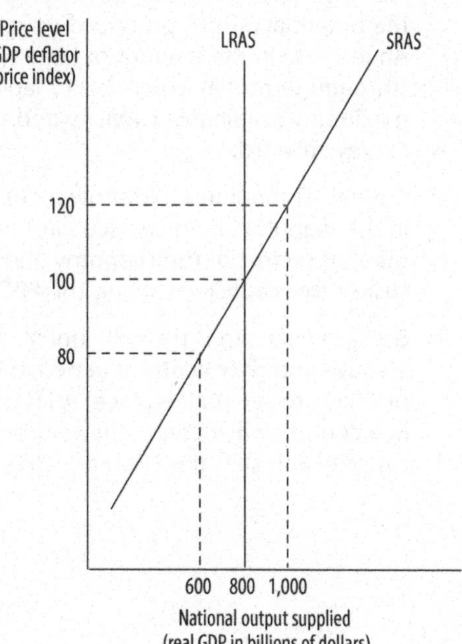

ii. In the preceding graph, the LRAS curve is vertical at an output of $800 billion, meaning that once wages and prices have fully adjusted and resources are fully employed, the country should produce this much output in the long run.

iii. In the short run, when wages are fixed, output will increase or decrease for the reasons outlined in the ACC example earlier in this chapter.

**B.** LRAS and the PPC. The LRAS curve corresponds to the production possibilities curve (PPC) because they both represent maximum sustainable capacity or full employment output. An increase in a country's maximum sustainable output will shift both the PPC and the LRAS curves outward.

1. Full employment output increases when there is an increase in either the quality or the quantity of a country's factors of production, including:

    i. Labor. An improvement in the productivity of labor or in the size of a country's workforce will increase a country's maximum sustainable capacity, shifting the PPC and LRAS curves outward.

    ii. Land. An improvement in the efficiency with which land resources are used through improved technology (better farming, mining, fishing, or logging techniques) will increase the potential output produced on a fixed amount of land. An increase in the amount of land available to a country (through territorial expansion or land reclamation) will increase maximum sustainable capacity and shift the PPC and LRAS curves outward.

    iii. Capital. Technological improvements increase productivity in the manufacturing, service, and primary (e.g., agriculture, mining) sectors of the economy and increase the maximum sustainable capacity, shifting the PPC and LRAS curves outward.

    iv. Entrepreneurship is the willingness of individuals to pursue creative and risky ventures aimed at introducing unique products to the marketplace. An increase in entrepreneurship in a country will increase the economy's maximum potential capacity and shift the PPC and LRAS curves outward.

2. An outward shift of LRAS and the PPC illustrates economic growth, or an increase in the actual and potential output of goods and services in a country over time.

   i. The following graphs depict the effect of economic growth in an AS model and in a PPC model.

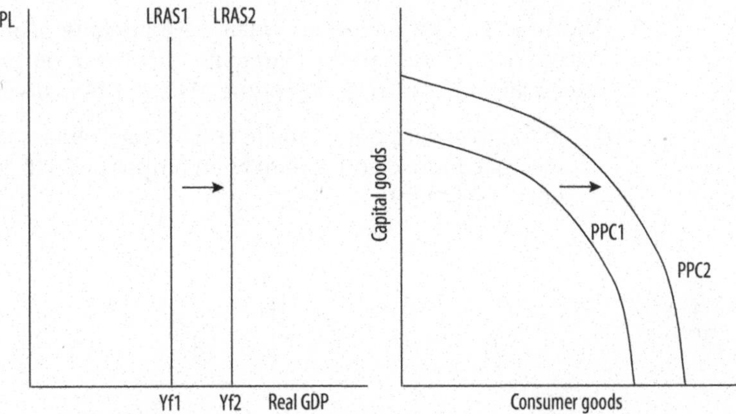


   ii. These graphs show that the country has experienced an increase in its potential output due to an increase in the factors of production.

   - In the LRAS model, output increases from "Yf1" to "Yf2" (Yf = full employment national output).
   - In the PPC, the curve has shifted outward, indicating a higher level of maximum sustainable output.

***Be familiar with the various determinants of aggregate supply. You should also know whether a change in a certain factor (such as business taxes, energy prices, or labor productivity) affects SRAS, LRAS, or both.***

## VI. Equilibrium in Aggregate Demand-Aggregate Supply (AD-AS) Model

**A.** Short-Run Equilibrium. The macroeconomic equilibrium real output and price level are what an economy achieves at a particular time given the level of AD and AS in the economy.

1. Short-run equilibrium occurs when the aggregate quantity of output demanded and the aggregate quantity of output supplied are equal, at the intersection of the AD and SRAS curves.

   i. In the following graph, the fictional Snowlandia is in a macroeconomic equilibrium at an output of $650 billion and a price level of 90.

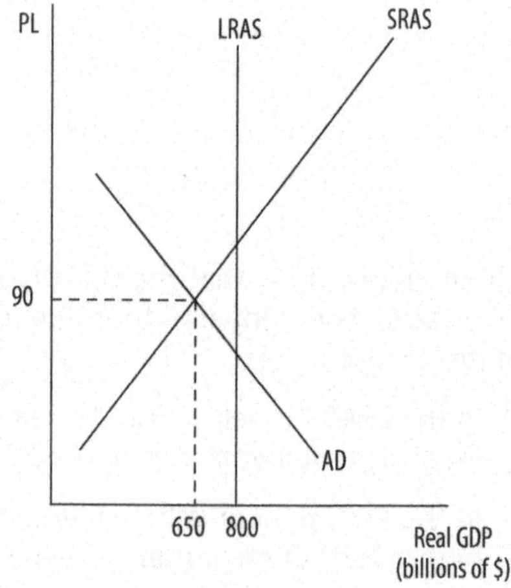


   ii. In this scenario, the Snowlandia economy is experiencing a short-run equilibrium level of output that is below its long-run equilibrium level of output.

   - The AD curve intersects the SRAS curve at a real GDP of $650 billion, which is less than the long-run equilibrium output of $800 billion.
   - Snowlandia is underutilizing its resources experiencing cyclical unemployment.

**B.** Long-Run Equilibrium. A country's full employment level of output is its maximum sustainable output assuming all resources are efficiently employed, and unemployment is at its natural rate.

1. Long-run equilibrium occurs when the AD and SRAS curve intersect on the LRAS at the full-employment level of real output.

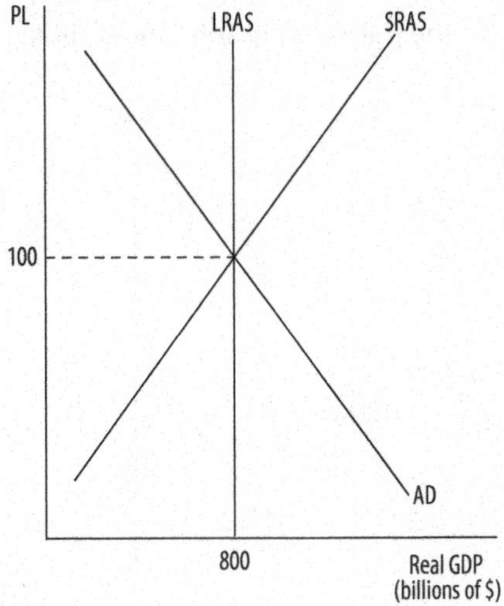


2. In the preceding graph, Snowlandia's production is at its full-employment level of output. AD intersects the SRAS curve along the LRAS curve.

   i. The price level is stable at a CPI of 100, and equilibrium output is the full employment level of real GDP.

   ii. The economy is experiencing only its natural rate of unemployment.

C. Output Gaps. When an economy's short-run equilibrium output is above or below the full-employment level, positive or negative output gaps are created.

1. When short-run equilibrium output is below full-employment output, an economy is experiencing a negative output gap (also called a recessionary gap).

   i. In the following graph, Snowlandia is in a recession.

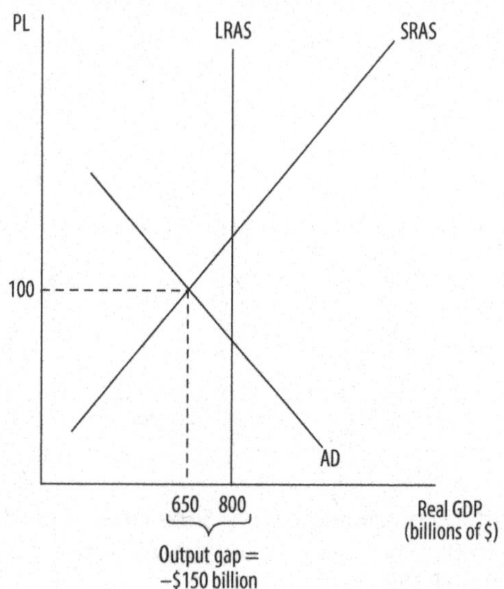


   ii. Due to some macroeconomic shock (examples of which are found in Part VII of this chapter), Snowlandia's economy is producing at a level $150 billion below its full-employment level.

   iii. With the recessionary gap, the economy also experiences a higher rate of unemployment than its natural rate, since cyclical unemployment occurs when an economy's output falls below full employment.

2. An economy can also produce beyond its full employment in the short run due to the stickiness of wages.

   i. In the following graph, Snowlandia has a positive output gap (also called an inflationary gap).

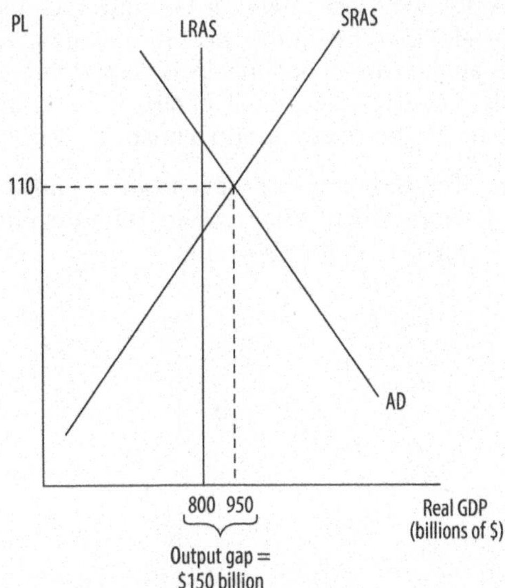


ii. Snowlandia's economy is producing at a level of output $150 billion greater than its full-employment output.

iii. Unemployment at $950 billion is lower than the Natural Rate of Unemployment (NRU), meaning labor markets are especially tight, and resources, extremely scarce.

iv. Inflation has accelerated in the economy, indicated by the CPI rising from 100 to 110.

***Many multiple-choice questions will ask you to determine how certain changes in AD and AS will affect employment, price levels, output, etc. In preparation, practice shifting the curves and determining how different macroeconomic indicators are affected.***

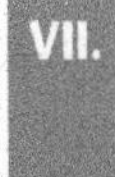


## Changes in AD-AS Model in the Short Run

**A.** Aggregate Demand (AD) Shocks. Output gaps are the result of shocks to either AD or AS. A shock occurs when one of the components of AD or the determinants of SRAS change. This causes the level of total spending or of total production to increase or decrease and short-run equilibrium price level and real GDP to change.

1. A positive shock in AD causes output, employment, and the price level (PL) to rise in the short run. Assume, for example, that there is an increase in national income and therefore, an increase in AD in Snowlandia. National income is the value of goods and services a nation produces during a financial year.

   i. The economy will move from an equilibrium at full employment to one where both the price level and output increase in the short run.

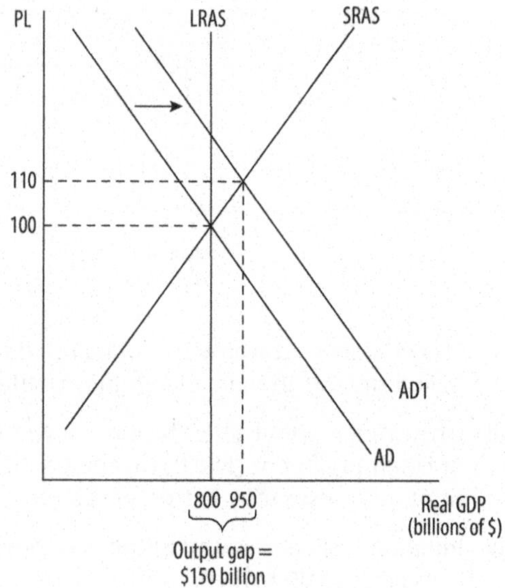


   ii. Because of a positive demand shock, Snowlandia's economy is temporarily producing at a short-run equilibrium level of output that is beyond its full employment output.

   iii. Note that the CPI (Consumer Price Index), has increased from 100 to 110, equating to a 10% inflation rate. (CPI quantifies the aggregate price level in an economy and thus measures the purchasing power of a nation's currency.)

   iv. The gap between its equilibrium output and full employment level of output is called the inflationary gap.

   v. The economy is essentially overheating; the unemployment rate is below the natural rate of unemployment and inflation is higher than desired.

2. Negative Demand Shocks. Assume that Snowlandia increases income taxes and reduces government expenditures, leading to a fall in AD.

   i. The following graph shows the effect this contractionary fiscal policy has on the country's macroeconomic equilibrium in the short run.

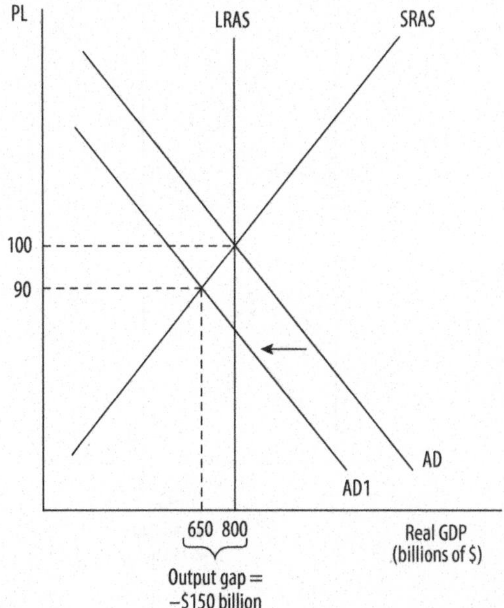


   ii. Due to sticky wages, firms are forced to lay off workers and reduce their output as the price level falls from a CPI of 100 to 90.

   iii. Costs must be cut in the face of falling prices, and the only way to reduce costs is to reduce output and employment since wages cannot be lowered in the short run.

   iv. The fall in output causes a recessionary gap of $150 billion, representing the amount by which equilibrium output is below the country's full employment output.

**B.** Aggregate Supply (AS) Shocks. A supply shock occurs when there is a change in a determinant of SRAS, causing output, employment, and the price level to change. Consider the effect of a sudden increase in energy prices. Higher costs will lead the economy's producers to reduce output and raise prices, shifting the SRAS curve to the left.

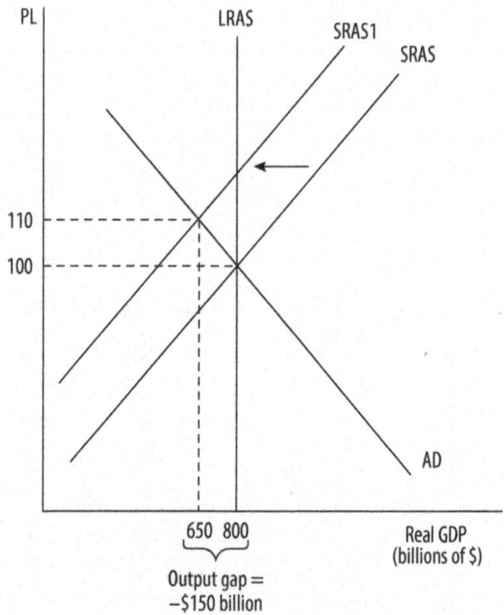


1. A negative supply shock has led to higher production costs, which have been passed to consumers through higher prices.
   i. Because wages are sticky, firms must fire workers to compensate for the higher energy prices, so unemployment increases as inflation increases.
   ii. A negative output gap results along with a higher price level.
2. Positive supply shocks occur when the costs to businesses are reduced, shifting the SRAS curve to the right. Assume, for example, Snowlandia's government reduces environmental and health regulations on all producers, resulting in lower production costs.
   i. SRAS will shift outward, employment and output will increase, and the price level will decrease.

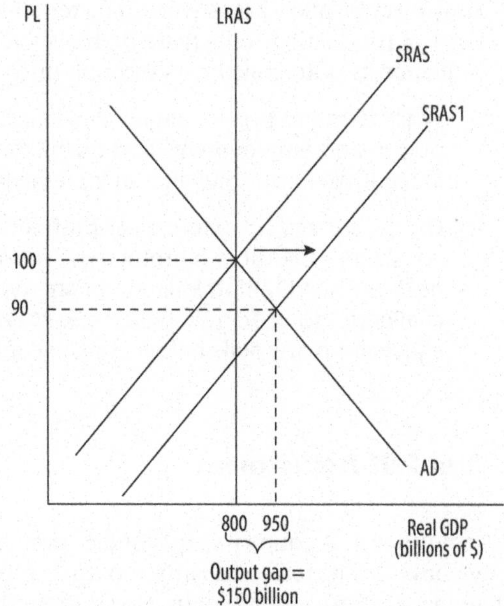


ii. Reduced regulation has led to a positive supply shock, allowing Snowlandia to produce beyond its previous full employment level of output.

iii. There is a positive output gap and a lower price level due to the lower cost of doing business in the economy.

iv. Unemployment has fallen below its natural rate, as firms have scrambled to hire more workers due to the firm's desire to increase output during the period of deregulation.

C. Inflation, an increase in the general price level of a nation's output over time, can be caused by changes in either AD or AS. An analysis of demand and supply shocks reveals that inflation can result from either a positive or a negative demand shock.

1. Demand-pull inflation results when a component of AD increases in an economy already producing at or near its full employment level of output. Increased consumption, investment, government spending, or net exports creates demand-pull inflation as resources become increasingly scarce and producers find that consumers are willing to pay more for their output.

2. Cost-push inflation arises when a factor affecting SRAS causes the costs of production to increase. In the short run, firms will pass higher costs onto consumers through price increases.
   i. While demand-pull inflation will be accompanied by rising output and employment, cost-push inflation is characterized by a negative output gap and an increase in unemployment.
   ii. On the surface, therefore, cost-push inflation could be considered the more harmful type; however, as we will see next in Part VIII, high inflation of any type poses serious challenges to economic policymakers and can have detrimental effects on many stakeholders in an economy.

## VIII. Long-Run Self-Adjustment

**A.** Self-adjustment. A country's equilibrium level of output can be above or below its full employment output in the short run, creating inflationary or recessionary gaps. However, in the long run, when wages and other input costs have fully adjusted to the price level, national output will return to its full employment level.

1. This process of self-correction is the foundation of the classical theory of long-run AS, which is vertical at full employment output. In the long run, there is no trade-off between unemployment and inflation.
2. The unemployment rate will always settle at the natural rate of unemployment, even as inflation rises and falls with changes in the level of AD.
3. From a positive output gap. Snowlandia's inflationary gap is a short-run phenomenon. The gap exists because wages are sticky and therefore, firms compete for the few available workers in order to increase output in response to rising prices.
   i. While wages remain fixed, firms demand more labor and increase their output in the short run.
   ii. However, in the long-run, nominal wages will begin to rise in response to the increased labor demand and limited labor supply.
      - Workers will have more bargaining power as the labor market tightens; they will begin to demand pay hikes to keep up with the rising cost of living.

- As the nominal wage rate rises, firms will find it less attractive to continue employing more workers and some firms will be forced to cut back on output and employment.
- Notably, as the nominal wage rate is a determinant of short-run AS, the SRAS will decrease in the long run, pushing prices up further and causing output to fall back to its full employment level.

iii. The following graph illustrates how Snowlandia's economy will adjust in the long run after the initial, positive demand shock.

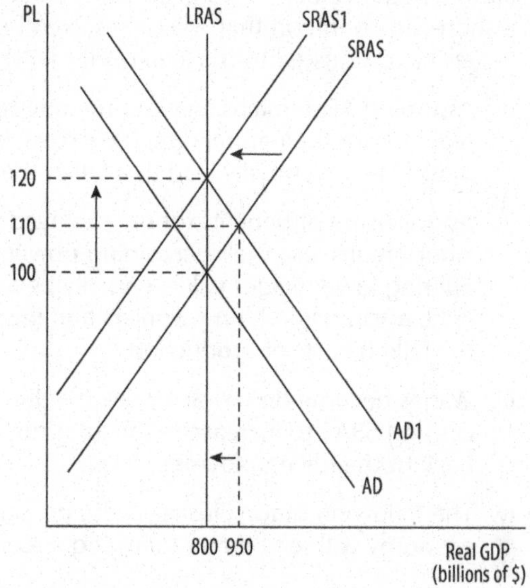


- The initial increase in output to $950 billion proved unsustainable as tight labor markets led to rising wages and a reduction in output and employment back to the full employment level of $800 billion.
- The price level is driven up initially by demand-pull inflation, and later by cost-push inflation. In the long run, Snowlandia's output is limited by its available resources of land, labor, and capital.
- The short-run boost in output caused by stronger export demand proves temporary as the economy cannot sustain its higher output due to limited resources.

iv. The process of self-correction following the positive demand shock described earlier in this part is the result of the flexibility of wages in the long run.

v. An economy will return to its full employment level of output following any shocks to aggregate demand or aggregate supply once wages and other input costs have adjusted to the price level.

vi. A similar scenario unfolds following a negative demand shock and a recessionary gap.

4. From a negative demand shock. Snowlandia's recessionary gap is a short-run condition that will be resolved in the long run once wages have adjusted to the lower price level.

    i. Assuming AD remains low and the unemployment rate remains higher than the natural rate, the excess supply of labor in the market will eventually lead to a fall in the nominal wage rate.

    ii. As government benefits for unemployed workers expire and labor unions lose their bargaining power, new contracts offering lower wages will eventually be accepted and firms will once again begin hiring workers and increasing output due to the falling costs of production.

    iii. Wages become downwardly flexible during a recession, causing SRAS to increase in the long run, and increasing output back to the full employment level.

    iv. The following graph illustrates the process by which the economy will self-correct following a recessionary gap.

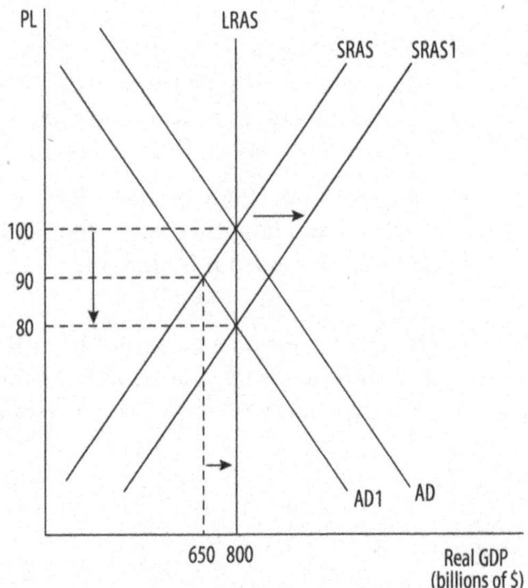

v. The recession caused by the government's contractionary fiscal policy eventually ends as falling wages and other input costs motivate firms to increase their output and lower prices even further.

- While the nominal wage rate falls, real income and output are restored to the full employment level as lower wages are offset by lower prices across the economy.
- Real output returns to its full employment level of $800 billion.

**B.** Shifts in LRAS. Economic growth occurs when there is an increase in a country's actual and potential output of goods and services over time.

1. From our analysis of changes in the AD-AS model, we can conclude the following:

   i. Changes in AD alone will not cause economic growth.

   - A decrease in AD causes a recession in the short run.
   - An increase in AD causes demand-pull inflation and an overheating economy.
   - In both cases, output returns to full employment once wages and other input prices have fully adjusted.

   ii. Changes in SRAS can cause a short-run decrease in output (if resource costs increase) or increase in output (if resource costs decrease).

   iii. In other words, shifts in AD and SRAS alone will not cause an increase in an economy's potential output, only in its actual output (its short-run equilibrium real GDP).

   iv. In order for potential output to increase, there must be an outward shift in the long-run aggregate supply (LRAS) curve.

2. Increase in potential output. LRAS will increase if there is an increase in the quantity of factors of production (more workers, more capital, or more land resources) or if there is an increase in the quality of the factors of production (a more educated or higher skilled workforce, greater productivity, or improvements in technology).

   i. Increases in a nation's potential output through advances in human capital or technology cause the LRAS curve to shift out.

   ii. Typically, such changes also result in increased AD and SRAS as well (due to new investment and consumption or increased government spending on human or physical capital).

iii. Assume that due to a combination of increased immigration and improvements in the education system, Snowlandia's labor force has increased both in quantity and quality. More, better skilled workers increase LRAS and the country's full-employment level of output.

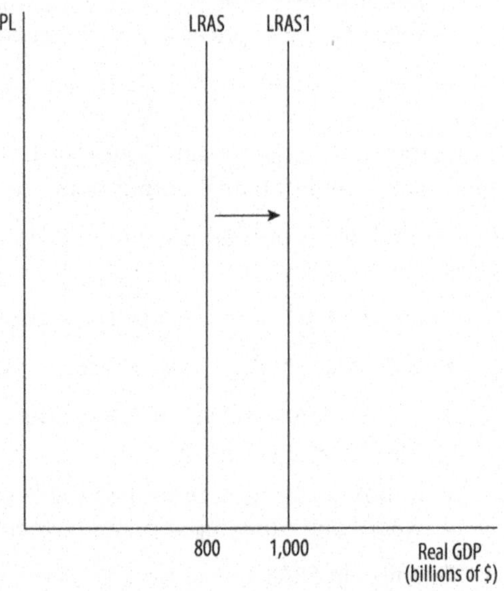

***Understanding the difference between how a change in aggregate demand affects an economy both in the short run and in the long run is commonly tested in both sections of the AP® Macro exam. Be able to explain that in the long run, because wages and prices are flexible, an economy will always return to its full employment level of output following any increase or decrease in aggregate demand.***

## IX. Fiscal Policy

A. Tools of Fiscal Policy. Governments implement fiscal policies to achieve macroeconomic goals, such as full employment, price-level stability, economic growth, and reductions in income inequality. The tools of fiscal policy are government purchases, transfers, and taxes.

1. Government purchases include all public-sector expenditures on goods and services, such as infrastructure, schools and universities, national defense, healthcare services and hospitals, national parks, and fire and police protection.
2. Transfers, such as social security payments, unemployment insurance, welfare spending, college financial aid, and producer subsidies, differ from government spending on public goods because no new good or service is provided when a transfer payment is made.
   i. Transfer payments simply transfer income from one group in the country to another and thus do not count as government purchases.
   ii. An increase in transfers, all else being equal, will increase AD as recipients of the transfers will use the income to increase their own consumption (in the case of households) or investment (in the case of firms).
3. Taxes come in many forms, including direct taxes, such as the income tax and indirect taxes, such as sales and excise taxes (placed on particular goods).
4. Changes in government purchases affect AD directly, and changes in taxes and transfers affect AD indirectly.
   i. When a government spends *x dollars* on a new bridge, new defense equipment, or to build new schools, the money is directly injected into the country's circular flow of income as workers are hired to build or construct the new public goods.
   ii. However, when the same government cuts taxes by *x dollars* or transfers *x dollars* from one group of citizens to another, a smaller stimulus results as only a proportion of the tax cut or transfer will be spent on new goods and services, while some proportion will be saved by those who receive the money.

**B.** Multipliers. Earlier in this chapter, we introduced the concept of the spending multiplier, which tells us the magnitude by which real GDP will change as a result of a particular change in spending in the economy.

1. The spending multiplier is a function of the marginal propensities to consume and save, and is determined using the formula:

$$\text{Spending multiplier} = \frac{1}{1-\text{MPC}}$$

i. For example, in a country with a marginal propensity to consume 0.5, the spending multiplier is:

$$\text{Spending multiplier} = \frac{1}{1-0.5} = 2$$

ii. A $100 million increase in government spending would stimulate the country's GDP by $200 million.

2. The government spending multiplier is greater than the tax multiplier. To determine the approximate effect of a tax cut of a particular amount, the tax multiplier must be used.

   i. A tax cut affects AD only indirectly, since it is left up to those who receive it to determine how much of it they will spend on new goods and services and how much they will save.

   ii. The formula for determining the tax multiplier is:

$$\text{Tax multiplier} = \frac{-\text{MPC}}{\text{MPS}}$$

   iii. Note that the tax multiplier is negative; this is because a change in taxes (an increase or a decrease) will have the opposite effect on spending in the economy.

   iv. For example, an increase in taxes causes disposable incomes and consumption to decrease, while a tax cut causes disposable incomes and consumption to *increase.*

   v. In our country introduced above with an MPC of 0.5, the MPS also equals 0.5. Therefore, the tax multiplier is:

$$\text{Tax multiplier} = \frac{-0.5}{0.5} = -1$$

3. If the government cuts taxes by $100 million, the country's GDP could be expected to increase by $100 million.

   i. Compare this to the effect of the $100 million increase in government spending, which would have stimulated GDP by $200 million.

   ii. What accounts for the smaller stimulus effect of the tax cut of $100 million? The answer is that households will *save half of the tax cut,* and the initial increase in spending will therefore only be $50 million, resulting in a much smaller increase in overall GDP compared to the increase in government spending.

**D.** The table below shows the spending multipliers and the tax multipliers associated with various levels of marginal propensities to consume and save.

| MPC* | Spending multiplier | Tax multiplier |
|---|---|---|
| 0.9 | $\frac{1}{0.1} = 10$ | $\frac{-0.9}{0.1} = -9$ |
| 0.6 | $\frac{1}{0.4} = 2.5$ | $\frac{-0.6}{0.4} = -1.5$ |
| 0.5 | $\frac{1}{0.5} = 2$ | $\frac{-0.5}{0.5} = -1$ |
| 0.4 | $\frac{1}{0.6} = 1.67$ | $\frac{-0.4}{0.6} = -0.67$ |
| 0.2 | $\frac{1}{0.8} = 1.25$ | $\frac{-0.2}{0.8} = -0.25$ |

*Marginal propensity to consume

1. Note that the magnitude of the tax multiplier is always less than that of the spending multiplier. Policymakers should be aware of this when determining the best fiscal policy response to a macroeconomic shock such as a recessionary or an inflationary gap.
2. Understanding the different effects of changes to government spending or taxes allows policy makers to determine the appropriate size of a fiscal policy to deal with the challenge at hand.

**E.** Correcting Output Gaps. Expansionary or contractionary fiscal policies are used to restore full employment when the economy is in a negative or positive output gap.

1. Negative output gaps. Assume our country is in recession and economists estimate its equilibrium real GDP is $80 million below its full employment GDP.
    i. We can determine the size of an increase in spending or a decrease in taxes needed to achieve the desired increase in GDP:

$$\text{Needed } \Delta \text{ in spending} = \frac{\text{Needed } \Delta \text{ in GDP}}{\text{spending multiplier}}$$
$$= \frac{\$80 \text{ million}}{2} = \$40 \text{ million}$$
$$\text{Needed } \Delta \text{ in taxes} = \frac{\text{Needed } \Delta \text{ in GDP}}{\text{tax multiplier}}$$
$$= \frac{\$80 \text{ million}}{-1} = -\$80 \text{ million}$$

ii. To achieve the needed $80 million increase in GDP, the government must either increase spending by $40 million or cut taxes by $80 million.

2. Fiscal policy can influence AD, real output, and the price level. The AD-AS model can be used to demonstrate the immediate effects of fiscal policy. The following graph shows the economy experiencing a recessionary gap of $80 million.

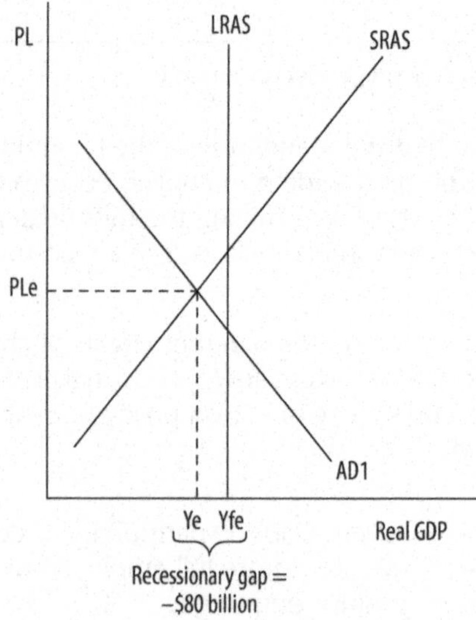


i. Assume the government decides to enact an expansionary fiscal policy and increases spending by $40 million in order to boost AD and end the recession.

 - The initial increase in spending will shift the AD curve out by $40 million, but once household incomes rise they begin spending half of what they earn, further boosting AD until the final increase in expenditures is twice the initial change in government spending.

- The immediate and final impact on AD of the fiscal stimulus is shown in the following graph.

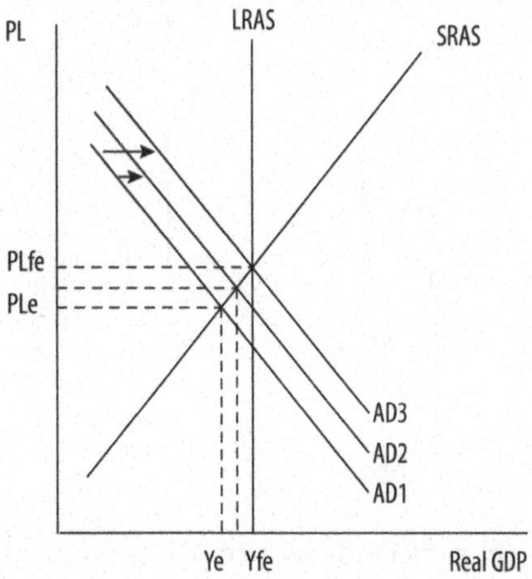


- The fiscal stimulus has increased AD, the price level, and the level of real output. Unemployment falls as the recession ends and those who were cyclically unemployed at Ye are rehired.
- At Yfe, unemployment is at its natural rate.

3. Positive output gaps. Contractionary fiscal policies can be employed to cool down an overheating economy and close an inflationary gap.

   i. Assume that the fictional country of Mellondia has an inflationary gap of $150 million and that inflation is higher than desired at 5% and unemployment is at an all-time low of 2.5%.

   ii. The government fears that any further decrease in unemployment will drive inflation to even greater heights, so it decides to cool down the economy by raising income taxes.

   iii. Assume also that the marginal propensity to consume is 0.75.

   iv. The following graph shows the economy before the contractionary fiscal policy is enacted.

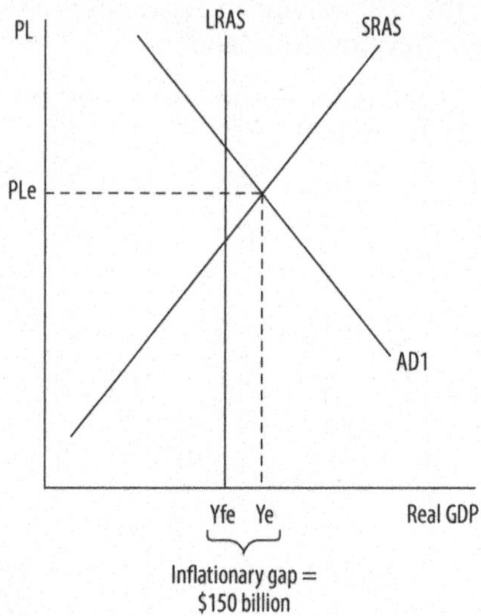


v. To sufficiently reduce AD through a tax hike, the government needs to consider the size of the tax multiplier.

$$\text{Tax multiplier} = \frac{-\text{MPC}}{\text{MPS}} = \frac{-0.75}{0.25} = -3$$

- With this information the government can determine the amount by which taxes should be raised.

$$\text{Needed } \Delta \text{ in taxes} = \frac{\text{desired in GDP}}{\text{tax multiplier}}$$

$$= \frac{-\$150 \text{ million}}{-3} = \$50 \text{ million}$$

- Mellondia should raise taxes by $50 million to achieve a $150 million decrease in its GDP.
  - The initial increase in taxes will reduce disposable income by $50 million, which will in turn reduce consumption by 75% of the $50 million, or by $37.5 million.
  - The $37.5 million fall in spending is then multiplied four times throughout the economy, leading to an ultimate fall in aggregate expenditures of $150 million.
  - The effect of the contractionary fiscal policy is seen in the following graph.

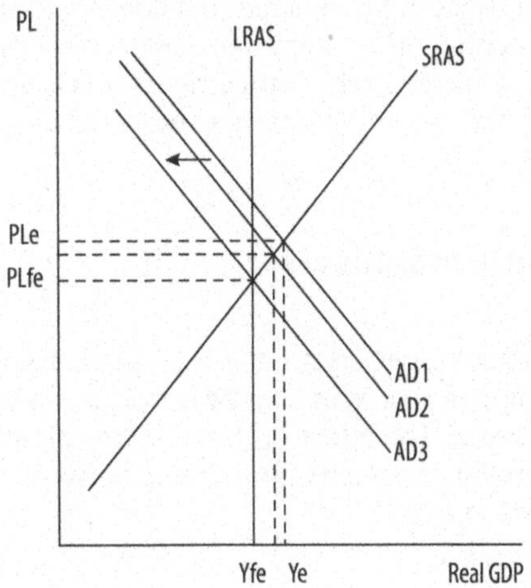


- The increase in income taxes had led to a decrease in disposable incomes and consumption among households, reducing AD, the price level, and the equilibrium level of national output.
- Unemployment, which had been a troublesome low of 2.5% at Ye, has returned to its natural rate at the full employment level of output of Yfe.

F. Time Lags. There are expected time lags to discretionary fiscal policy caused by factors such as the time it takes to decide on and implement a policy action.

1. Government officials may take several months or longer to decide on and enact fiscal policies.
2. In democracies like the U.S., votes must be taken in both chambers of the legislature and bills must be signed by the executive branch before they can be enacted into law.
3. By the time an appropriate package of spending and/or tax changes can be enacted into law, the country's macroeconomic conditions may have changed.
    i. For example, during a recession it would be expected that over time nominal wages will fall and firms will begin hiring unemployed workers without any government intervention.
    ii. If the government adds a fiscal stimulus, an undesirable outcome may result. For example, a tax cut or an increase in

spending is enacted in a country that is automatically self-correcting during a recession. This fiscal stimulus may result in an unfavorable outcome in which unemployment falls below the natural rate rather than returning to it.

## X. Automatic Stabilizers

**A.** Automatic stabilizers are the built-in changes in transfers and taxation that happen when an economy's output and employment increase or decrease. The effect of these automatic stabilizers is to prevent an economy from overheating that otherwise might do so following an increase in AD.

**B.** Discretionary Fiscal Policies. Government policymakers who change fiscal policy to either contract or expand AD are implementing discretionary fiscal policies.

**C.** Triggering Automatic Fiscal Stabilizers. When changes in output or employment trigger automatic increases or decreases in spending and taxation, an economy is employing automatic fiscal stabilizers.

**D.** Negative Demand Shock. Consider what happens following a negative demand shock resulting from a decrease in foreign incomes and net exports:

1. As AD falls, workers in the export sector are laid off due to sticky wages and other input costs in the short run.
2. Unemployed workers who have lost their income stop paying income taxes, so there is an automatic decrease in the taxes collected by the government.
3. As long as AD remains weak, workers will remain unemployed and many will begin collecting unemployment benefits from the government; therefore, there is an automatic increase in transfers as AD falls.
4. During a demand-deficient recession, tax revenues decrease automatically as GDP falls, preventing consumption and the economy from falling further.
5. At the same time, transfer payments increase, helping maintain consumption among those who have lost their jobs.

6. The effect of these automatic stabilizers is to steady AD and prevent it from falling as much as it would if these effects had not contributed.

E. Positive Demand Shock. Consider what happens when an economy already producing at full employment experiences an increase in investment spending.
    1. As AD increases, workers who were structurally or frictionally unemployed will be hired by firms producing capital goods, causing unemployment to fall below its natural rate.
    2. Newly employed workers start paying income tax, automatically increasing tax revenues for the government.
    3. Since they are no longer unemployed, the same workers will stop collecting unemployment benefits from the government, automatically reducing the amount government pays in transfers.
    4. During an expansion, tax revenues increase automatically as GDP rises, slowing consumption and preventing the economy from overheating.
    5. At the same time, transfer payments decrease, helping prevent consumption from rising more than it otherwise would.

F. The following graph shows the relationship between the level of GDP, tax revenues, and government expenditures.

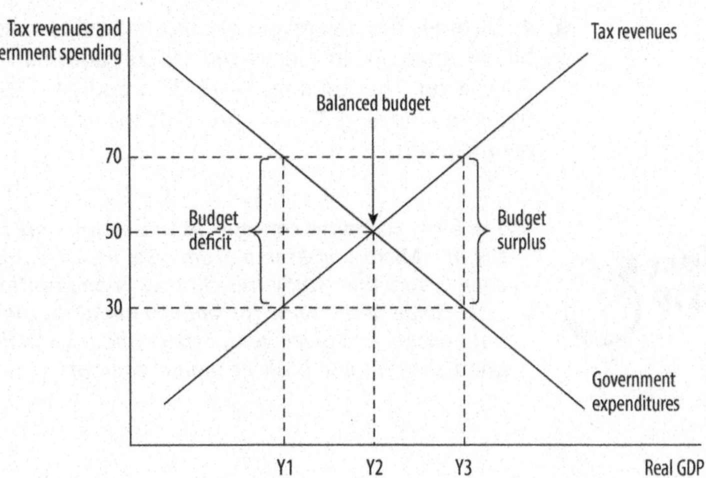

1. In the economy depicted in the preceding graph, three combinations of real GDP, tax revenues, and government expenditures are depicted.

    i. At output of Y1 (Year 1), the economy is in a recession; tax revenues are down to $30 billion due to reduced output and employment, while government expenditures are at $70 billion due to increased transfer payments to unemployed workers and to households who have slipped below the poverty line.

    ii. The resulting budget deficit of $40 billion represents an automatic stimulus to the economy; no new policies were enacted by the government, rather, the built-in stabilizers of the country's social safety nets have resulted in increased government spending and reduced tax revenues, mitigating the recessionary effects of the fall in AD.

    iii. At Y2, the economy is producing at a level where tax revenues and government expenditures are equal at $50 billion. The budget is "balanced," meaning spending equals taxation.

    iv. The increase in output from Y1 to Y2 has meant more revenues have come in due to higher incomes and more economic activity, while less money has gone out in the form of unemployment and welfare benefits.

    v. At Y3, the economy is producing beyond full employment, perhaps due to a positive demand shock such as an increase in private sector investment.

    vi. As incomes rise, tax revenues automatically increase to $70 billion while government expenditures automatically fall to $30 billion. The resulting $40 billion budget surplus dampens the effect of rising AD and prevents the economy from overheating.

***The basic economic concepts in this chapter are tested on both the AP® Micro and Macro exams. So, if you're taking the two courses together, study this chapter in preparation for both tests. Some of the same (or similar) questions may appear on both exams in a given year. Expect about six multiple-choice questions on these basic economic concepts.***

Chapter 6

# UNIT 4 Financial Sector

## I. Financial Assets

A. Definition. A financial asset is any non-physical asset whose value is derived from a contractual claim.

1. Money is the most familiar financial asset. Money comes in many forms, depending on its liquidity, which refers to the degree to which an asset can easily be bought or sold.

   i. Cash is the most liquid form of money, as it is universally accepted as a means of payment for goods and services.

   ii. Cash's value is based on the contractual agreement between its owner and the government that issued it.

   iii. Belief in the value of cash is tied to confidence that the issuing government will manage its supply responsibly.

2. Other financial assets. Assets that can be held in place of cash include deposits at banks (called demand deposits), bonds (interest-bearing assets), and equities (also called stocks).

   i. Along with cash, which includes both coins and paper money, demand deposits are the next most liquid financial asset.

      - Demand deposits refer to money kept in an account at an institution such as a commercial bank against which checks can be written or a debit card can be used to buy goods and services.

      - In a checking account, the money figure on your account statement is your demand deposits. This money, while it is not necessarily held as cash by the bank, can be spent just like cash by using a debit card.

ii. Besides cash and demand deposits, other, less liquid financial assets include bonds and equities (stocks).

- Bonds are interest-bearing debt contracts that are issued by governments or corporations. They cannot be used as a means of payment and cannot be converted to cash easily enough to be considered a form of money.
- Equities or stocks are ownership shares in a corporation. They are not considered money because they cannot be directly exchanged for goods and services.

**B.** Role of Bonds in the Financial Sector. Governments and private companies can issue and sell bonds as a way of borrowing money to invest in public goods or capital.

1. To attract investors to their bonds, the issuer must offer a yield (or interest rate), which is inversely related to the price of the previously-issued bonds.

i. For example, assume the U.S. government wishes to borrow $1 billion from the public to finance a budget deficit (a shortfall of tax revenue compared to government spending).

- To raise the money, the government issues one million 1-year bonds with a face value of $1,000 each (1 million × $1,000 = $1 billion).
- A bond represents a promise to pay the person who buys it the face value of the bond exactly one year in the future.
- No rational investor would be willing to pay the face value of the bond today, because it would not be profitable to lend the government $1,000 today only to get repaid exactly $1,000 in the future.
- To make the investment attractive, therefore, at the time of issue, the government must sell the bond for something less than $1,000.
- The lower the price of the bond, the higher the yield (the interest rate) earned by the bond investor.

2. The following graph shows the market for 1-year, $1,000 U.S. government bonds (bonds that will pay their holders $1,000 in one year from the date of purchase).

   i. The bond's price is determined by the supply (based on the number of bonds issued by the government, which in turn is based on the government's need for borrowing), and the demand for bonds (which is based on the price of and the return on alternative assets investors could buy, such as savings accounts and equities).

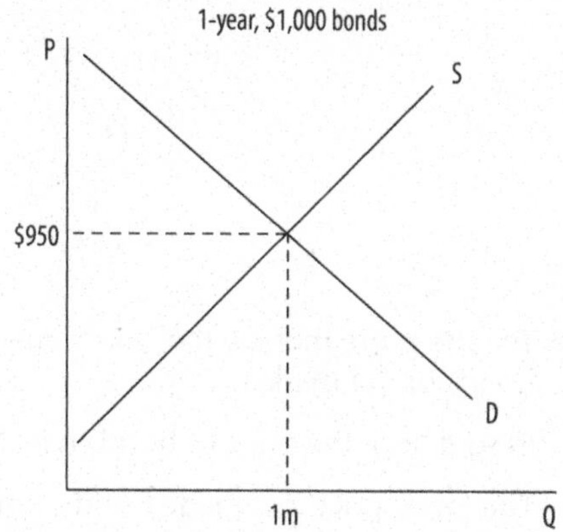


   ii. At a price of $950, the government is able to sell 1 million bonds that promise to pay buyers $1,000 in exactly one year.

   iii. We can determine the interest these bonds will yield for the investors who buy them, knowing that one year after purchasing a bond an investor will receive a $1,000 payment from the government.

   - Investor's purchase price = $950
   - Payment from government after one year = $1,000
   - Investor's return = $50
   - $\text{Interest on investment} = \dfrac{\text{Investor's return}}{\text{Purchase price}} \times 100 = \dfrac{\$50}{\$950} \times 100 = 5.26\%$

   An investor who pays $950 for a $1,000, 1-year bond will earn interest of 5.26%.

3. What happens if the government needs to issue more bonds to finance an even larger budget deficit? The supply of bonds will increase and in any market, the equilibrium price will decrease.

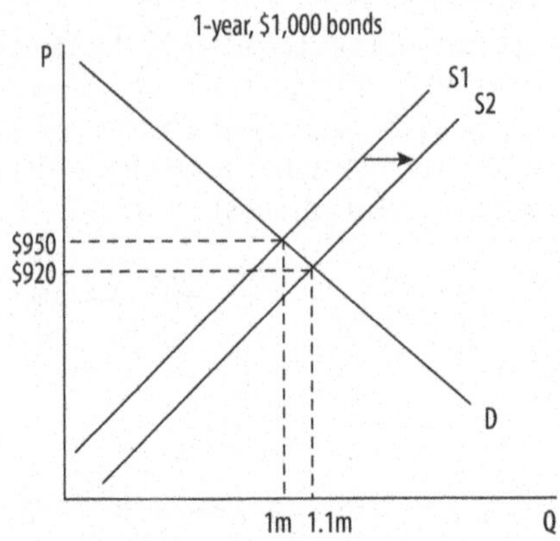


   i. To raise more money, the government has supplied more bonds to the market.

   ii. In so doing, the price of bonds has decreased.

   iii. The lower price has made bonds a more attractive investment to investors, who will now enjoy a higher yield.

   iv. We can calculate the new interest rate on 1-year, $1,000 government bonds:

      - Investor's purchase price = $920
      - Payment from government after one year = $1,000
      - Investor's return = $80
      - Interest on investment = $\frac{\$80}{\$920} \times 100 = 8.69\%$

   As prices of bonds fall, the interest rate investors can earn increases. Now, instead of earning just over 5% on their investment, bond investors enjoy a nearly 9% return on the money lent to the government.

4. An individual or institution's demand for money as an asset, therefore, is inversely related to the interest rate in the economy.

   i. At higher interest rates, less money is demanded by households as an asset, since the opportunity cost of holding money is greater.

ii. At lower interest rates, more money is demanded as an asset, since the opportunity cost of holding money is lower.

## II. Nominal vs. Real Interest Rates

**A.** The *nominal interest* rate is the annual rate a borrower must pay back a lender for the use of borrowed money or the annual rate a lender receives in payment for their investment. The *real interest rate* is the nominal interest rate adjusted for inflation.

1. Lenders and borrowers will establish nominal interest rates based on their desired rate of return and the expected rate of inflation.

   i. For example, a bank lends money to Rahim at a real return of 5% each year the loan is paid back. Then the bank and Rahim must establish a nominal interest rate that takes into account the expected inflation rate, in this case, 3%.

      - Desired real return = 5%
      - Expected inflation rate = 3%
      - Nominal interest rate = 5% + 3% = 8%

   ii. To earn a real return of 5%, the bank must charge a nominal interest rate of 8%, since inflation is expected to reduce the value of the money Rahim repays by 3%.

   iii. The formula is:

   Nominal interest rate = desired real rate + expected inflation rate

2. A real interest rate can be calculated in hindsight by subtracting the actual inflation rate from the nominal interest rate:

   Real interest rate = nominal interest rate – inflation rate

   i. Lenders charge an inflation premium by adjusting the nominal interest rates they charge borrowers by the anticipated inflation rate.

      - Higher expected inflation will lead banks to raise the inflation premium and increase the nominal interest rate on new loans.
      - This way, banks are protected from the diminished purchasing power of the money they are repaid.

- The nominal interest rate established is the desired real return rate plus the expected inflation rate.

ii. Nominal interest rates are determined in the money market, where the money supply is determined by a country's central bank policy and the demand for money is determined by anyone who needs money as an asset or to purchase goods and services, including households, firms, governments, and foreign nationals.

iii. Real interest rates are determined in the market for loanable funds, where the supply of savings and the demand for investment establish equilibrium interest rates in the economy.

## III. Definition, Measurement, and Functions of Money

A. Money is any asset that is widely accepted as a means of payment. Money can be either commodity money (whose value comes from the commodity from which it is made, such as a silver coin), or fiat money (which has no intrinsic value, such as paper currency). As long as the asset is generally recognized as payment for goods and services, it can be considered money.

1. Any asset used as money must serve three basic functions:

i. Medium of exchange. Money must be widely accepted as a means for purchasing goods, services, or other assets. Therefore, money is best when it is portable and durable, able to remain in circulation for a long period of time without deteriorating. While coins are particularly durable, paper money is exceptionally portable. Both are universally accepted as a medium of exchange by sellers of goods and services.

ii. Store of value. Any asset that can transfer purchasing power from the present to the future is a store of value. When a person chooses not to spend $1 million today but instead saves it for future consumption, she puts faith in the money's ability to store value for the future.

iii. Unit of account. Money is used to express the value of something. When we say "this car cost $30,000" or "this car cost $3,000," we have a pretty good understanding of which car is nicer than the other. In this case money (dollars) is used as a unit of account; we know how much something is worth based on how much money one is willing to spend on it. Dollars, yen, euros, or any other currency acts as a convenient common denominator for accounting purposes (e.g. for calculating GDP or comparing individuals' incomes or wealth levels).

**B.** A nation's money supply has several components, ranging from the most liquid types of money (M0 and M1) to less liquid types (M2).

1. M0: Also called the "monetary base," M0 includes currency in circulation and commercial banks' reserves held at the central bank.
2. M1: The M1 money supply includes the monetary base (M0) plus all the demand deposits of the nation's households.
3. M2: The M2 money supply includes M1 plus less liquid forms of money, including savings accounts, small-denominated time deposits, and money market mutual funds. M2 is the broadest measure of the money supply reported by the United States Federal Reserve System.
4. Note that not all financial assets are included in the money supply. Bonds, equities, and other relatively illiquid assets are not considered "money" since they do not fulfill all of money's requisite functions.

**C.** Consider the following table, which includes the value of different types of money in Country X.

| Type of asset | Value |
|---|---|
| Cash, coins, and bank reserves | $200 million |
| Demand deposits | $300 million |
| Savings deposits | $300 million |
| Small-denominated time deposits | $50 million |
| Money market mutual funds | $150 million |

1. From this table, we can determine the size of each of the components of the country's money supply.
   i. M0: Cash, coins, and bank reserves = $200 million
   ii. M1: M0 + demand deposits = 200 million + $300 million = $500 million
   iii. M2: M1 + savings deposits, small-denominated time deposits, and money market mutual funds = $500 million + $300 million + $50 million + $150 million = $1 billion

2. Country X's total money supply is $1 billion. This includes all forms of money, from the most liquid forms in the monetary base (M0) and demand deposits (M1) to the less liquid forms included only in M2.

3. Note that excluded in the money supply are non-money financial assets such as the value of stocks and bonds.

## IV. Banking and Expansion of the Money Supply

**A.** Depository institutions, mainly banks, serve a crucial role in modern economies.

1. Functions. By accepting deposits in checking and savings accounts, banks protect households' financial assets. By making loans to businesses and other households, banks provide money for investments in infrastructure, capital equipment, and housing for the economy. Banks act as the primary intermediary between households seeking to earn interest on their savings and businesses looking to borrow money for investment.

2. Assets and liabilities. Whenever a bank accepts a deposit from a household, that money is considered a liability for the bank.

   i. A liability is created when someone owes money to someone else because of a past transaction.

   ii. For the depositor, the money is an asset, which means it is something of value that someone owns or that someone is owed sometime in the future.

      - If Joseph deposits $1,000 in a bank, that money is an asset for Joseph and a liability for the bank.

      - On the other hand, if a bank loans $1,000 to Carlo, that $1,000 is an asset for the bank and a liability for Carlo, since it is he who owes the bank money sometime in the future.

3. Accounting. Banks organize their assets and liabilities into balance sheets, which are accounting tools for visualizing and keeping track of the money coming and going into and leaving a bank.

   i. The following table is a simple bank balance sheet for the Bank of White Oak.

**Bank of White Oak's Balance Sheet**

| Assets | | Liabilities | |
|---|---|---|---|
| Reserves | $5,000 | Demand deposits | $20,000 |
| Loans | $15,000 | Owner's equity | $5,000 |
| Government bonds | $3,000 | | |
| Property | $2,000 | | |
| Total assets | $25,000 | Total liabilities | $25,000 |

ii. A bank's assets always equal its liabilities. Here are more details about the different parts of the Bank of White Oak's balance sheet. First, the liabilities:

- Demand deposits = $20,000. This is the money bank customers have deposited and are able to write checks against or use their debit cards to make purchases. Demand deposits are a liability for the bank because they are other people's money. The bank is obliged to provide the depositors with these funds upon request.
- Owner's equity = $5,000. Owner's equity is the money the bank's founders (or investors) pitched in to start the bank with. This is a liability for the bank because if any investor sought to withdraw their equity and invest it elsewhere the bank would owe the individual his or her share of the equity.
- The bank's total liabilities are the money it owes people, either depositors or the bank's investors.

Here are the assets:

- Reserves = $5,000. Reserves are the portion of the bank's total deposits that the bank has not loaned out. This is "cash on hand" at the bank (or, more likely, at the central bank in whatever country the Bank of White Oak operates).
- Loans = $15,000. Loans are the money the bank has loaned to private borrowers (such as businesses or households who have borrowed to invest in capital or housing). Loans are an asset because they represent money owed to the bank.
- Government bonds = $3,000. Government bonds are bank loans to the government. As discussed earlier, bonds are certificates of debt owed to the holder of the bond by the issuer of the bond. Since the government owes the bank this money, it is an asset for the bank.
- Property = $2,000. The bank's property is the physical capital of the bank itself. This includes any buildings, land, computers, desks and chairs, and all other physical assets owned by the bank.
- The bank's total assets are the money it is owed by others, the money it has on hand (reserves), and the bank's physical property.

**B.** Money Creation. By accepting deposits from households, then lending those deposits to borrowers, which end up being deposited and lent again and again, banks *create new money* through their daily financial activities.

1. Commercial banks must keep a certain percentage of deposits in reserve. Required reserves are the portion of a bank's deposits the bank is required by the country's central bank to keep in reserve. For example:

    i. A reserve requirement of 20% means that a bank with total deposits of $1 million would have to keep $200,000 on reserve at the central bank. This money may not be loaned out by the commercial bank.

    ii. With the other $800,000, the bank can make loans and charge interest on those loans. The bank's business model is to charge a higher interest rate to borrowers than it pays to households saving money with the bank.

2. Excess reserves are a bank's actual reserves minus required reserves. Banks are allowed to make loans only from their excess reserves.

   i. The following table highlights the balance sheet of the Bank of YourTrust.

**Bank of YourTrust Balance Sheet**

| Assets | | Liabilities | |
|---|---|---|---|
| Required Reserves | $15,000 | Demand deposits | $30,000 |
| Excess reserves | $3,000 | Owner's equity | $4,000 |
| Loans | $8,000 | | |
| Government bonds | $5,000 | | |
| Property | $3,000 | | |
| Total assets | $34,000 | Total liabilities | $34,000 |

- The Bank of YourTrust has $30,000 in total deposits and it is required to keep $15,000 in reserve.
- The *reserve requirement* (also called the required reserve ratio) can be determined by dividing the bank's required reserves by its total deposits:

$$\text{Reserve requirements} = \frac{\text{required reserves}}{\text{total deposits}}$$
$$= \frac{\$15,000}{\$30,000} = 0.5$$

- The Bank of YourTrust as well as other U.S. banks is required to keep 50% of its total deposits in reserve.
  - Typically, the actual money will be stored at the country's central bank, which is the national bank that sets bank regulations and controls the country's money supply (discussed later in this chapter).
- Note that the bank has excess reserves of $3,000. This is money the bank can use to make new loans.
- Excess reserves are the basis of the expansion of the money supply by the banking system and will be explained further below.

C. Money Multiplier. Whenever a bank makes a loan to a borrower, new money is actually being created by the banking system. It sounds strange, but it really does happen.

1. Assume that the Bank of White Oak receives a deposit of $100 and that the central bank requires all commercial banks to keep 20% of their total deposits on reserve (the required reserve ratio is 0.2).

   i. The following graphic illustrates how this $100 deposit will lead to the creation of new money across the banking system.

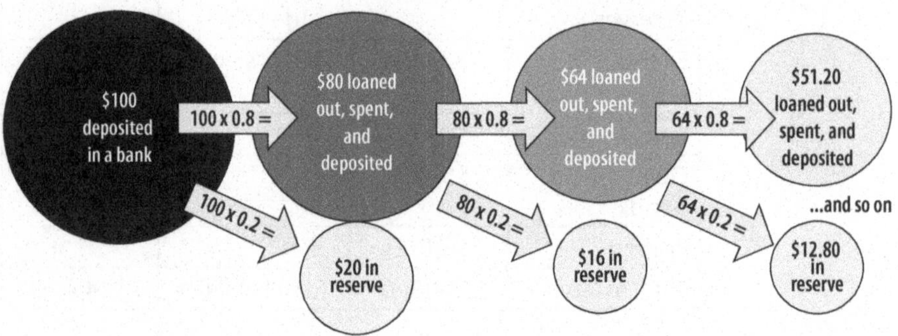


   ii. Money deposited in one bank creates *excess reserves*, which can be loaned to borrowers, which can be spent and deposited in other banks, creating more excess reserves which can be loaned out again.

   iii. In this way, an initial change in bank deposits will lead to a greater change in the overall money supply in an economy.

   iv. The degree by which the money supply will be affected depends on the size of the money multiplier.

$$\text{The Money Multiplier} = \frac{1}{\text{Required Reserve Ratio}}$$

2. To determine the total impact on the money supply of an initial change in a bank's deposits, multiply the initial change in excess reserves by the money multiplier. For example, when $100 is deposited in the Bank of White Oak:

   i. Required reserves increase by $20.

   ii. Excess reserves increase by $80.

   iii. Assuming the bank loans out all of its excess reserves, multiply the change in excess reserves by the money multiplier:

$$80 \times \frac{1}{0.2} = 80 \times 5 = \$400$$

iv. The initial deposit of $100 will lead to the creation of $400 of new money throughout the banking system.

3. The amount predicted by the simple money multiplier may be overstated because it does not account for a bank's desire to hold excess reserves or the public's desire to hold onto currency as an asset.

    i. One assumption in the preceding calculation is that the bank loans all of its excess reserves, that borrowers spend all of the borrowed money, and that its recipients deposit all of what they earned in the bank.

    ii. Banks may hold some of their excess reserves as cash and households may hold some of their savings as cash. The technical term for these actions is liquidity preference.

    iii. Depending on the degree of banks' and the public's liquidity preference, the money multiplier will be smaller than that predicted by the preceding simple equation.

4. The money multiplier is the ratio of the money supply to the monetary base. To understand why, let's revisit our money supply table from earlier in the chapter.

    i. Consider the following table, which includes the value of the different types of money in Country X.

| Type of asset | Value |
|---|---|
| Cash and bank reserves | $200 million |
| Demand deposits | $300 million |
| Savings deposits | $300 million |
| Small-denominated time deposits | $50 million |
| Money market mutual funds | $150 million |

ii. The total money supply (M2) in this country was $1 billion.

- The monetary base (M0), which includes cash and bank reserves), is $200 million.
- The money multiplier can be calculated as the ratio of M2 over M0.

$$\text{Money multiplier} = \frac{\text{M2}}{\text{M0}}$$
$$= \frac{\$1\text{ billion}}{\$200\text{ million}} = 5$$

- There is just $200 million of actual cash in this economy. Yet, from this relatively small amount, there is a money supply of $1 billion.

iii. All the demand deposits, savings deposits, and money in small-denominated time deposits and money market mutual funds is money that was created through the lending activities of commercial banks from the reserves created through households' deposits.

*Practice using the required reserve ratio and the money multiplier to calculate the effects of changes in checkable deposits in the banking system on required reserves, excess reserves, and the total reserves in the banking system. Typically, there will be four or five multiple-choice questions phrased in various ways requiring the use of the required reserve ratio (RRR) and the money multiplier.*

*Carefully read the multiple-choice questions before answering. For example, the following question can be misinterpreted. "Assume the required reserve ratio is 20%, and a bank receives a new deposit of $1,000. How much is the increase in the bank's required reserves?" A similar question may conclude with "How much is the increase in the bank's excess reserves?" While only one word has changed in the question, the answer will be clearly different. Read carefully to determine exactly what a question is asking.*

## V. The Money Market

A. The demand for money shows the inverse relationship between the nominal interest rate and the quantity of money people want to hold. The public demands money for one of two reasons: either as an asset or to purchase goods or services.

1. The *asset demand* for money is inversely related to the interest rate.

    i. At higher interest rates less money is demanded as an asset, because the opportunity cost of holding cash is higher due to the interest income foregone by holding money instead of investing it in savings accounts, government bonds, or other interest earning assets.

    ii. At low interest rates the asset demand for money is greater, since there is less opportunity cost of holding cash since alternative financial assets (savings accounts, bonds) would earn less interest income.

    iii. Recall that there is an inverse relationship between bond prices and interest rates. At higher interest rates bonds are cheaper and therefore a more attractive asset than money.

    iv. When interest rates are lower, bonds are more expensive and thus holding money as wealth is more desirable.

2. The *transaction demand* for money depends on the level of output produced in the nation and the interest rate.

    i. At lower interest rates, households are more willing to spend money on goods and services due to the lower opportunity cost of spending rather than saving.

    ii. At higher interest rates, the public demands less money for transactions, since the opportunity cost of making purchases is higher when more interest can be earned in financial assets.

    iii. As national income rises, the demand for money for transactions increases at every interest rate, as people wish to consume more when their incomes are higher.

    iv. During a recession, when national income falls, the transaction demand for money decreases at every interest rate due to the fall in income and consumption.

3. The inverse relationship between the demand for money as an asset and for transactions, and the nominal interest rate, is illustrated in a money demand curve.

    i. The following graph shows the money demand curve for the fictional country of Mogulia.

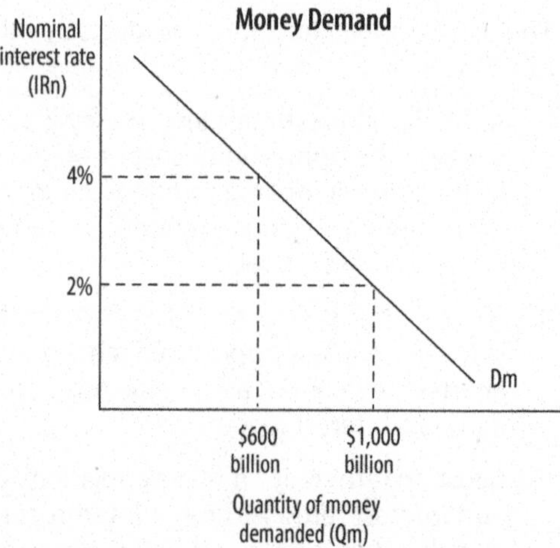


    ii. The money demand curve above shows that at a 4% interest rate, Mogulian households choose to hold $600 billion as an asset and for transactions, while at 2%, $1,000 billion (i.e., one trillion dollars) is demanded.

    iii. A change in national income and consumption would cause a shift in the money demand curve.

        - For example, assume Mogulia enters a recession and household incomes fall, leading to a fall in consumption of goods and services. Now, at every interest rate, consumers demand less money for transactions.

➤ The decrease in money demand is shown as an inward shift of the Dm (money demand) curve in our graph.

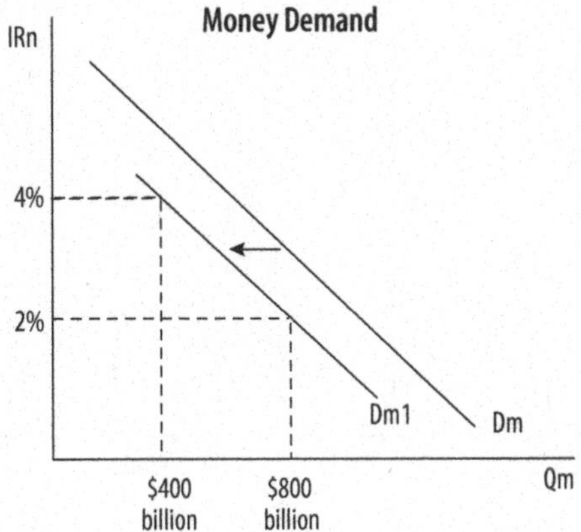


➤ Due to falling income and consumption, money demand has decreased. Now, only $400 billion is demanded at an interest rate of 4% and $800 billion at 2%.

**B.** The money demand curve is just one side of the money market model. Money supply is determined by a country's central bank and is independent of the nominal interest rate.

1. The central bank controls a country's money supply through its monetary policy, increasing or decreasing it in order to influence the equilibrium interest rate and promote certain macroeconomic objectives, the primary one being low and stable inflation.

2. The money supply curve is vertical at the central bank's desired quantity of money.

   i. For example, assume the central bank of Mogulia sets the M1 money supply (cash and demand deposits) at $800 billion. The money supply curve is shown in the following graph.

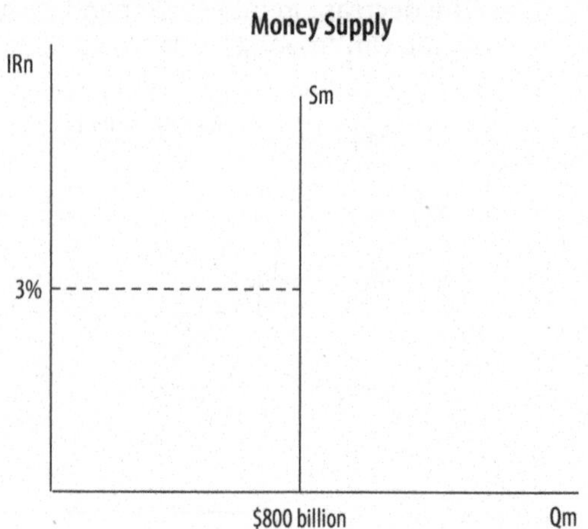


ii. Mogulia's money supply, established by the central bank's monetary policy, is vertical at $800 billion.

C. Equilibrium. The interest rate does not affect the money supply; rather, the equilibrium interest rate is achieved where the quantity of money demanded is equal to the quantity supplied by the central bank.

1. To determine the equilibrium interest rate in Mogulia, consider both the money supply and money demand in the following graph.

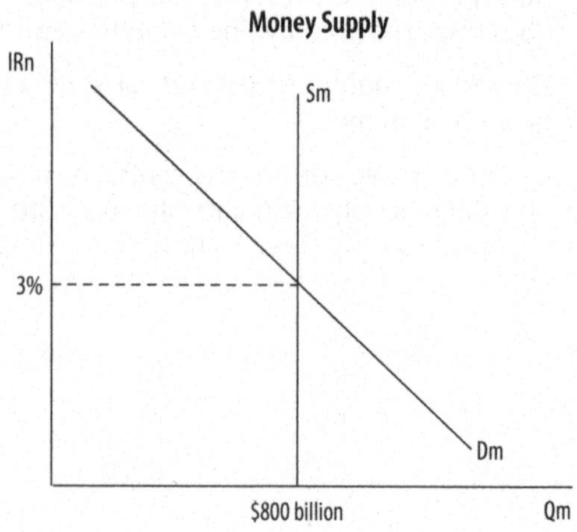

i. By including Mogulia's money demand and money supply in the same graph, we can see the equilibrium interest rate is 3%.

ii. At this rate Mogulian households demand $800 billion for transactions and as cash to hold onto as an asset.

iii. At 3% the quantity of money demanded is equal to the quantity supplied.

The 3% interest rate referred to here is the prime lending rate, or the rate that banks charge their most creditworthy borrowers. All other interest rates (the rate offered to savers and charged to borrowers with poor credit) are based off this prime rate and will be either lower (for savers) or higher (for borrowers with poor credit).

**D.** Disequilibrium. Disequilibrium nominal interest rates create surpluses and shortages in the money market.

1. For example, assume commercial banks attempted to charge borrowers 4% instead of 3%. The impact on the market can be shown in the following graph.

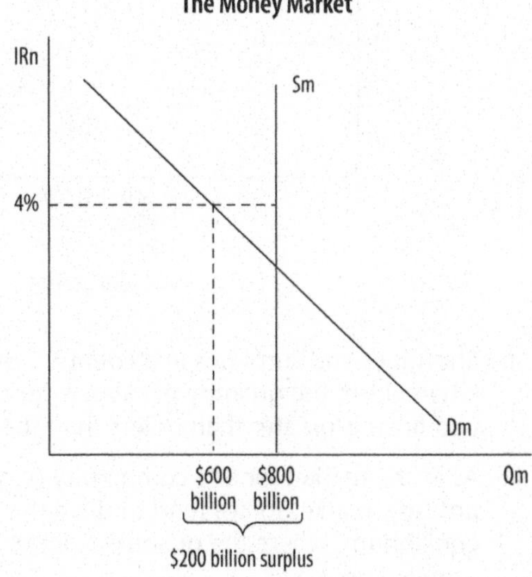


i. At 4%, there is a money surplus in the system; the amount supplied ($800 billion) exceeds the amount demanded ($600 billion).

ii. Market forces would drive nominal interest rates toward equilibrium, as banks must lower rates to incentivize borrowers to withdraw and spend the extra $200 billion that banks hold in reserve.

2. At a rate below equilibrium, a shortage of money arises and market forces would drive nominal interest rates up as banks would be unable to meet the demand from households and firms that want to hold more money for transactions or as an asset than there is available.

   i. At 2%, for example, the shortage would be $200 billion in Mogulia, as seen in the following graph.

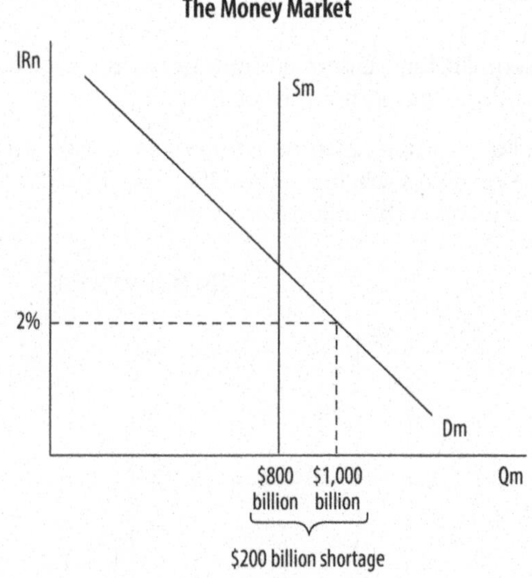


   ii. Shortages and surpluses in a country's money market exist when either the quantity of money demanded by households and firms is greater than or less than the quantity supplied.

   iii. As in the market for any commodity (e.g., cars, toys, food, houses), market forces tend to drive the money market toward equilibrium, where the quantities of money demanded and supplied are equal.

   iv. The equilibrium nominal interest rate is where households and firms demand just as much money as the central bank supplies.

**E.** Changes in Equilibrium. The equilibrium nominal interest rate can be changed by factors that shift the demand for money, such as fluctuations in national income or the price level, and by factors that shift the supply of money, such as monetary policy. Earlier we explained how a change in national income can shift the demand for money. Recessions cause money demand to fall, while expansions cause it to rise.

1. Changes in the price level can have similar effects on money demand.

   i. Inflation, which occurs when there is an increase in the price of consumer goods and services, causes money demand to increase and drives up the nominal interest rate (when things cost more, more money is needed to buy them).

   ii. Deflation, on the other hand, causes money demand to fall and nominal interest rates to decrease.

   iii. The following graphs show the effect of recession or deflation (on the left) and economic expansion or inflation (on the right) on the equilibrium interest rate. In both cases, we assume the central bank holds the money supply constant at $800 billion.

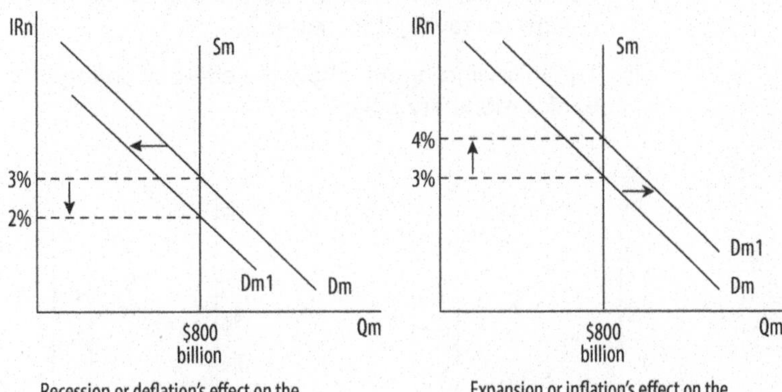


Recession or deflation's effect on the equilibrium interest rate

Expansion or inflation's effect on the equilibrium interest rate

- ➤ A decrease in money demand caused by falling income or falling prices causes the nominal interest rate to fall.
  - – Banks must lower interest rates in order to maintain the quantity demanded at the same level as the quantity supplied.

- Without a drop in interest rates, excess money would be available in the system and banks would not be able to loan out all the money they have in reserve.

➤ An increase in money demand from rising incomes or rising prices causes the nominal interest rate to increase.

- Banks must raise interest rates to maintain the quantity demanded at the same level as the quantity supplied.
- Without a rate hike, there would be a shortage of money in the system. Borrowers could not access the money they demand for transactions and for use as an asset.

2. A change in a central bank's monetary policy causes the money supply to shift and leads to a change in the equilibrium interest rate.

   i. When a country's supply of money increases as the result of an expansionary monetary policy, the nominal interest rate falls in order to maintain equilibrium in the market.

   ii. A decrease in the money supply, known as contractionary monetary policy, causes interest rates to rise as money becomes scarcer. Thus the cost of borrowing money or the reward for saving it increases.

   iii. The following graphs show the effect of changes in a central bank's monetary policy.

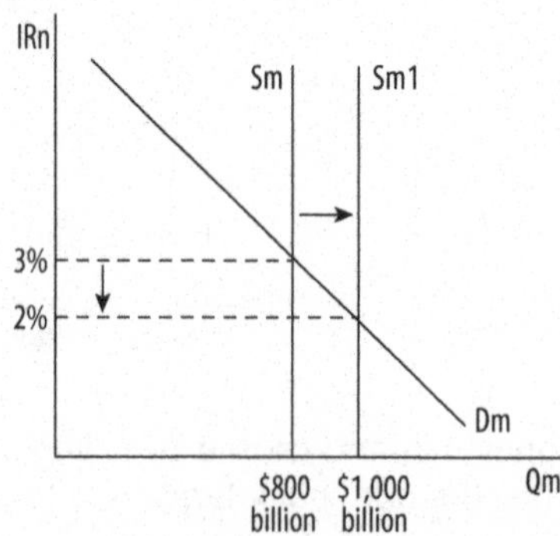

Expansionary monetary policy's effect on the equilibrium interest rate

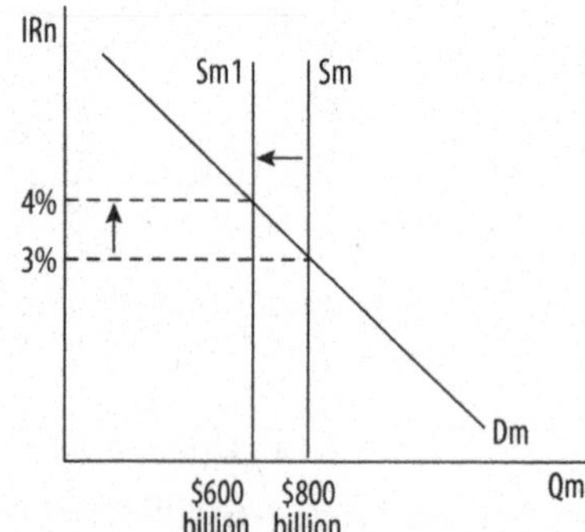

Contractionary monetary policy's effect on the equilibrium interest rate

- Changes in the money supply are the result of a central bank's deliberate intervention in the money market through the use of monetary policy.

## VI. Monetary Policy

A. Tools of Monetary Policy. A central bank's manipulation of the money supply and nominal interest rates is known as *monetary policy*. Central banks implement monetary policies to achieve macroeconomic goals, such as price stability, full employment, and economic growth.

1. A central bank is the institution in most modern market economies that controls the overall supply of money in the nation's economy.

    i. Most central banks act independently of the nation's government and are thus, in theory, insulated from political agendas and influences. They include:

    - The Federal Reserve System, the "Fed" (U.S.)
    - The Bank of England (U.K.)
    - The People's Bank of China (China)
    - The Bank of Japan (Japan)
    - The European Central Bank in the eurozone

    ii. Every major world economy has a central bank. Following is a snapshot of one central bank and its role in the nation's banking system and wider economy.

| The Federal Reserve System of the U.S. | |
|---|---|
| **Overview** | The Fed includes 12 bank branches located in different regions. It is coordinated by the Fed's seven-member board of governors (including the chairperson). The Fed provides banking services to commercial banks, including accepting deposits from and lending money to commercial banks.<br><br>The Federal Open Market Committee (FOMC) is made up of the presidents of five of the 12 banks and the seven members of the Fed's board of governors. The FOMC's job is to determine how and when to increase or decrease the money supply and interest rates in the economy to promote certain macroeconomic objectives, primarily low and stable inflation. |
| **Functions of the Fed** | The Fed has several functions, including the issuing of currency into the commercial banking system. The Fed can inject new currency into the money supply by issuing Federal Reserve Notes (dollars) to commercial banks to be loaned out to the public.<br><br>The Fed also sets the reserve requirements, which tells commercial banks the fraction of their total deposits they must keep in reserve.<br><br>The Fed also lends money to commercial banks through what's called the "discount window." As the "lender of last resort," the Fed typically only loans to banks that are distressed or unable to borrow from other commercial banks to meet their reserve requirement.<br><br>Finally, the Fed controls the money supply by either buying government bonds from commercial banks (increasing the supply of liquid money) or selling bonds to commercial banks (decreasing the supply of money). Through its "open market operations" (or OMO) the Fed can cause the nominal interest rate to decrease (buying bonds) or increase (selling bonds). |

2. By increasing or decreasing the money supply, a central bank can cause interest rates to change, which can then influence the level of aggregate expenditures in the economy. A central bank has *three tools* for increasing or decreasing the supply of money in an economy:

i. Buying and selling of government bonds (OMO, open market operations). Every commercial bank will invest some of its depositors' money in illiquid government bonds (remember our balance sheets from earlier in this chapter?) Bonds are not money.

   - If a central bank wishes to increase the supply of money in the economy, it can buy bonds from commercial banks using newly printed cash (which *is* money!).
   - If the goal is to reduce the money supply, a central bank can sell bonds to commercial banks, which results in less money in circulation and more illiquid government bonds on banks' balance sheets.

ii. Changing the required reserve ratio. The required reserve ratio (RRR) is the percentage of a bank's total deposits it is required to keep in reserve.

   - By reducing the RRR, a central bank immediately increases commercial banks' excess reserves, which frees up money for new loans.
   - By increasing the RRR, a central bank immediately reduces the amount of excess reserves in the banking system and commercial banks must raise interest rates to meet the higher reserve requirement.

iii. Changing the discount rate. The discount rate is the interest rate the central bank charges commercial banks for short-term loans.

   - If this rate is lowered, banks will be more willing to make loans to private borrowers and interest rates will fall.
   - If the discount rate is increased, banks will be less willing to loan to private borrowers and the interest rate will increase.

**B.** Open market operations refer to a central bank's buying and selling of bonds in the bond market and are the most commonly employed monetary policy tool.

1. Open market operations can be employed as either an expansionary monetary policy (one that increases the money supply and reduces interest rates) or as a contractionary monetary policy (one that reduces the money supply and increases interest rates).

2. In order to reduce interest rates, a central bank will buy bonds from commercial banks and the public. An open market purchase of government bonds will cause the money supply to increase by a magnitude determined by the money multiplier.

    i. For example, assume the central bank of the fictional country Wahoovia seeks to reduce interest rates by increasing the money supply by $10 billion.

    ii. The reserve requirement is 20% in Wahoovia. The money multiplier can thus be calculated:

$$\text{Money multiplier} = \frac{1}{\text{RRR}} = \frac{1}{0.2} = 5$$

    iii. If the central bank wishes to increase the money supply by $10 billion, it must purchase $2 billion in government bonds from the public. Doing so will increase banks' excess reserves by $2 billion, which will increase the money supply based on the money multiplier.

Desired $\Delta$ in money supply = $\Delta$ in excess reserves × money multiplier

$2 billion × 5 = $10 billion

    iv. A $2 billion purchase of government bonds by the central bank of Wahoovia will increase the money supply by $10 billion.

        - Banks will loan out the initial $2 billion increase in their excess reserves.
        - This will create new deposits and new loans across the banking system until the initial increase in the money supply is multiplied five times.

3. To raise interest rates, the central bank must reduce the money supply.

    i. To decrease the money supply, the central bank must sell bonds on the open market.

    ii. Recall that there is an inverse relationship between bond prices and bond yields (see Chapter 6, Part V); as the central bank sells bonds, their prices fall and commercial banks (looking for a profit) are attracted to them.

    iii. To buy the higher-yield bonds, banks will take some of their customers' deposits and rather than make loans, will buy government bonds instead.

iv. Assume the central bank seeks to reduce the money supply by \$15 billion and the reserve requirement is 0.2. The money multiplier is 5, therefore an open market sale of bonds must take place:

$$\text{Needed sale of bonds} = \frac{\text{Desired } \Delta \text{ in money supply}}{\text{money multiplier}}$$

$$\frac{-\$15 \text{ billion}}{5} = -\$3 \text{ billion}$$

- To reduce the money supply by \$15 billion, the central bank must sell \$3 billion of government bonds on the open market (reducing banks' reserves by \$3 billion).
- As the preceding equations show, the effect of an open market purchase or sale of government bonds by the central bank on the money supply is greater than the effect on the monetary base because of the money multiplier.

***Be familiar with the three tools of monetary policy. Many multiple-choice questions will test your understanding of these tools. The most commonly used is OMO, so expect several questions asking about the central bank's sale or purchase of government bonds, and be able to calculate the effect on the money supply of a bond sale or purchase of a particular size.***

C. Target Interest Rates. Most modern central banks target an interest rate that commercial banks charge one another for short-term loans (called the interbank overnight lending rate in some countries and the federal funds rate in the U.S.).

1. Commercial banks continually borrow money from one another to meet their reserve requirements. At the end of each business day, some banks will have made new loans that have resulted in their actual reserves falling below their required reserves, while others may have excess reserves that they were not able to loan out.

   i. To cover their shortfalls, banks will borrow "overnight" from others that have excess reserves.

   ii. The interest rate banks charge one another for these short-term loans is known as the federal funds rate, and the central bank (the Fed in the U.S.) can manipulate this nominal interest rate through its open market operations, which in turn will affect investment and consumption.

- An open market bond purchase by the central bank will increase overall reserves in the banking system and lead commercial banks to lower the rate they charge one another for short-term loans, and thus lower the rates they charge customers looking to borrow to finance investments and consumption.
- A bond sale by the central bank will reduce bank reserves and lead banks to charge one another higher nominal rates for their now limited reserves, driving up the market interest rate charged to borrowers.

2. Through their interventions in the bond markets, central banks thus target a nominal interest rate between commercial banks, which in turn affects the commercial rates charged to households and businesses, affecting the level of aggregate expenditures in the economy.

**D.** Output Gaps. Expansionary or contractionary monetary policies are used to restore full employment when the economy is in a negative or positive output gap.

1. Assume for example, that the U.S. economy is in recession with lower than desired inflation; because output is falling and prices are rising more slowly than usual, business investment has declined and household savings have increased as business and consumer sentiment are low.

   i. To stimulate spending and restore full employment, the Fed engages in an open market purchase of government bonds.

   ii. The effect of the Fed's expansionary monetary policy can be seen in the following graphs.

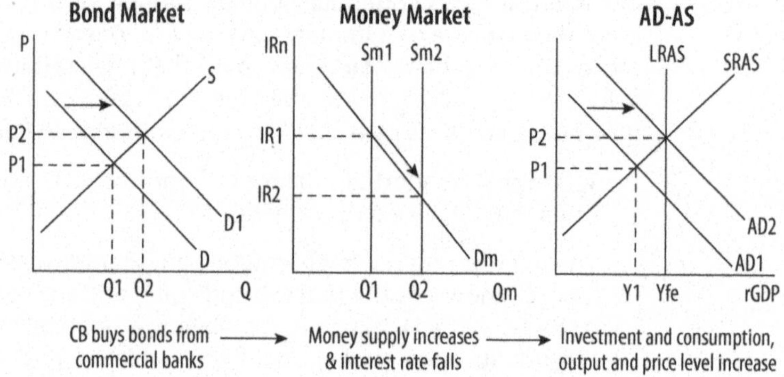

iii. The central bank's purchase of government bonds resulted in a fall in the nominal and the real interest rate, an increase in investment and interest sensitive consumption (e.g., buying a luxury car), and an increase in AD.

- Note that before the expansionary monetary policy this country had a recessionary gap of Yfe – Y1.
- However, after the stimulus, AD has increased to the full employment level.

2. A contractionary monetary policy will have the opposite effect on output, employment, and the price level.

   i. Assume that rather than a recession, the U.S. is facing high inflation.

   ii. An open market sale of government bonds by the Fed will reduce the money supply, raise interest rates, and reduce interest sensitive spending in the economy.

   iii. The effect of a contractionary monetary policy can be observed in the following graphs.

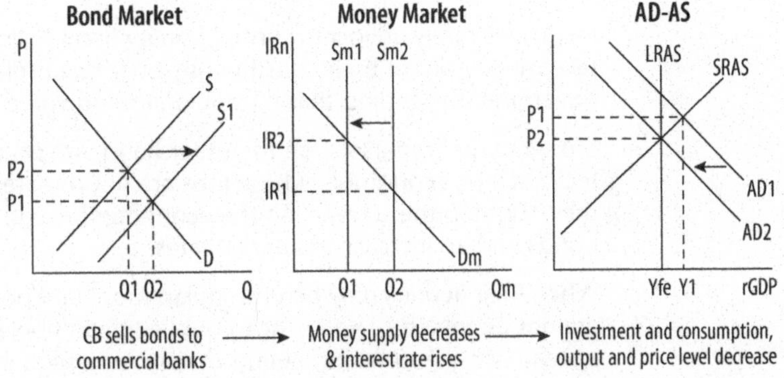


3. The sale of government bonds by the central bank has resulted in an increase in the nominal and the real interest rate, a decrease in investment and interest-sensitive consumption, and a decrease in AD.

   i. Note that before the expansionary monetary policy this country had an inflationary gap of Y1 – Yfe.

   ii. However, after the stimulus, AD has fallen to the full employment level.

**E.** Time lags. Similar to fiscal policy, there are time lags to monetary policy. These lags are caused by the time it takes to recognize a problem in the economy added to the time it takes for the economy to adjust to the policy action.

1. Central bankers may fail to identify macroeconomic issues like creeping inflation or a slowdown in GDP growth in time to enact policies to prevent an economy from overheating or dipping into recession. They may also spend too much time debating the correct response once the issue is identified. As a result, inflation can get out of control or recession can strike before monetary constraint or stimulus are enacted.

2. On the other hand, compared to fiscal policy, monetary policy is relatively nimble, and policymakers can respond more quickly to macroeconomic shocks. One reason is that in democracies (including the U.S.) monetary policymakers are not elected officials. So, their actions are generally sheltered from any potential political fallout.

   i. A legislator who proposes a large tax increase as a fiscal policy response to rising inflation, for example, would likely feel the anger of voters in the next election.

   ii. Politicians rarely advocate contractionary fiscal policies that take money out of their constituents' pockets or roll back government spending that is popular among voters.

   iii. Monetary policymakers, on the other hand, are usually technocratic economists whose jobs are not threatened when they "tighten the screws" on the economy through the sale of bonds and an increase in interest rates.

   iv. While their actions may be unpopular, monetary policymakers are not beholden to voters or to public opinion polls, and instead are tasked with meeting certain macroeconomic objectives regardless of public reaction.

3. Most central banks maintain a target inflation rate, usually around 2%–3% (although this could vary widely depending on the country in question).

   i. The Fed aims to achieve an inflation rate of 2%.

   ii. According to the Federal Reserve, "Communicating this inflation goal clearly helps keep longer-term inflation expectations firmly anchored, thereby fostering price stability and moderate long-term interest rates and enhancing the (Fed's) ability to promote maximum employment.[1]"

## VII. Loanable Funds Market

A. Demand and Supply. The loanable funds market illustrates how the real interest rate, which takes into account the effect of inflation, is determined. This model describes the behavior of savers and borrowers in an economy, illustrating the relationship between the real interest rate and the willingness to save funds and the willingness to borrow funds for investment among an economy's households and firms.

1. The demand for loanable funds shows the inverse relationship between real interest rates and the quantity demanded of loanable funds for investment in capital equipment by firms and in housing and property by households.

   i. At higher real interest rates, less funds are demanded since the cost of repaying any borrowed funds is higher.

   ii. At lower real interest rates, more funds are demanded since the cost of repaying loans is lower.

   iii. The following graph shows the demand for loanable funds.

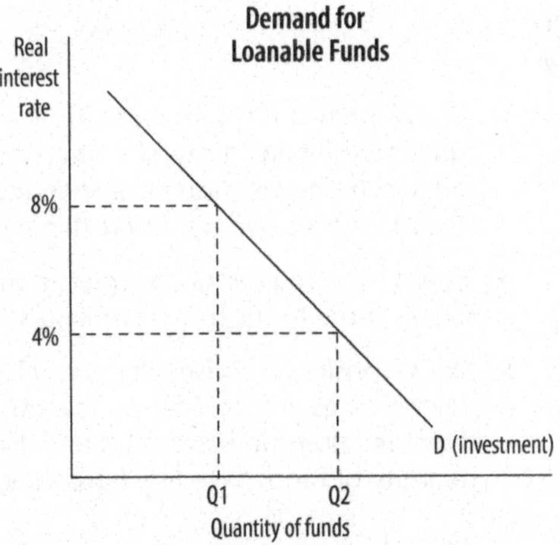


[1] Source: "What are the Federal Reserve's objectives in conducting monetary policy?", The Board of Governors of the Federal Reserve System. *https://www.federalreserve.gov/faqs/money_12848.htm*

- At a real interest rate of 8%, less funds are demanded for investment than at 4%.
- The higher the interest rate, the higher the cost of repaying any money borrowed by a household or firm, while at lower rates the cost of repaying borrowed funds is lower.

2. The supply of loanable funds describes the relationship between the real interest rate and the quantity of funds supplied by a nation's households and firms to the banking sector.

   i. The following graph shows the supply of loanable funds.

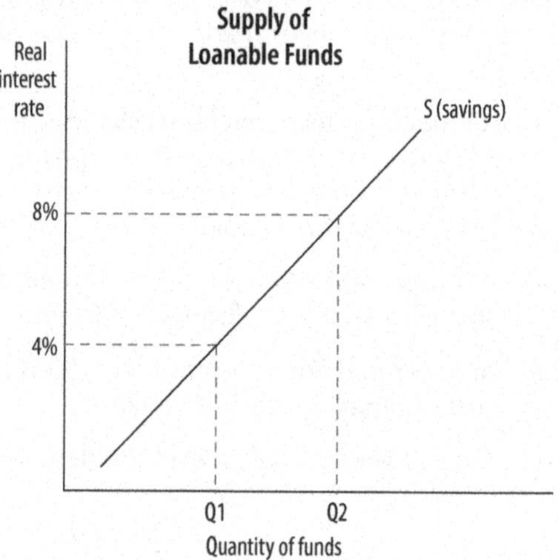


- At low interest rates, households are willing to supply less funds to the banking sector, since the opportunity cost of holding money as cash or of spending their money is lower (they'll miss out on less interest income).
- However, at higher interest rates households are willing to supply more funds to the banking sector.
- Not surprisingly, households are willing to save more at high interest rates and save less at low interest rates. There is a direct relationship between the real interest rate and the quantity of funds saved by households.

**B.** Net Capital Flows. Assume a country with a closed economy does not trade with other countries or engage in international borrowing and lending. Its supply of loanable funds would represent the level of national savings at a different real interest rate.

1. In a closed economy, national savings is the sum of both private sector and public sector savings.

   i. Recall from Chapter 4 that national income (Y) equals total spending in the economy. In a closed economy, this included only consumption (C), investment (I), and government purchases (G).

   $$Y = C + I + G$$

   ➤ From the preceding equation, observe that investment is equal to the share of national income made up of business spending, or national income (Y) minus consumption (C) and government purchases (G).

   $$I = Y - C - G$$

   ➤ National savings is whatever is left after consumer spending and government purchases have been subtracted from national income. Savings, therefore, is equal to national income (Y) minus consumption (C) and government purchases (G).

   $$S = Y - C - G$$

   ➤ In a closed economy, national income minus consumption and government spending equals savings.

   – Investment is also equal to national income minus consumption and government spending.

   – Therefore, national savings is equal to investment.

   $$I = Y - C - G$$

   and . . .

   $$S = Y - C - G$$

   Therefore,

   $$S = I$$

   ➤ In a closed economy, the amount of savings and investment are equal. Funds that are saved by the private and public sectors are invested by households and firms.

   ii. Consider the following table, which shows the expenditures in Scrubland, an isolated country that does not trade with other countries.

| Category | Amount (millions of $) |
|---|---|
| Consumption | 600 |
| Investment | 300 |
| Government spending | 100 |

- Scrubland's total GDP (Y) is the sum of C, I, and G.

Y = C + I + G = 600 + 300 + 100 = $1,000 million or $1 billion

- To determine the amount of savings in Scrubland, subtract consumption and government spending, which leaves investment.

National savings (S) = Y – C – G
= $1,000 m – $600 m – $100 m
= $300 million

- The country's savings of $300 million equals its investment of $300 million.
- Why do savings equal investment? Because every dollar the country invests must first have been saved by a household, firm, or the government.

2. In an open economy (one that trades goods and services and engages in foreign investment with other countries) investment equals the sum of national savings and net capital inflows.

   i. Net capital inflows measure investment into an economy's assets by other countries minus investment into other countries' assets by domestic investors.

   - If foreigners invest more in the domestic economy than is invested abroad by domestic investors, net capital inflows will be positive.
   - If domestic investors spend more on foreign capital than foreigners spend in the home economy, net capital inflows are negative (a negative net capital inflow is also called a capital outflow).

   Investment (I) = National savings (S) + net capital inflows

ii. The effects of net capital inflows and capital outflows on the market for loanable funds is further illustrated and explained later in this chapter.

C. Equilibrium. Returning to the loanable funds market graph, we can see that the equilibrium in the loanable funds market occurs where the quantity of funds supplied by savers equals the quantity of funds demanded by investors. In other words, the market is in equilibrium when savings equals investment.

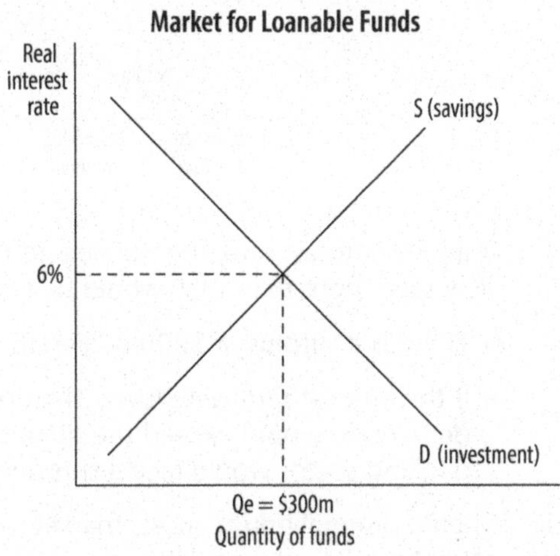


1. In Scrubland's loanable funds market, the equilibrium interest rate is 6%.

   i. At this rate, national savings and investment are equal at $300 million.

   ii. Given the current level of demand for loanable funds and the supply of loanable funds, any interest rate other than 6% would result in a disequilibrium in which the amount of funds demanded and supplied would be different from one another.

D. Disequilibrium and Changes in Equilibrium. Disequilibrium real interest rates create surpluses and shortages in the loanable funds market.

1. Assume, for example, banks in Scrubland charged borrowers a real interest rate of 8%. The result is captured in the following graph.

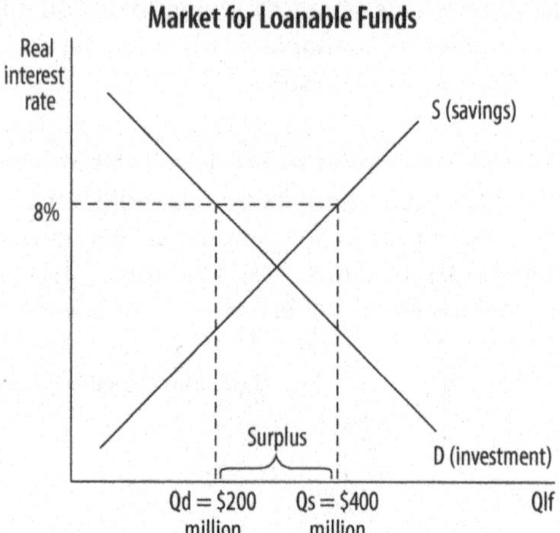


i. At an 8% interest rate, the public and private sectors would likely save more than they would be willing to invest.

   ➤ There is a surplus of $200 million in loanable funds.

   ➤ If the interest rate were lower than 6%, the quantity demanded would exceed the quantity supplied and the banking sector would face a shortage of loanable funds.

ii. When a disequilibrium arises, market forces drive the real interest rate toward equilibrium.

   ➤ In the preceding graph, interest rates will decrease. This rate decrease will lead borrowers to demand more funds and savers to supply less, until the quantities supplied and demanded are once again equal at $300 million.

2. The equilibrium real interest rate will change when there is a change in the demand for, or supply of, loanable funds. Factors that affect the demand for loanable funds include changes in the determinants of investment in the economy, including a change in business confidence, expected future inflation or deflation, the degree of excess capacity in the economy, investment tax credits or business subsidies, and changes in technology.

   i. For example, an investment tax credit which gives tax relief to purchasers of new capital will increase the demand for loanable funds and drive up the equilibrium real interest rate.

ii. The following graph shows the immediate effect of an investment tax credit.

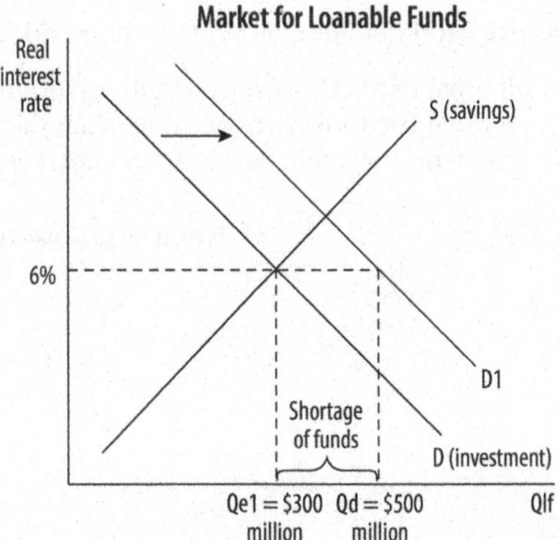


iii. Increased demand for funds to invest in new capital has resulted in a temporary shortage of funds as at a 6% rate firms now demand $500 million of funds for investment. Interest rates must rise to restore equilibrium in the market.

iv. Higher rates encourage households to save more, which leads to more funds being supplied to businesses for capital investment.

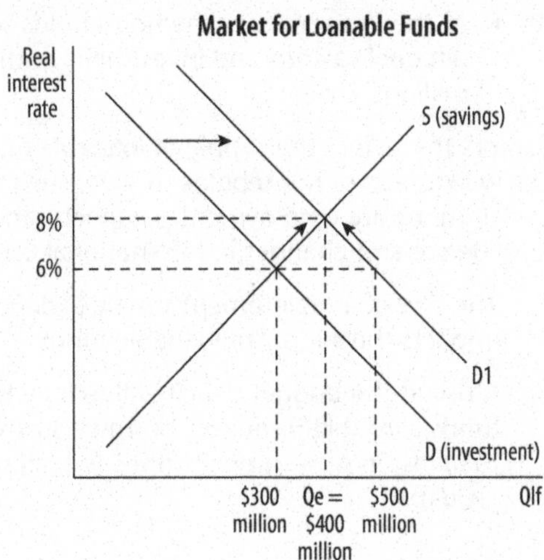

v. When the interest rate rises, market equilibrium is restored at a new higher interest rate of 8% and a greater equilibrium level of savings and investment of $400 million.

3. Anticipated deflation also affects demand for loanable funds.

   i. If firms expect a lower price in selling their output, they will reduce their investment in new capital. As a result, overall demand for loanable funds will decrease.

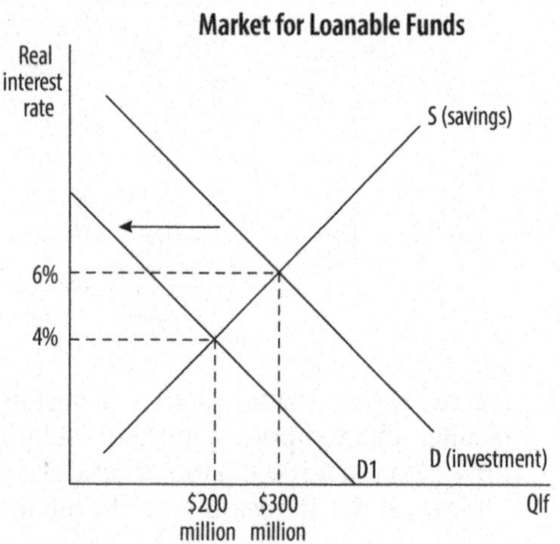


   - Expected deflation has caused current investment demand to fall, lowering the equilibrium interest rate to 4%.
   - At the lower rate, many households will save less, so national savings and investment both decrease to $200 million.

4. Factors that affect the supply of loanable funds include changes in the willingness of households to save, such as expected inflation or deflation, future employment prospects, and the level of consumer confidence and changes in international capital flows.

   i. The size of a government's budget deficit or surplus also impacts the supply of loanable funds.

   ii. A rise in the budget deficit will reduce the supply of loanable funds available to private borrowers as savers withdraw funds to invest in government bonds (which would now offer higher yields).

iii. Deficit reductions or budget surpluses will increase the supply of loanable funds as investors sell the now lower yield government bonds and put their funds back into the private market for loanable funds.

iv. Net capital inflows also affect the supply of loanable funds.

v. When net exports are negative, a country spends more through trade than it earns.

vi. To balance its international accounts, countries with which the home country trades will invest in domestic assets.

vii. The resulting net capital inflow increases the supply of loanable funds in the domestic market, reducing interest rates at home.

viii. The effect of a negative trade balance (X<M) and a net capital inflow is reflected in the following graph.

**Market for Loanable Funds**

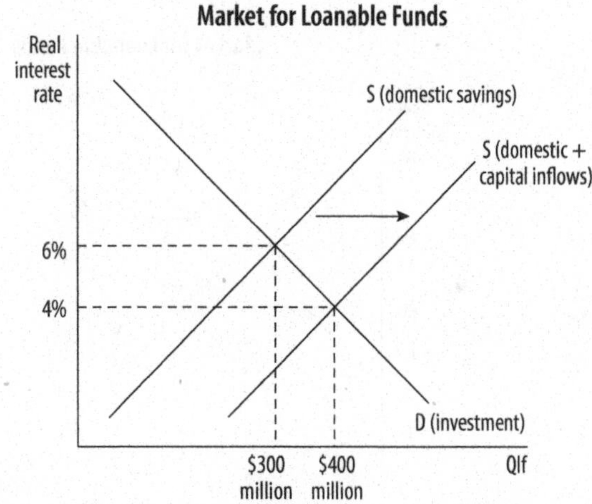


- Assume Scrubland is now open to trade with other countries and has a trade deficit resulting in more money leaving Scrubland to purchase imports than entering the country for the sale of exports.
- Foreigners invest more in Scrubland's assets than Scrubland entities invest in foreign assets.
- The inflow of foreign capital increases the supply of loanable funds and drives down the real interest rate, increasing the equilibrium quantity of funds demanded.

- In an open economy, investment equals domestic savings ($300 million) plus net capital inflows ($100 million).

  Investment (I) = National savings (S) + net capital inflows

5. When net exports are positive, a country earns more from trade than it spends.

   i. To balance its international accounts, the country will supply funds to the countries buying its goods for investment in those economies.

   ii. The resulting capital outflow reduces the supply of loanable funds in the domestic market, driving up interest rates at home.

   iii. Assume that Scrubland's trade balance moves into surplus, meaning its exports now exceed imports. The effect of a positive trade balance (X>M) and a capital outflow is seen in the following graph.

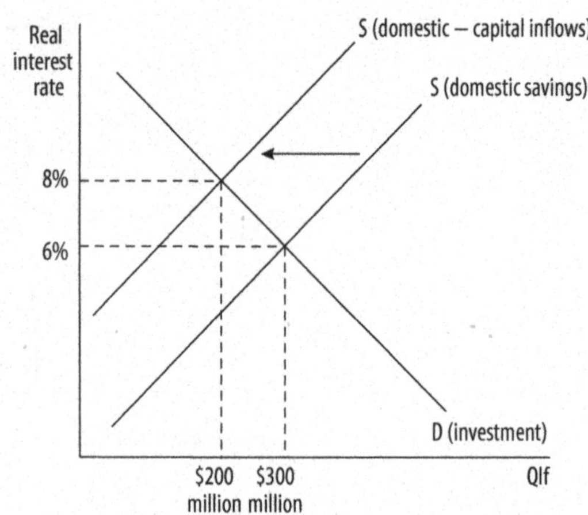


- Investment in Scrubland ($200 million) equals domestic savings plus net capital inflows (which in this case is –$100 million).
- The outflow of capital into foreign economies reduces the domestic supply of loanable funds and drives up the equilibrium interest rate, reducing the amount of domestic investment.

Chapter 7

# UNIT 5 Long-Run Consequences of Stabilization Policies

## I. Short-Run Fiscal and Monetary Policy Actions

A. Demand-side Policies

1. Effects of fiscal and monetary policies. A combination of fiscal and monetary policies may be used to restore full employment when the economy is in a recessionary or inflationary gap. Both fiscal and monetary policies are typically described as demand-side policies, since their primary objective is to either increase or decrease the level of aggregate demand in the economy. By impacting aggregate demand, fiscal and monetary policies can affect real output, the price level, and interest rates.

   i. Expansionary policies, including lower taxes, increased government purchases or transfers, or an increase in the money supply, cause AD to increase. This leads to a short-run increase in real output, employment, and the price level. Expansionary policies are used to close a recessionary gap.

   ii. Contractionary policies, including higher taxes, reduced government purchases or transfers, or a decrease in the money supply, cause AD to decrease. This leads to a short-run decrease in real output, employment, and the price level. Contractionary policies are used to close an inflationary gap.

2. Expansionary policies in the short run. If a government or central bank undertakes an expansionary fiscal or monetary policy in an economy that was already producing at its full employment level of real output, there would be a short-run boost in output, employment, and the price level. This would create a positive output gap, as shown in the following chart.

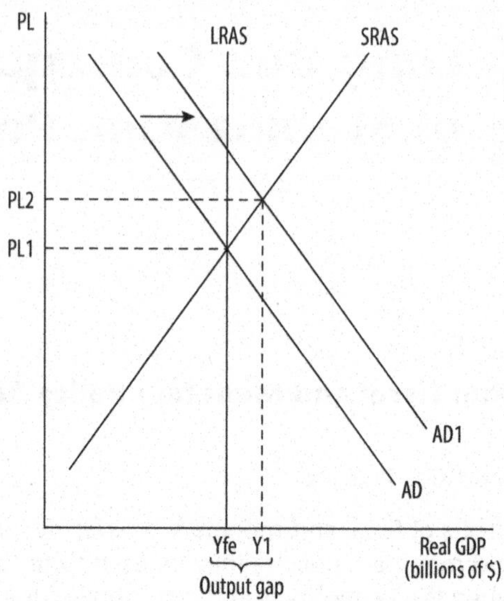


i. Following fiscal and monetary stimulus, the economy is producing beyond its full employment level.

ii. However, in the long run any economy's output is constrained by its available factors of production.

- In the economy illustrated here, land, labor, and capital are over-employed; the demand for resources exceeds their supply, which in the long run will drive up wages and other resource costs.
- As wages and other costs increase, firms will reduce output and further raise prices, causing output to return to its full employment level.

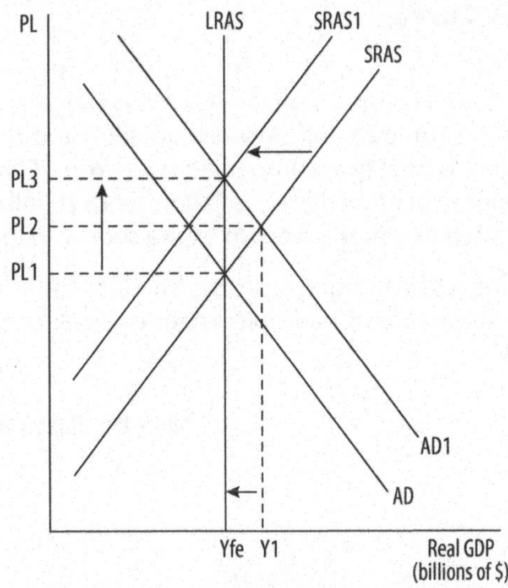


**B.** Conclusions. Demand-side policies are effective at closing output gaps but not at achieving long-run economic growth.

1. Changes in aggregate demand alone will not impact the economy's potential output or its level of long-run aggregate supply. Changes in AD do, however, impact equilibrium output and the price level.
2. Changes in an economy's long-run output are made possible through the factors that create economic growth, a concept that will be explored later in this chapter.

***In the free-response section, you may be asked to show the short-run and the long-run effects of particular fiscal or monetary policies. Such analysis is simple if you remember that in the long run an economy will always return to its full-employment level of output regardless of the demand-side policies of the government and the central bank.***

## II. Phillips Curve

A. Short-Run Phillips Curve (SRPC). When aggregate demand shifts, there is a short-run trade-off between inflation and unemployment. Rising inflation is usually accompanied by a drop in unemployment; but when unemployment increases, inflation tends to fall. This trade-off can be illustrated in a model known as the short-run Phillips curve.

1. The following graph shows an SRPC for a country in which the natural rate of unemployment is 5% and the target inflation rate is 3%.

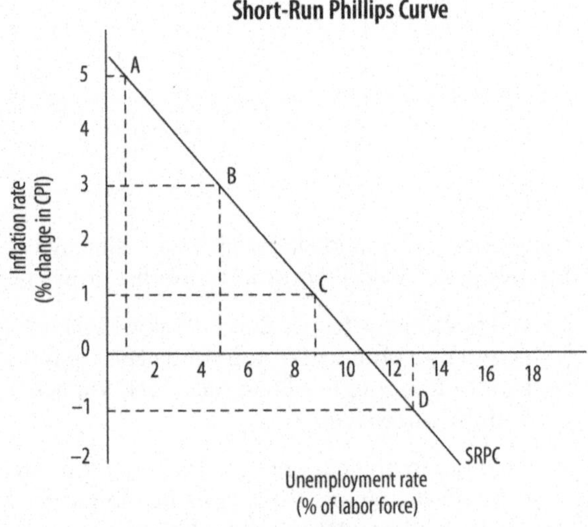


i. A country that is producing at its full employment output will be at point B on the Phillips curve.

ii. If AD were to increase, then the higher output the country achieves in the short run would lead to a lower unemployment rate, a higher inflation rate, and a movement along the Phillips curve up and to the left to point A.

iii. A decrease in AD would cause a recession and a negative output gap, resulting in higher unemployment and lower inflation. The country would move to point C or D on its Phillips curve.

iv. In the short run, lower unemployment comes with higher inflation as greater demand for a country's output causes prices to rise. Higher unemployment comes with lower inflation as falling AD causes output and employment to fall and pushes the price level down.

***Think of the short-run Phillips curve as a mirror image of the short-run aggregate supply curve. Anything that shifts SRAS left will shift the SRPC right. Anything that increases SRAS will shift SRPC to the left.***

**B.** Long-Run Phillips Curve (LRPC). In the long run, wages and prices are perfectly flexible and a country's output will return to its full employment level following negative or positive demand shocks.

1. In the long run, a recession would cause wages and prices to fall and output to increase back to full employment at a lower price level.
2. A positive demand shock and an inflationary gap would cause prices and wages to rise in the long run and result in output returning to full employment at a higher price level.
3. The LRPC is thus vertical at the natural rate of unemployment, to which an economy will always return over time once wages and prices have adjusted to the level of aggregate demand. The following graph shows the same country's LRPC.

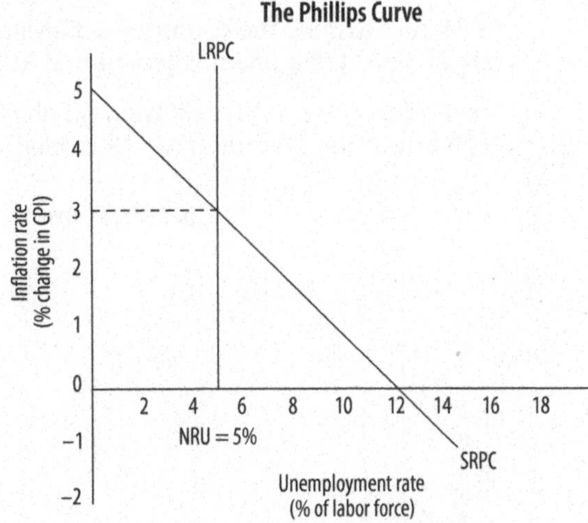


4. The LRPC is vertical at 5% unemployment because this is the unemployment rate that is consistent with the full employment level of output, to which the economy will return in the long run following any negative or positive demand shocks.

C. Demand and Supply Shocks and Output Gaps. Changes to aggregate demand cause a movement along a country's SRPC.

1. For example, assume a country is producing at its full employment level and is in its long-run equilibrium in both the AD-AS model and the Phillips curve model.

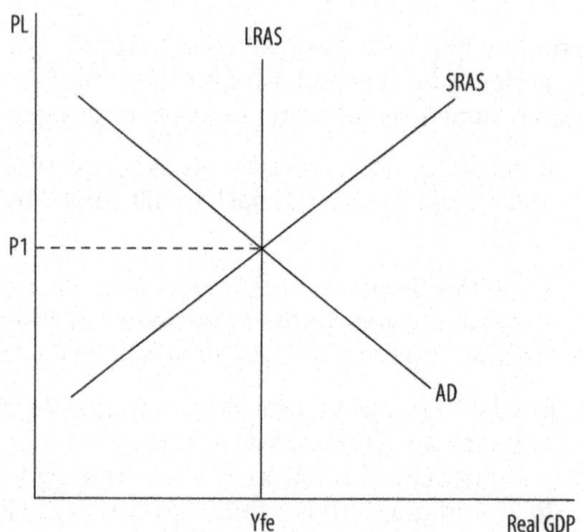


i. At P1, let's assume the country is achieving its target inflation rate of 3%. At Yfe, unemployment is at its natural rate of 5%.

ii. The Phillips curve in the following graph represents the same economy as the preceding AD-AS model.

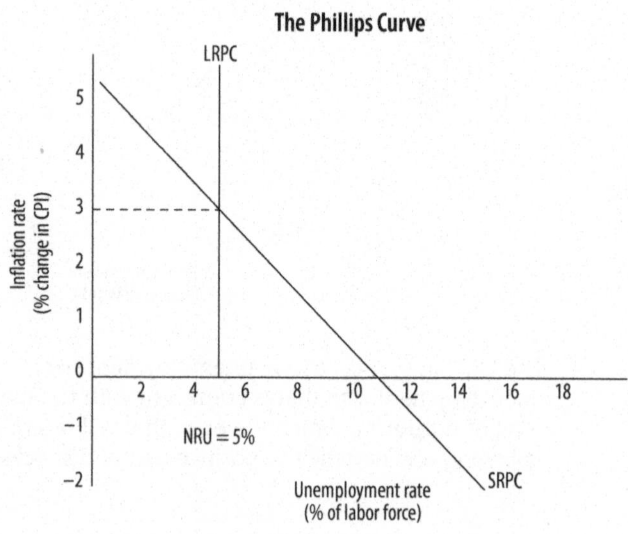

2. Assume there is an increase in aggregate demand in the economy, creating positive demand shock. This results in an increase in output, employment, and the price level in the AD-AS model and a movement up and to the left along the SRPC in the Phillips curve model.

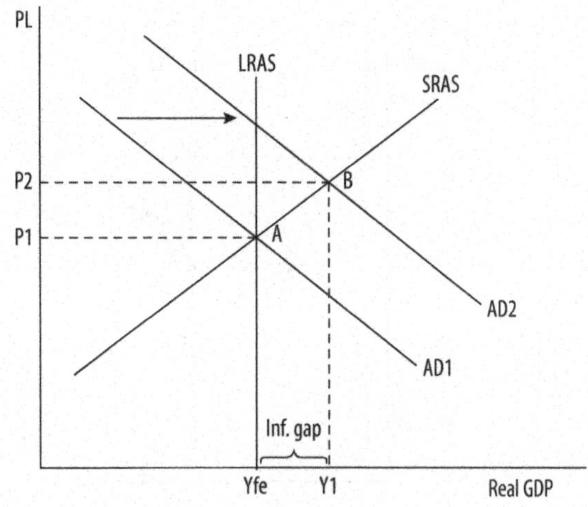


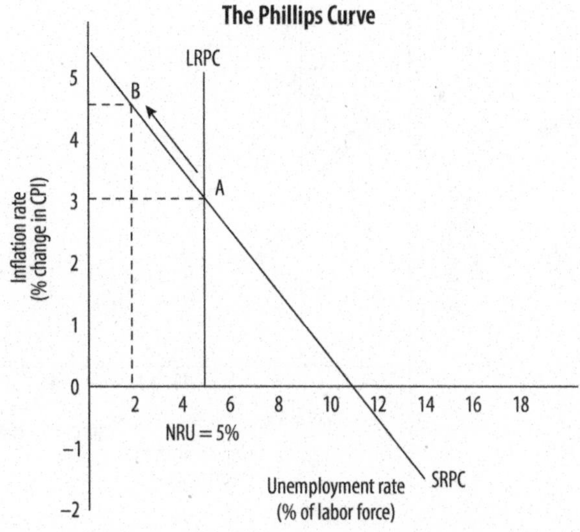


i. The increase in AD caused output, the price level, and employment to increase (A to B in the AD-AS model), a decrease in unemployment, and an increase in inflation (A to B in the PC model).

ii. In the long run, an economy producing at point B (beyond full employment) will experience rising wages and input costs, causing the SRAS to decrease and output to return to the full employment level. As this happens, inflation will increase and unemployment will return to the NRU in the Phillips curve model.

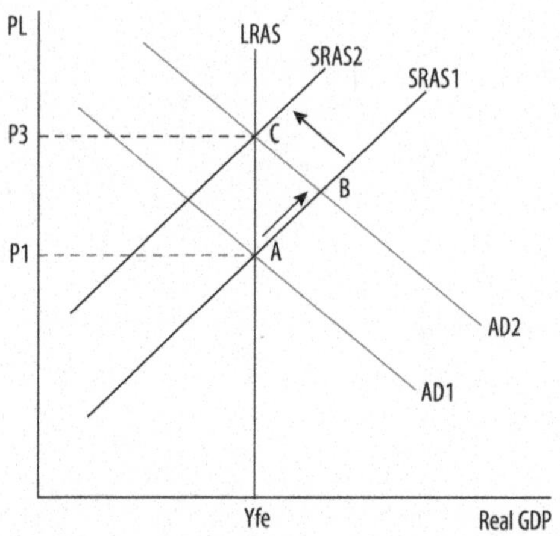


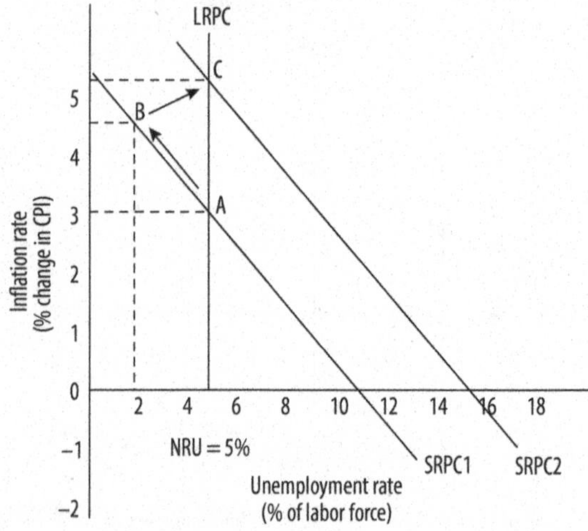


iii. Rising wages and other input prices cause the SRAS to shift in, moving the economy from equilibrium at point B in the AD-AS model to a new equilibrium at point C.

iv. Inflation has increased while unemployment has returned to its natural rate.

v. In the Phillips curve, higher inflation and higher unemployment are shown as an outward shift of the SRPC which causes the equilibrium in the Phillips curve model to move from B to C.

vi. As output returns to its full employment level in the AD-AS model, unemployment returns to its natural rate in the PC model.

3. A negative demand shock will cause a decrease in output, employment, and the price level in the AD-AS model, and a movement down and to the right along the SRPC in the Phillips curve model.

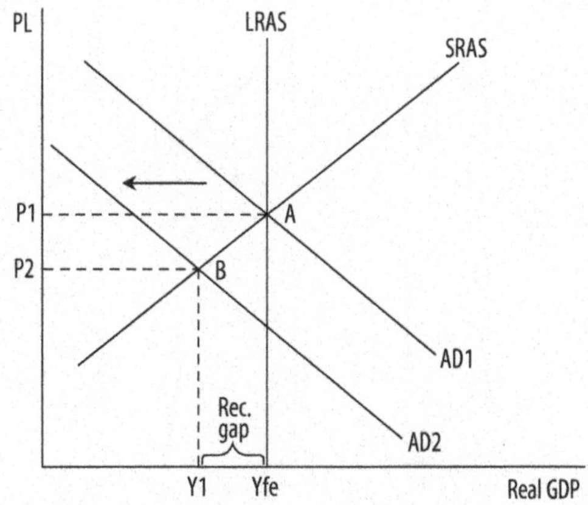


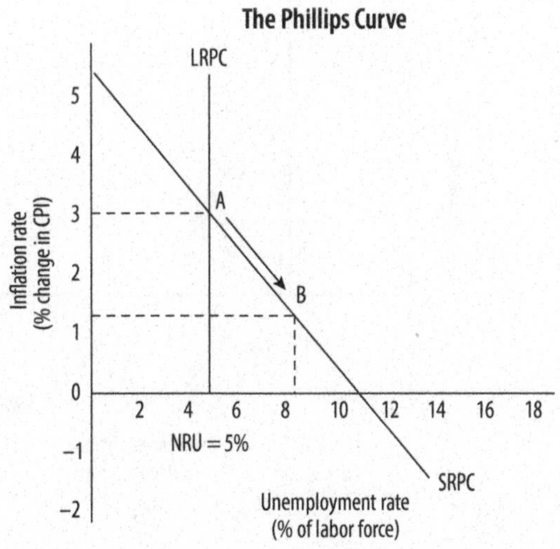

i. A move from point A to B in the AD-AS model corresponds with a move from point A to point B in the Phillips curve model. (See preceding graphs.)

ii. In the long run, an economy producing at point B (below full employment) will experience falling wages and input costs, causing the SRAS to increase and output to return to the full employment level.

iii. As the foregoing happens, inflation will decrease and unemployment will return to the NRU in the Phillips curve model. (See the next two graphs.)

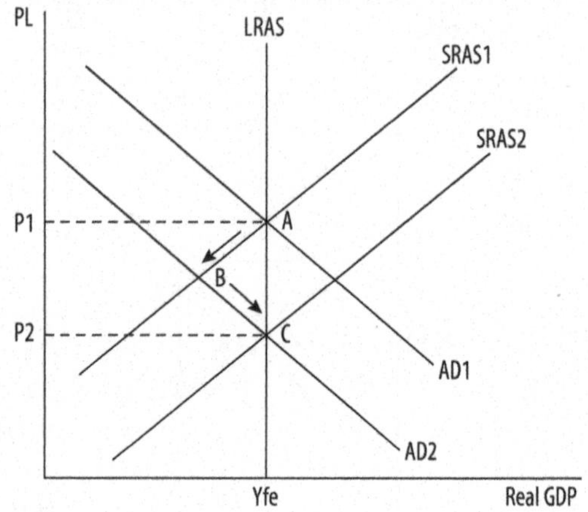


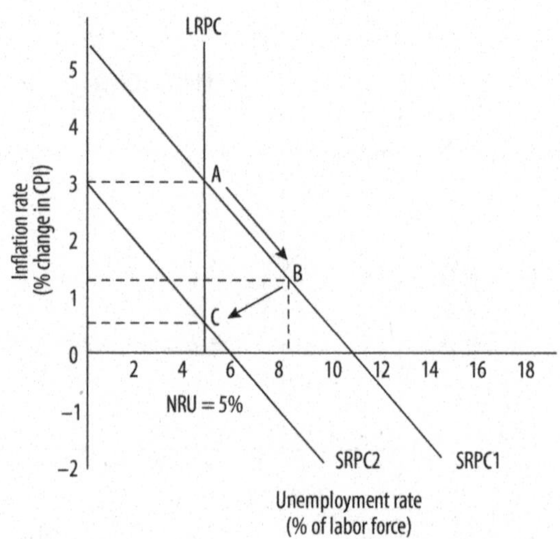

iv. Falling wages and other input prices cause the SRAS to shift out, restoring full employment in the AD-AS model at a lower price level.

v. The outward shift of the SRAS corresponds with an inward shift of the SRPC, restoring the NRU in the Phillips curve model at a lower inflation rate.

4. A supply shock occurs whenever a factor leads to a shift in the short-run aggregate supply (SRAS) curve. A shift in SRAS in one direction causes a shift in the SRPC in the opposite direction.

   i. A negative supply shock causes both higher inflation and higher unemployment. For example, assume there is an unexpected increase in energy prices.

      - SRAS will shift in as the cost of producing output increases.
      - Firms reduce both employment and output, while raising prices to consumers. (See the following two graphs.)

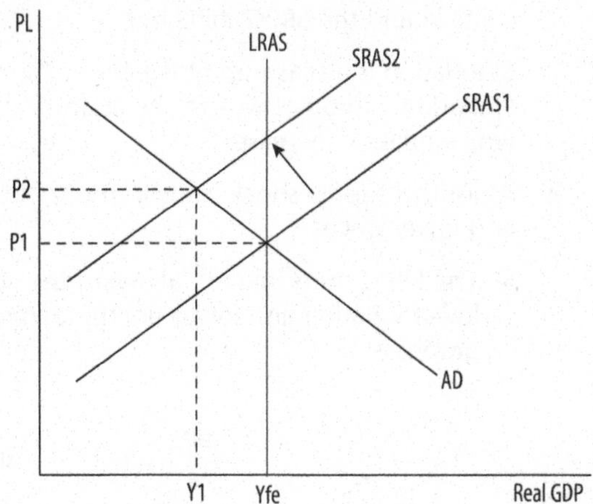

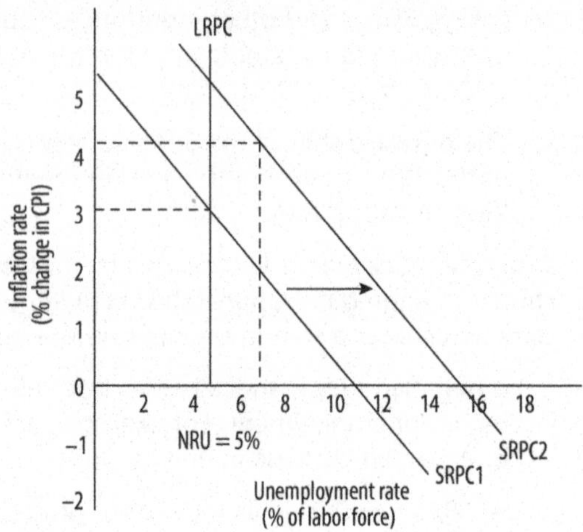


ii. A negative supply shock causes higher inflation and higher unemployment. A country experiences stagflation when SRAS shifts in and the SRPC shifts out.

iii. Stagflation is a mash-up of the terms "stagnant" and "inflation." In other words, the country's economy stagnates while inflation increases.

iv. A positive supply shock leads to more output and employment and lower prices.

- The SRPC shifts inward, allowing the country to enjoy both lower inflation and lower unemployment. (See the next two graphs.)

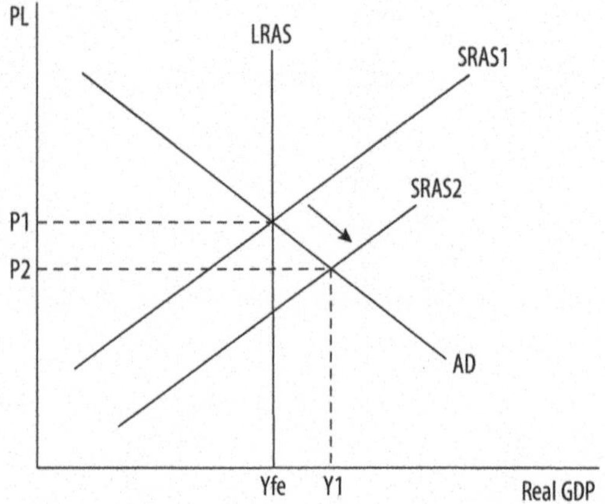

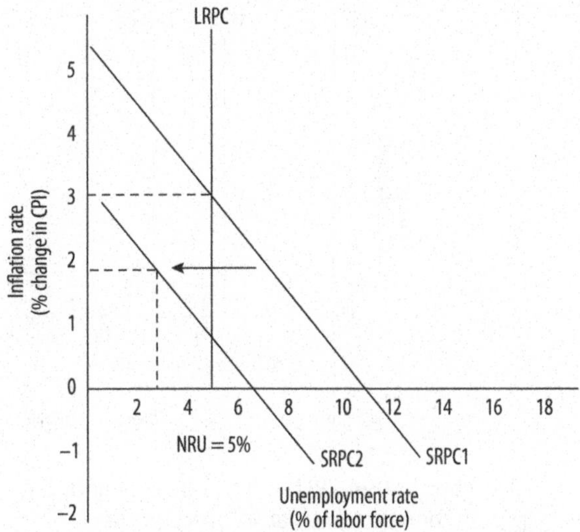


➤ A positive supply shock causes output to increase and the price level to fall. More output means lower unemployment and a lower price level means lower inflation.

**D.** Natural Rate of Unemployment and the LRPC. Factors that cause the natural rate of unemployment (NRU) to change will cause a shift of the long-run Phillips curve (LRPC).

1. Recall that the NRU consists of two types of unemployment:

   i. Structural unemployment arises due to changing technology or other factors that result in a mismatch between the skills of a nation's workforce and the needs of employers.

   ii. Frictional unemployment arises from workers who are in between jobs and cannot quickly and easily be matched up with firms that demand labor.

2. Increase in the NRU. Changes to the NRU are rare. They result from shifts in society's attitudes toward work, changes in technology, or from policies that change the incentives around being unemployed.

   i. For example, if globalization and automation slowly displace a country's factory labor, then structural unemployment will increase and the LRPC will move outward to a higher NRU, as represented in the following graph.

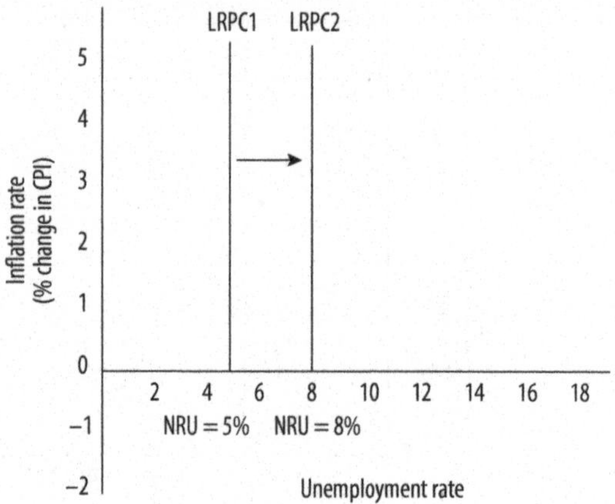


3. Decrease in the NRU. On the other hand, a government might reduce benefits to unemployed workers.
   i. Over time a cut in benefits would likely lead to fewer workers choosing to remain unemployed, instead taking jobs at lower wage rates.
   ii. In such a case the levels of frictional and structural unemployment would fall in the long run and the LRPC would shift inward as the country's NRU decreases.
   iii. A decrease in structural or frictional unemployment causes an inward shift of the LRPC and a lower natural rate of unemployment as shown in the following graph.

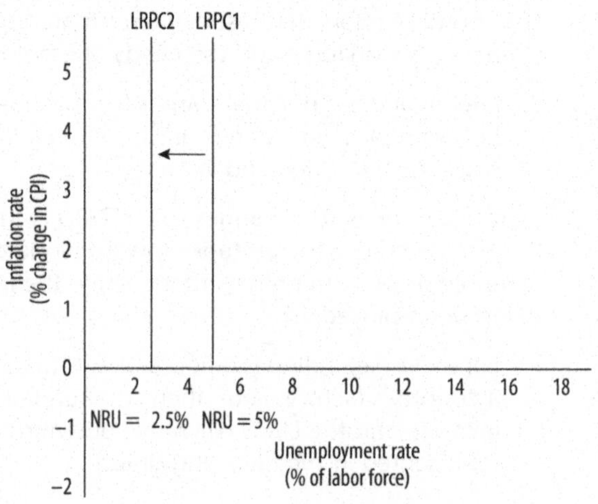

## III. Money Growth and Inflation

A. Expansionary monetary policies can stimulate aggregate demand and lead to short-run changes in output and inflation. But these policies will not affect the long-run growth rate of an economy. If the money supply increases faster than the rate of long-run economic growth, inflation would follow.

1. Excess monetary growth. Assume the country represented in the following graph has full employment. Also, the country's long-run rate of economic growth (the increase in potential output over time) is 2% per year.

   i. If the country increases the money supply at about the same rate as the economic growth rate, then policymakers should expect low and stable inflation to accompany the country's rising output.

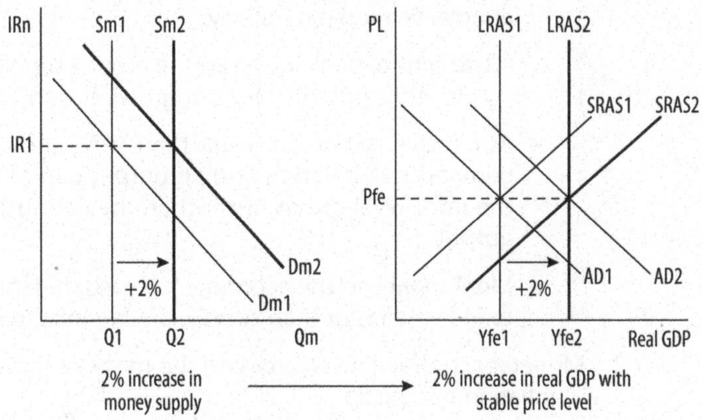


   ii. In the preceding graphs, the money supply is increasing at the same rate as the real GDP over time. Therefore, the country enjoys price level stability (low and stable inflation).

   iii. However, if a central bank pursues an overly aggressive monetary policy and increases the money supply faster than the long-run rate of economic growth, the country can expect aggregate demand to increase faster than aggregate supply. The result is an increase in inflation over time.

      ➤ The following graphs show the effect of central bank policy that increases the money supply at a rate faster than the country's long-run economic growth rate.

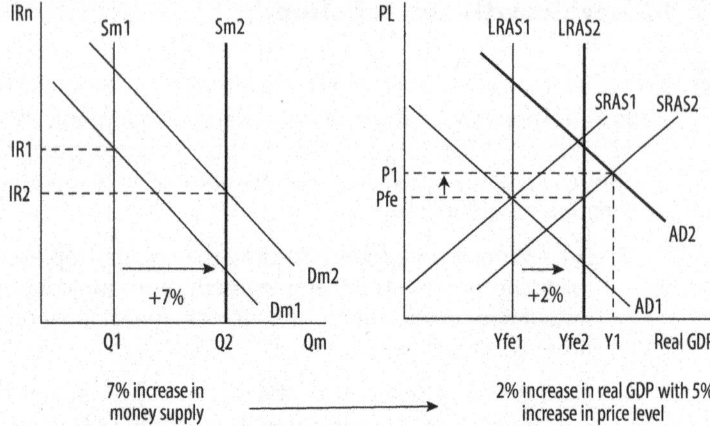


- In the country's economy represented in the preceding graphs, we can observe the consequences of overly aggressive monetary policy.
  - The central bank increases the money supply at 7% per year, while potential output grows at only 2% per year.
- As a result, AD grows faster than SRAS and LRAS, causing demand-pull inflation and an output gap of Y1-Yfe2, as the price level grows faster than the country's potential output.
- More money in the economy has caused demand for output to increase faster than supply, driving inflation up.

2. Monetary contraction. Decreasing the money supply causes disinflation or deflation.
   i. Assume that in the same economy, which averages 2% increase in its potential output year after year, the central bank decides to decrease the money supply between two years.
   ii. The following graphs show the consequence of contractionary monetary policy in a country in which potential output grows 2% per year.

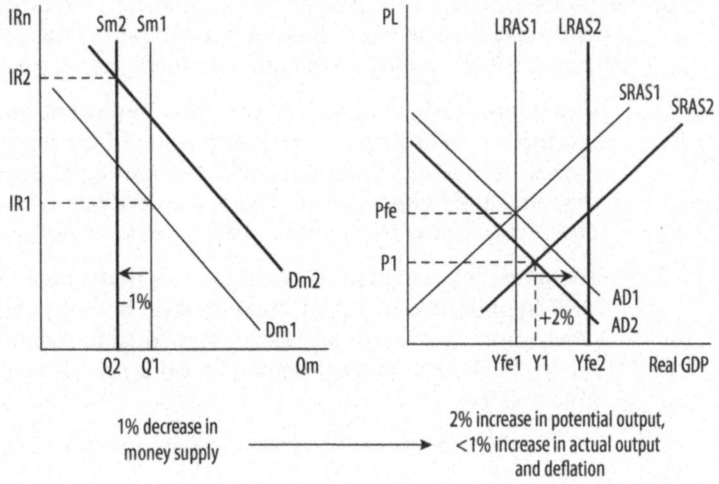


- Even as the economy's potential output increases (due to increase in the factors of production), the amount of money available to buy the growing output decreases, causing interest rates and aggregate demand to fall.
- The result is a large recessionary gap (Yfe2-Y1) and falling prices (Pfe to P1).

3. Monetary growth does not equal economic growth. As can be seen from the preceding analysis, changes in the money supply have no effect on the long-run economic growth rate when a nation is at full employment.
   i. Increasing the money supply at a rate faster than the rate at which potential output increases only causes inflation.
   ii. Decreasing the money supply when potential output increases causes deflation and possibly a recession, as aggregate demand would not be able to increase with aggregate supply, creating a negative output gap.
   iii. Economic growth in the long-run is achieved only through increases in the quantity or the quality of the factors of production: land, labor, and capital. Recall from Chapter 6 that money is only a medium of exchange that facilitates trade between buyers and sellers; it is not a factor of production itself.
   iv. Supplying more money to an economy, therefore, only facilitates more transactions, but it does not create more transactions.

**B.** Monetary Equation of Exchange. In the long run, the growth rate of the money supply determines the growth rate of the price level (inflation rate) according to the quantity theory of money.

1. Under monetarist economic theory, the nominal output a country produces at in any given time is a function of the amount of money in circulation and the velocity of money, i.e., which measures the frequency with which a unit of money is spent (in other words, how many times in a year a single dollar is spent).

2. The monetary equation of exchange says that a country's nominal GDP (represented as *PQ*, or the price level times the quantity of newly produced goods and services) is equal to the amount of money in circulation (represented by *M*) times the velocity of money (*V*).

   The monetary equation of exchange: $MV = PQ$

   i. According to monetarist theory, the velocity of money (*V*) and the quantity of newly produced goods and services (*Q*) are constant and grow at equal fixed rates.

   ii. Therefore, the inflation rate (the rate of change in the price level, *P*) exactly equals the growth rate of the money supply (*M*).

   iii. The implication of monetarist theory is that increasing the money supply, all else being equal, only causes inflation, not an increase in actual output.

3. Monetary rules. Noted economist Milton Friedman advocated monetary rules which would require central banks to target the growth rate of the money supply to equal the growth rate of real GDP.

   i. Increasing the money supply only at the rate of growth in real GDP would leave the price level unchanged while providing the money necessary to facilitate the exchange of a nation's growing output of goods and services over time.

***The monetary equation of exchange is seldom tested on the AP® Macro exam. Still, it is important to know the implications of the theory on policymakers. For example, know that increasing the money supply rapidly will lead to inflation and little change in output.***

## IV. Government Deficits and the National Debt

### A. Government Budget

1. A government budget which records the balance of its expenditures and revenues can be in either a surplus or a deficit.
   i. A budget surplus means a government's total receipts from tax revenues are greater than its total spending on public goods and transfers.
   ii. A budget deficit occurs when a government's total spending on public goods and transfers is greater than its total receipts from tax revenues.
2. A budget surplus or deficit can be measured over a given period. The following chart shows the U.S. federal budget position between 1996 and 2016.

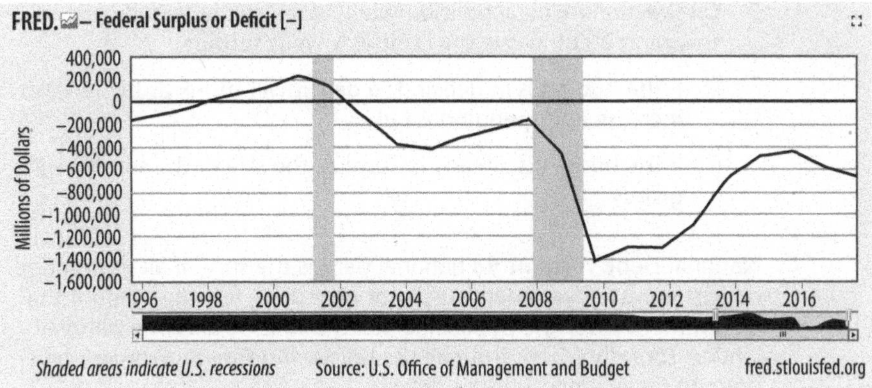


Source: FRED Economic Data—Federal Surplus or Deficit. *https://fred.stlouisfed.org/series/FYFSD*

   i. The horizontal line represents a balanced budget, i.e., when tax receipts equal government expenditures.
   ii. When the budget line is above the horizontal line, the budget is in surplus. When it's below the horizontal line, the budget is in deficit.
   iii. Gray areas indicate the years in which the U.S. economy was in recession. Observe the following from the chart:
      - The federal budget was in deficit in 1996–1997, and then in every year since 2003.

- The budget was balanced in 1998 and 2002.
- The budget was in surplus in 1999, 2000, and 2001.
- During the 2008–2009 recession, the budget deficit ballooned from $200 billion to $1,400 billion (or $1.4 trillion).

**B.** Effect of Fiscal Policy. A government's fiscal policy has a direct and immediate impact on its budget balance.

1. Expansionary fiscal policies, when taxes are cut or government spending is increased, move the budget toward deficit.
   i. If the budget is in surplus, the surplus will shrink or move to deficit.
   ii. If the budget is already in deficit, the size of the deficit will increase.
2. Contractionary fiscal policies, when taxes are increased or spending is cut, move the budget toward surplus.
   i. If the budget is in deficit, the deficit will shrink as tax receipts increase and spending is cut.
   ii. If the budget is already in surplus, the size of the surplus will grow.

**C.** National Debt. A country's national debt is the sum of all past budget deficits minus government surpluses over time. It is the amount the government owes the public, including domestic and international lenders (bondholders), from all the borrowing the government has done to finance past budget deficits.

1. If there is a budget deficit, the government must borrow funds to finance the deficit, just like persons must do who spend more than their income.
   i. In years when a government has a deficit, its total debt increases.
   ii. When the budget is in surplus, the government has the opportunity to reduce its debt by paying back past lenders.
   iii. The following graph tracks the U.S. government's total debt from 1996 to 2016.

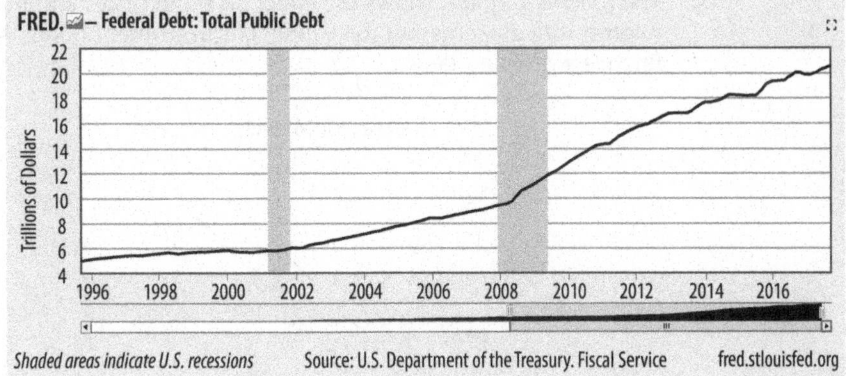


Source: FRED Economic Data—Federal debt: total public debt

- Note that in the years in which the budget was balanced or in surplus (1998–2002), the total public debt remained constant, at about $6 trillion.
- However, beginning in 2003, when the budget was in deficit every year, total debt grew steadily to over $20 trillion in 2016.
- During the Great Recession (2009), the rate of increase in total debt was at its greatest. The main reason is that during this period the budget experienced its largest deficits in history (over $1 trillion).
- The U.S. government's expansionary fiscal policy in 2009 and the years that followed saw deficit-financed spending increase while tax revenues declined due to lower incomes and slow economic growth.

**D.** Cost of Deficits. Borrowing funds from the public to finance budget deficits comes with an opportunity cost for the government. As with everything in life, there's no such thing as free debt.

1. As discussed in Chapter 6, the bond market is where the government supplies bonds, i.e., certificates of debt, to investors who buy and sell bonds and determine the price and the yield (interest rate) a government must pay its lenders.

   i. As a government in deficit spends, more bonds must be issued to investors who lent it money.

ii. The following graph shows the effect on bond prices and the interest rate of increasing the supply of government bonds to finance a growing deficit.

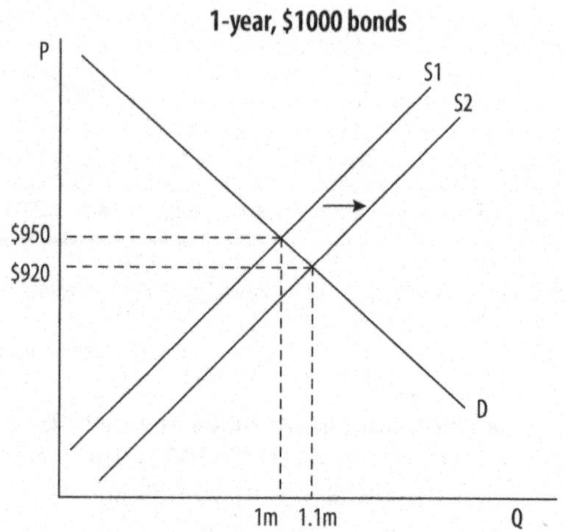


2. Recall that the interest rate on bonds is inversely related to bond prices. Before the government supplies more bonds (S2), the interest rate the government must pay its lenders can be calculated:

   i. Investor's purchase price = $950

   ii. Price government pays after one year = $1000

   iii. Investor's return = $50

   iv. Interest on investment = $\frac{50}{950} \times 100 =$ **5.26%**

3. Once the government increases the supply of bonds to finance a growing deficit, the interest rate the government must pay investors rises.

   i. Investor's purchase price = $920

   ii. Price government pays after one year = $1000

   iii. Investor's return = $80

   iv. Interest on investment = $\frac{80}{920} \times 100 =$ **8.69%**

4. As total debt increases, the government must pay interest on that debt just to maintain confidence among lenders that it is a reliable debtor.

5. A government's total interest payments in a year can be roughly estimated by multiplying the total amount of debt by the interest rate expressed as a percentage.
   i. For example, assume the U.S. government has $20 trillion in debt.
   ii. If interest rates on government bonds are currently 2.5%, then annually, the United States must pay 2.5% of its $20 trillion in debt to lenders in interest payments.

   Interest payments = Total debt × interest rate (in hundredths)

   =$20 trillion × 0.025 = **$500 *billion***

   iii. The following chart shows the U.S. government's interest payments on public debt from 1996 to 2016.

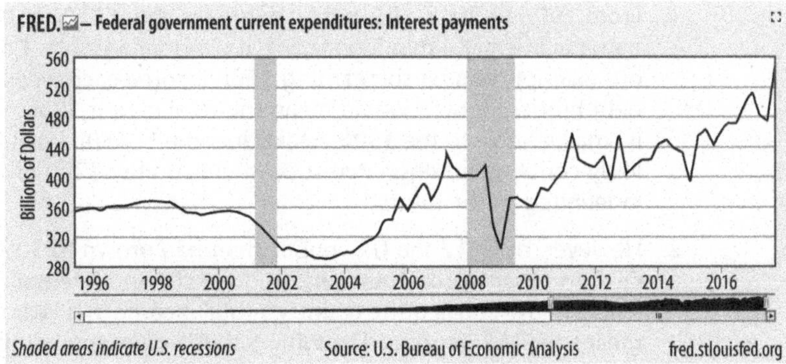


Source: FRED Economic database—Federal government current expenditures: interest payments

   iv. Notice that as the total debt increased over 20 years, interest payments increased to around $500 billion in 2016.

E. Debt as a Percentage of GDP. While America's $20 trillion debt sounds huge (and it *is!*), what really matters when considering the size of a country's debt is the ratio of its total debt to its total GDP. If any other country owed its lenders $20 trillion, the burden of the interest payments alone would likely wipe out the government's budget and bring the economy to a screeching halt. However, while America's debt is big, its GDP over the last 20 years has been much greater. The following chart shows the percentage of the U.S. GDP the total public debt made up from 1996 to 2016.

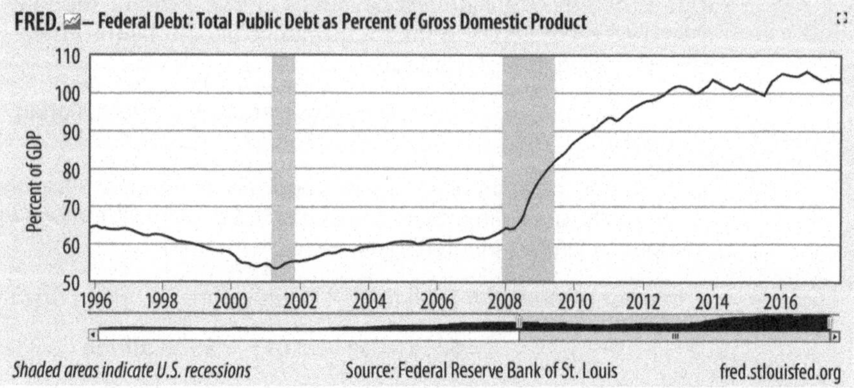


Source: FRED Economic database—Total public debt as a percentage of GDP

1. From 1996 to 2008, U.S. public debt was about 60% of the U.S. national income. While significant, it was manageable. Consider our example of a person earning $500 income each week. A debt burden of 60% would mean the total debt is $300, which is small relative to the $500 weekly income of $500. She can likely continue making interest payments on her $300 of debt indefinitely in the future.
2. However, by 2012 the U.S. public debt had grown to 100% of GDP. In other words, total debt to domestic and international lenders now equaled the country's total income in a year (which means the U.S. produced roughly $20 trillion of total output in 2016).
3. Once a country's total debt exceeds 100% of its GDP, fiscal policymakers must consider the future costs of further increases in spending or decreases in taxation.
4. As total debt grows, so do total debt payments. The interest rate on the debt must increase to attract lenders willing to put their faith in the government's ability to repay its debts as the size of the debt grows relative to its income.

## V. Crowding Out

"Crowding out" describes rising government spending, particularly borrowing, resulting in driving down private sector investment.

**A.** Fiscal Policy and the Government Budget. A government with an expansionary fiscal policy either increases spending or decreases taxes or does both simultaneously. Such a policy would be aimed at stimulating aggregate demand to achieve an increase in output and employment. This typically requires the government to borrow money to finance the resulting budget deficit (when tax revenues fall short of total government spending).

1. Fiscal policy's effect on the loanable funds market. When a government borrows money to pay for a tax cut or an increase in government spending (or both), the supply of loanable funds in the economy decreases.

   i. The increased supply of government bonds needed to finance the deficit causes bond prices to fall and bond yields to increase, making bonds a more attractive asset for households to invest in relative to a bank savings deposit.

   ii. The corresponding decrease in the supply of private sector savings causes an increase in the real interest rate and a decrease in the quantity of investment demand in the economy.

   iii. The following graph shows the crowding-out effect of government borrowing in an economy.

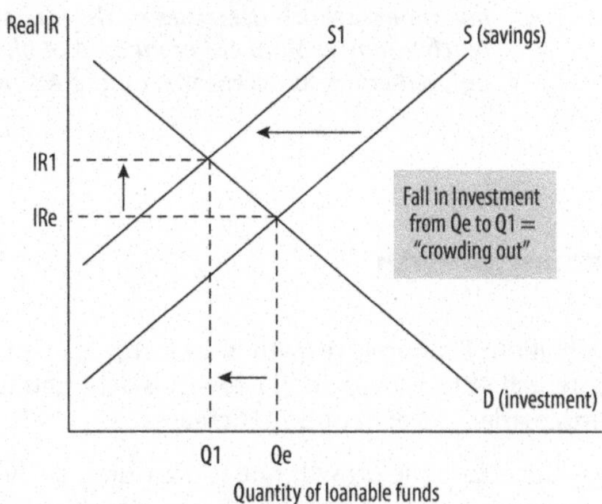


➤ As more households invest their savings in government bonds, the supply of loanable funds in the private sector decreases, leading to higher interest rates.

- As borrowing costs are now higher, households and firms that may have been willing to invest at lower rates are now "crowded out" of the market, and overall private sector investment falls.

2. Consequences of crowding out. The crowding-out effect highlights a potential downside of government intervention in an economy in recession.

   i. While the multiplier effects (described in Chapter 5) explain how an increase in government spending or a tax cut may result in a proportionally larger increase in total spending and GDP, if crowding out occurs, then the expansionary effect of a fiscal stimulus will be smaller than forecast.

   ii. A potential long-run impact of crowding out is a lower rate of capital accumulation and less economic growth as a result.

***The crowding-out effect can be illustrated in the loanable funds diagram in two ways. The preceding graph shows supply decreasing and the higher interest rates leading to a fall in private investment. However, the AP® Macro exam would also accept a diagram showing demand increasing due to government's demand for loanable funds. As the government enters the market for funds, the higher interest rate results in a fall in the level of private borrowing. While overall spending increases, it comes at the expense of private investment, which decreases as the interest rate rises. Your teacher may explain either method of illustrating crowding out; either one is acceptable on the AP® Macro exam.***

## VI. Economic Growth

A. Definition. Economic growth is an increase in an economy's actual and potential output over time. Growth is achieved when a country's full employment level of output increases.

   1. The economic growth rate is measured as the change in a country's potential real GDP between two time periods. The following graph shows U.S. real GDP from 2014 through 2018.

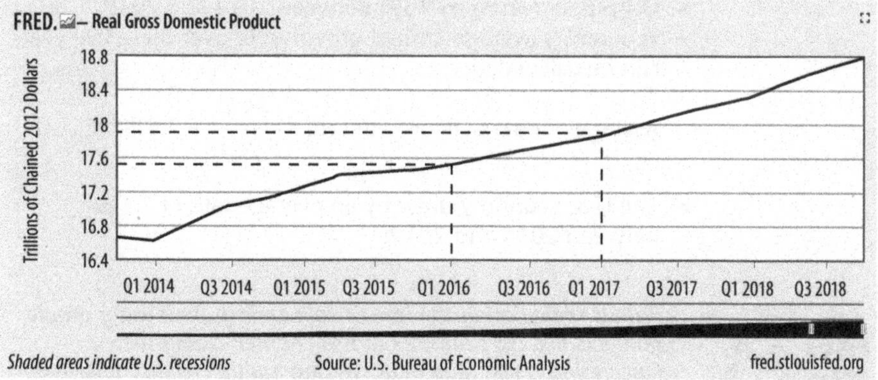


Source: FRED Economic Data—St. Louis Federal Reserve

i. From the chart, the economic growth rate between any two time periods can be calculated.

   - For example, between Q1 2016 and Q1 2017, U.S. output increased from $17.523 trillion to $17.863 trillion.
   - The GDP growth rate is calculated as the percentage change in real GDP between two time periods:

$$\text{GDP growth rate} = \frac{\text{GDP in year 2} - \text{GDP in year 1}}{\text{GDP in year 1}} \times 100$$

$$= \frac{\$17.863 - \$17.523 \text{ trillion}}{\$17.523 \text{ trillion}} \times 100$$

$$\text{GDP growth rate} = 1.94\%$$

   - The growth rate in real GDP between 2016 and 2017 was 1.94%.

ii. Over the five years as plotted on the graph, the U.S. had almost continuous economic growth.

   - From Q1 2014 to Q4 2018 output increased from $16.621 trillion to $18.784 trillion.
   - We can calculate the growth in GDP over five years:

$$\text{GDP growth rate} = \frac{\$18.784 - \$16.621 \text{ trillion}}{\$16.621 \text{ trillion}} \times 100$$

$$\text{GDP growth rate} = 13\%$$

- Output increased by 13% between 2014 and 2019. The economy's average annual growth rate over these five years can be calculated:

  $$\text{Average annual GDP growth rate} = \frac{13\%}{5 \text{ years}} = 2.6\% \text{ per year}$$

- The U.S. economy grew by an average rate of 2.6% between 2014 and 2019.

***Practice calculating the rate of economic growth using simple numbers like the examples in this chapter. Doing such a calculation is common in answering multiple-choice and free-response questions.***

**B.** Consequences of Growth. Economic growth has several desirable consequences.

1. More jobs. Total output and employment are directly related because firms need to employ more workers in order to produce more output. Therefore, economic growth creates more jobs, which in a population that is growing over time is necessary to keep unemployment low and assure that the typical household can sustain itself through work.
2. Higher living standards. A basic assumption of economics is that rising incomes lead to higher living standards and a better quality of life.
   - i. Since the Industrial Revolution of the 19th century, the living standards in countries that have experienced economic growth have also risen dramatically. This is evidenced not only by greater income, but also by increases in life expectancy, decreases in death rates and infant mortality rates, and the general alleviation of poverty.
   - ii. Economic growth is a driving factor in economic development, which is the general increase in standards of living over time.
3. Higher income. Per capita GDP measures the income of the average resident of a country, and per capita GDP growth is the best measure economists have of increased economic well-being. If real GDP increases faster than a country's population, it will result in an increase in a country's per capita GDP and higher living standards.

C. Productivity and Employment. The economic theory of an aggregate production function states that a country's rate of economic growth is a function of the allocation of the factors of production, including labor, capital, land, and technology.

1. According to the aggregate production function, real GDP is a function of the available inputs in a country, including:
   i. Physical capital, the machines and tools entities use to produce goods and services.
   ii. Labor, the amount of human work in the production of goods and services.
   iii. Human capital, the level of skills and education of the country's workforce.
   iv. Knowledge, the availability and accessibility of scientific and other know-how.
   v. Social infrastructure, the regulatory, business, legal, and cultural environment.
   vi. Natural resources, the availability of raw materials (minerals, forest resources, energy resources, etc.).
2. Increases in any of the preceding factors will bolster a country's real GDP and create economic growth; decreases in any of these will cause real GDP to fall.
3. Productivity is the amount of output attributable to a single unit of input (e.g., labor or capital).
   i. Labor productivity is the output per worker and is directly related to income. The more productive a country's workers, the higher their real income.
   ii. For this reason, investments in human capital can contribute to economic growth and increase a country's actual and potential output over time.
4. Human capital is generally the skills, knowledge, and experience of an individual or the people of a country.
   i. As human capital improves, productivity increases and the total output and income of a population will also rise.
5. Immigration. In addition to investing in human capital, adding to the labor force will also contribute to economic growth. Immigration can improve an economy's output by increasing the availability of labor.

6. The difference between economic growth from increases in the quantity of labor and growth from improvements in the quality of human capital is that while both will increase total output over time, only the latter will increase per capita real GDP. Greater productivity will drive up average incomes while more workers who are no more productive will only increase total income.

**D.** Physical Capital. Just as investments in human capital make labor more productive, investment in physical capital will make the tools, technologies, and machines employed in the production of a country's output more productive and increase the actual and potential output of the economy.

1. Physical capital is the man-made factors of production employed in the production of other goods and services in an economy. A rough synonym for physical capital is the "tools you can see or touch."
2. Technological advancements drive economic growth. So, when private firms invest in new and better capital equipment and technology, the potential and actual output of the economy should increase. Increasing the ratio of capital-to-labor in an economy will drive up labor productivity, further fueling economic growth.
   i. Investments in new technologies increase not just aggregate demand and short-run output through rising expenditures, but aggregate supply and full employment output through increasing the quantity and the quality of an economy's man-made factors of production.
   ii. When private sector investment in capital decreases or capital is allowed to depreciate without being replaced, the rate of economic growth can be expected to slow as the amount of capital or the productivity of capital is allowed to diminish over time.
   iii. A sustained period of low capital investment can trigger a recession as potential output decreases due to a diminished capital stock.
3. Research and development, or R&D, refers to the activities undertaken by private firms or by the government to improve existing technologies or products, or that lead to the introduction of new technologies or products.

i. R&D may focus on improving the means by which goods and services are produced or may investigate introducing new products.

   - Developing new or better products through R&D can open new markets for firms. When industries succeed in developing popular new products, it can lead to more employment and output.
   - The development of better production methods can increase productivity in already existing industries and drive economic growth.

ii. Governments also undertake R&D, often in industries that are under-researched by the private sector such as transportation, defense, energy, and healthcare.

   - Government-funded research can lead to breakthroughs that contribute to private-sector investment booms.
   - Examples include new developments in renewable energies and in more effective pharmaceuticals.

iii. There is a positive correlation between the level of private and public sector R&D and the extent of economic growth experienced in a country or region.

iv. The innovation resulting from R&D increases labor and capital productivity which in turn increases actual and potential output in the economy.

**E.** Illustrating Economic Growth. Three models demonstrate a country's long-run economic growth:

1. The PPC shows economic growth as an outward shift in the production possibilities of a country.
2. The business cycle represents economic growth as an increase in real GDP over time, shown by the "trend line" in the following graph.
3. The AD-AS model shows economic growth as an outward shift of long-run aggregate supply (LRAS) and an increase in the full employment level of output.

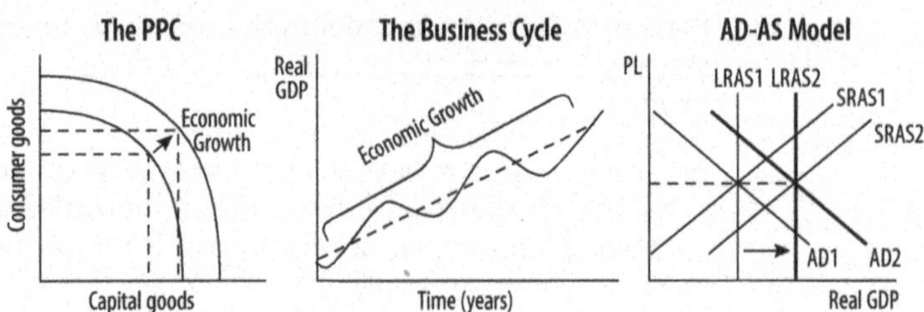


i. An outward shift of the PPC, the long-run growth line in the business cycle, and outward shifts of AD, SRAS, and LRAS all show that an economy's potential, full employment level of output is rising. Increases in the factors of production (land, labor, capital), productivity, or human capital are allowing the country to produce more output, creating economic growth.

## VII. Public Policy and Economic Growth

A. Supply-side policies are government measures aimed at increasing productivity, labor force participation, infrastructure or technology in the economy, and thereby increasing the level of aggregate supply.

1. Examples of government supply-side policies include:
    - i. Reducing business and income taxes
    - ii. Labor market reforms
    - iii. Deregulation of industries
    - iv. Trade liberalization
    - v. Investment in human capital
    - vi. Investment in physical capital
2. Supply-side policies increase productivity and reduce production costs, shifting SRAS and LRAS outward, increasing actual and potential output.
3. Reducing business and personal income taxes can positively impact aggregate supply in two ways.
    - i. Lowering taxes on firms reduces the cost of doing business. Allowing business owners to keep a larger share of their earned revenues should incentivize new investments in capital and

technology, which increase the productivity of labor and reduce costs, shifting AS outward.

ii. If tax rates are lowered, households may have a greater incentive to work, so labor force participation could increase and worker productivity could improve, increasing SRAS, LRAS, and potential output.

4. Labor market reforms that bring down the cost of labor will increase a nation's aggregate supply and lead to growth in national output. Supply-side labor market reforms include:

   i. Reducing or eliminating the minimum wage. The minimum wage is a price floor in the labor market set above the free market equilibrium wage rate. Minimum wage laws increase the cost of hiring workers in certain industries (typically the low-skilled sectors). Lowering or abolishing the minimum wage may lead firms to hire more workers and thereby produce more output at a lower per unit cost.

   ii. Weakening labor union power. Labor unions negotiate with employers for better worker benefits, such as higher wages, more paid vacation, better healthcare, and so on. Such benefits add to firms' production costs and keep aggregate supply lower than it might be otherwise. Reducing the power of unions will lower labor costs for producers and shift AS rightward.

   iii. Reducing government spending on unemployment benefits. Unemployment benefits are the money payments individuals receive during the period when they are out of work and seeking a new job. Lowering these benefits creates an incentive for unemployed workers to accept a new job more quickly and at a lower wage rate than they otherwise might accept. Firms will find more workers willing to work for lower wages.

5. Deregulation. Governments regulate certain activities of producers in the free market.

   i. The goals of regulation are often to reduce industries' impacts on the environment and on human health or safety.

   ii. The cost of complying with government regulations increases a firm's average costs and reduces the level of aggregate supply.

   iii. Deregulation (either removing or relaxing regulations) of industries will lead to lower costs and greater output, increasing aggregate supply.

- For example, the United States Environmental Protection Agency is often accused of imposing burdensome regulations on producers of goods ranging from cars to electricity to farm products.
- Environmental regulations reduce emissions of harmful toxins that damage human health and the environment.
- The cost of environmental regulations is the impact they have on employment and the price level of the goods or services provided.
- Reducing regulations will lead to more output and lower prices in deregulated industries, increasing actual and potential output in the country as a whole.
- However, the trade-off may be increased environmental degradation and reduced human health.

6. Trade liberalization is the relaxing of trade barriers between countries.
   i. Protectionism is the use of tariffs, quotas, or other measures aimed at making domestic producers more competitive with foreign producers by limiting imports into the nation.
   ii. The reduction or removal of protectionist policies will allow a country's firms to acquire cheaper inputs from abroad and increase the potential market for a country's producers by opening the market to international consumers.
   iii. Trade liberalization can provide a country's producers access to imported raw materials and other factors of production, reducing average production costs.
   iv. More foreign competition forces domestic firms to use their resources more efficiently, increasing productivity and output.
   v. Both lower production costs and increased competition increase the nation's aggregate supply and contribute to long-run economic growth.
7. Fiscal policies. Not all investment needed to promote economic growth comes from the private sector. Government investments in human and physical capital increase aggregate demand, aggregate supply, and potential output in the short run and long run by improving the quantity and the quality of physical capital and by improving human capital.
   i. Certain goods may not be readily available in the free market. Government provision or subsidizing of such goods can

improve efficiency in an economy and increase the country's potential output.

- Governments provide education through a public school system. A better educated workforce is more productive and provides businesses with higher-skilled workers, leading to greater tax revenues for government.
- Increased tax revenues allow the government to provide other public goods that further increase the economy's potential output.

ii. Governments provide certain types of infrastructure (roads, sanitation, electricity grids, communications) because private firms are unable or unwilling to do so.

- Better infrastructure reduces the costs for private businesses and allows them to operate more efficiently.
- Because these businesses do not bear these infrastructure expenses, they can produce and sell their products at lower costs.
- A modern, efficient infrastructure promotes economic growth and increases a country's potential output over time.

iii. The implementation of the supply-side fiscal policies described in this part can enhance a country's rate of long-run economic growth.

Chapter 8

# UNIT 6 Open Economy—International Trade and Finance

## I. Balance of Payments Accounts

A. Introduction to International Trade

1. International trade occurs when two or more countries engage in the exchange of goods and services and invest in one another's real and financial assets.

2. The study of international trade examines the flows of imports and exports into and out of a country, foreign investment at home and domestic investment abroad, and the determination of exchange rates on international currency markets.

B. Balance of Trade

1. The balance of trade is the most basic factor on the impact of foreign trade on a country's economy.

2. It is computed as the value of a country's exports minus the value of a country's imports and can be either positive (in surplus) or negative (in deficit).

The balance of trade = Export revenue (X) – Import spending (M)

i. The following chart shows the U.S. balance of trade in goods and services from 2000 through 2016.

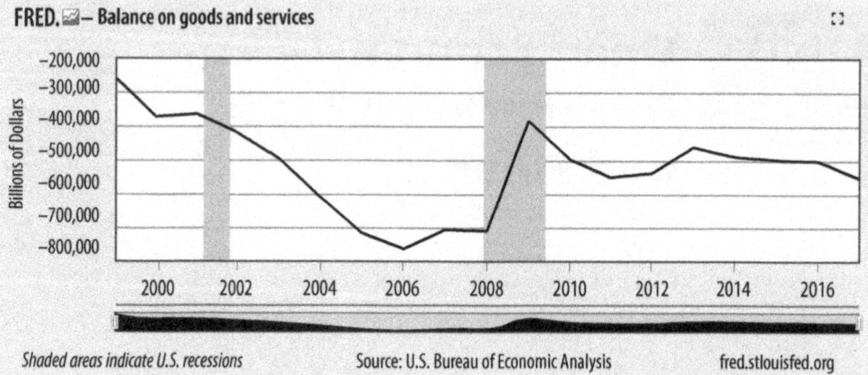


2. The U.S. had a balance of trade deficit with the rest of the world every year from 2000 to 2016, ranging from –$250 billion to as much as –$750 billion.
    i. So, the U.S. spent as much as $750 billion more on imports each year than it earned in revenue from its exports to the rest of the world.
3. Of course, as a result of this trade deficit, many U.S. trading partners experience a trade surplus with the U.S.
    i. A trade surplus yields a positive balance of trade value, as the country's export revenues are greater than the amount it spends on imports.

***The terms "surplus" and "deficit" often have either positive or negative connotations, but this should not be the case. A trade surplus, for example, has as many downsides as it does benefits for a nation.***

C. The Current Account of the Balance of Payments

1. The trade balance is one component of what economists refer to as the balance of payments, which is a broad measure of all the financial and goods transactions between one country and all other countries. In this chapter, we will closely examine the different accounts that make up a country's balance of payments.
2. A country's balance of trade is actually just one component of the current account of its balance of payments, which records the

values of net exports, net income from abroad, and net unilateral transfers (monetary gifts or grants between the country and other countries). The current account has many parts, including:

i. the goods balance (also called the visible trade balance), which measures the value of goods exported to other countries (recorded as a credit) and the value of goods imported from other countries (recorded as a debit).

ii. the services balance (or invisible balance), which measures the value of exported services (a credit) and imported services (a debit).

iii. the income balance, which measures the flow of income from domestic citizens working abroad and income from domestic investors' overseas assets into the country (a credit) and income earned in the country by foreign workers and investors but sent abroad (a debit). The income balance is also called the "net foreign factor income" (NFFI) and is what differentiates a country's GNP (gross national product) from its GDP. NFFI = GNP – GDP.

iv. the transfers balance, which records payments made from one nation to another that are not in exchange for any good or service, such as gifts or grants. Payments made to the country are recorded as a credit while payments made to other countries are a debit.

3. The sum of all the credits and debits in all of the sub-accounts determine the current account balance, which can be either positive (in surplus) or negative (in deficit). The chart below shows Canada's current account balance for the years from 1998–2013.

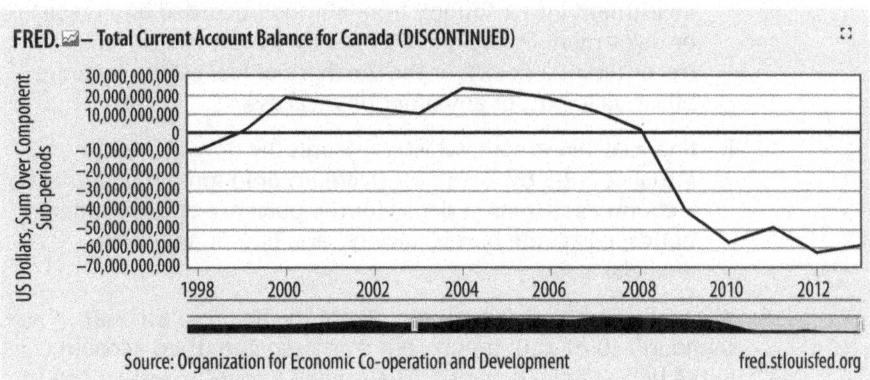

i. Note that Canada's current account ranged from a $10 billion deficit in 1998 to a surplus of $24 billion in the mid-2000s, to a deficit of $60 billion by 2012.

ii. In the surplus years from 1999 to 2008, more money flowed into Canada from trade in goods and services, income flows, and transfers than flowed out.

iii. However, in the deficit years more money flowed out than flowed in for these transactions with the rest of the world.

**D.** Capital and Financial Accounts in Balance of Payments

1. The second account in a country's balance of payments is the capital and financial account, which measures the flow of money between a country and all other countries for the purpose of buying or selling real and financial assets and the transfer of capital between countries.

   i. Real assets include tangible property such as factories, office buildings, and real estate like houses or apartment buildings. Real assets also include any other physical property bought by a country's citizens abroad or bought by foreigners in the home country.

   ii. Financial assets are "non-tangible" investments such as government and corporate bonds (certificates of debt), equities (shares in companies), and money put into bank accounts.

2. The financial account has several components or sub-accounts including:

   i. investments in physical assets, which measure the flow of investment into a country from abroad (recorded as a credit) or investment in foreign countries by a country's citizens (recorded as a debit) for the purchase of real estate, factories, office buildings, or any other physical asset.

   ii. financial investment, which measures the flow of investment into a country by foreigners (a credit) or in foreign countries by a country's citizens (a debit) for the purchase of government bonds, corporate bonds, savings, equities, or any other financial assets.

3. The capital account is a component of the financial account (although some countries record it as a separate third account in the balance of payments). The capital account measures the transfer of capital goods, money for the purchase of capital goods, and debt forgiveness between one country and other nations.

i. Money transferred by the citizens of foreign countries to another country for investments in physical or real assets, for debt forgiveness, or for capital acquisition is recorded as a credit and moves the capital and financial accounts toward a surplus.

ii. Money transferred from the home country to a foreign country for investments in physical or real assets, for capital acquisition, or for debt forgiveness in a foreign country is recorded as a debit and moves the capital and financial account balance toward a deficit.

4. The capital and financial account measures the flow of money into and out of a country for the ownership of real and financial assets.

   i. When foreigners take ownership of a country's assets, whether physical assets like buildings or financial assets like government bonds, that country's capital and financial account moves toward a surplus.

   ii. When citizens of that country invest in foreign assets (physical or financial), the capital and financial account moves toward a deficit.

   iii. Basically, any transaction that causes money to flow into a country is a credit toward its capital and financial account, and any transaction that causes money to flow out is a debit. The following chart shows the U.S. financial account from 1997 through 2012.

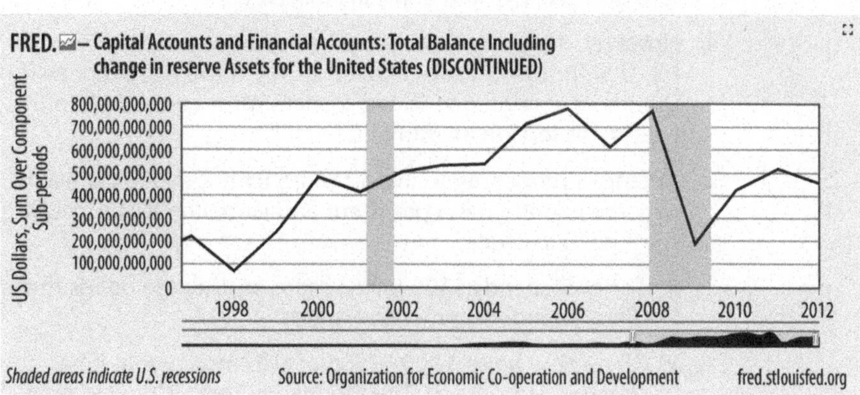


➤ The U.S. financial account was in surplus for every year from 1997 through 2012 and has been in surplus every year through 2019.

- The surplus ranged between $100 billion and $800 billion. More money flowed into the U.S. for investments than flowed out.

***Only recently has the AP® Macro exam referred to the account measuring the flow of financial transactions and ownership of assets abroad as the* financial account*. Formerly, it was known as the* capital account*. Be familiar with both terms because they may be used interchangeably on the exam.***

E. Balance of Payments. Note the relationship between the current account and the capital and financial account. When one is in deficit, the other must be in surplus. The two accounts will roughly balance out so that their combined value equals zero.

$$\text{Balance of Payments} = \text{current account} + \text{capital and financial account} = 0$$

1. A dollar spent by a country on a foreign good or service must come back to the country purchasing the imports in one way or another.

   i. If foreigners spend as much on a country's goods and services as it spends on foreign goods, then its current account balance will roughly equal zero and there will be little money left for foreigners to invest in domestic assets.

   ii. However, if a country has a current account deficit, as has the U.S. for the last several decades, then the extra money it spends on foreign goods and services must come back to the country as foreign investment.

   iii. America's propensity to import more than it exports explains why the country has a persistent and large financial account surplus. To illustrate:

   - The U.S. spends $300 billion more on Chinese goods than China spends on American goods.
   - China now holds $300 billion of U.S. money that it has not spent on U.S. goods. The rational thing for China to do is invest that money in assets that will earn Chinese investors a return.

- The alternative is to hold those dollars as cash (which China also does, holding U.S. dollars as foreign exchange reserves in the country's central bank).
- As Chinese investors invest the dollars earned from their trade surplus with the U.S. into the U.S. economy, America's financial account moves toward surplus.
- The result of these transactions is that nationals of China and other countries with which the U.S. has a current account deficit own an increasing share of American assets, both physical and financial, over time.
- One consequence is that by 2018 almost 30% of America's publicly held government debt was owed to foreign nationals.

iv. The following chart plots the amount of U.S. government debt owed to international investors.

- From 1998 to 2018, foreign ownership of U.S. government debt increased from $1 trillion to over $6 trillion, or 28.6% of the total federal debt of $21 trillion.
- This increase was caused by the U.S. running trade deficits with other countries year after year; surplus income earned by America's trading partners has come back to the U.S. as foreign investment.
- In addition to U.S. government debt, foreign investors are taking ownership in American companies and over U.S. property, and factors of production, such as office buildings and factories, through their investments in the financial account.

2. When a current account balance moves toward surplus, the country is earning more from exports than it spends on imports, thus more money flows into the country through trade than flows out. The country then has two options:

   i. it can hold its surplus money as cash, which moves its financial account toward deficit (since cash is an asset of another country that it has, in essence, imported).

   ii. it can invest that cash into assets in the country with which it has trade surpluses, in which case the country essentially "imports ownership of foreign assets," moving its financial account into deficit.

3. The current account and the capital and financial account balance one another out.

   i. When one account moves toward surplus, the other moves toward deficit, and vice versa.

   ii. The sum of the two accounts must therefore equal zero, meaning a country's balance of payments will always be "balanced."

## II. Exchange Rates and the Foreign Exchange Market

A. Demand for and Supply of Foreign Currency. When nations with different currencies trade or invest across borders, an exchange of currencies must take place.

1. The market in which different currencies are exchanged is called the foreign exchange market, or forex market.

   i. Forex markets exist for every currency in the world; there is a market for U.S. dollars in the U.K. and one for British pounds in the U.S., for Japanese yen in South Korea and for Korean won in Japan, for Australian dollars in Canada and for Canadian dollars in Australia, and so on.

2. Forex markets determine different currencies' exchange rates, i.e., the price of a currency in terms of another currency.

   i. When the price of a currency increases against another currency, it is called appreciation.

      ➤ If the price of one U.S. dollar to a British investor increases from 0.75 British pounds to 0.8 British pounds, the dollar has appreciated in the U.K.

ii. When the price of a currency decreases against another currency, it is called depreciation.

- If the price of a British pound decreases from 1.33 dollars to 1.25 dollars, it means that the pound has depreciated against the dollar.

3. Currency demand. Exchange rates are determined by the demand for and supply of, a currency, just as prices for goods and services are determined by demand and supply.

i. The following graph shows the demand for U.S. dollars in the U.K. The vertical axis shows the dollar exchange rate and the horizontal axis the quantity of dollars demanded in the U.K. at each value.

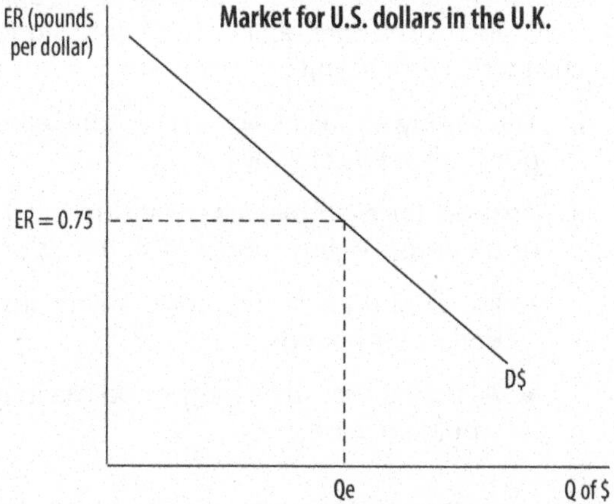


ii. Who in the U.K. demands U.S. dollars and why?

- British consumers who buy goods produced in the U.S. and imported into the U.K.
- British travelers visiting the U.S.
- British investors who wish to buy U.S. assets (bonds, stocks, real estate or property in the U.S.)
- The Bank of England (the U.K.'s central bank), which holds U.S. dollars in its official reserves of foreign currency
- If any of these groups' demand for dollars increases, the market demand for U.S. dollars increases in the U.K.

iii. There is an inverse relationship between the exchange rate and the quantity of dollars demanded by U.K. consumers and investors.

- When the dollar becomes cheaper, U.K. consumers demand more dollars to buy more imported American goods, which now appear cheaper to British consumers.
- Investors demand more U.S. assets which appear cheaper when the dollar depreciates.
- While British consumers and investors demand U.S. dollars, those dollars are supplied by Americans who exchange them for pounds to buy British goods and invest in British assets.

3. Currency supply. The supply of dollars is upward sloping; at higher exchange rates, Americans are willing to supply more dollars to the U.K., since a stronger dollar makes British goods and assets appear cheaper to American consumers and investors.

i. The supply of dollars will shift if Americans' demand for British goods or assets changes.

ii. Assume, for example, Americans demand more British goods, or they wish to buy more British bonds or equities.

- For all of these transactions, Americans must exchange dollars for pounds.
- As they do so, the supply of dollars in the U.K. forex market would increase.

**B.** Equilibrium. The equilibrium exchange rate is determined by the demand, and supply for, a currency in the forex market.

1. The following graph represents both demand for, and supply of, dollars in the U.K. The equilibrium exchange rate can thus be determined.

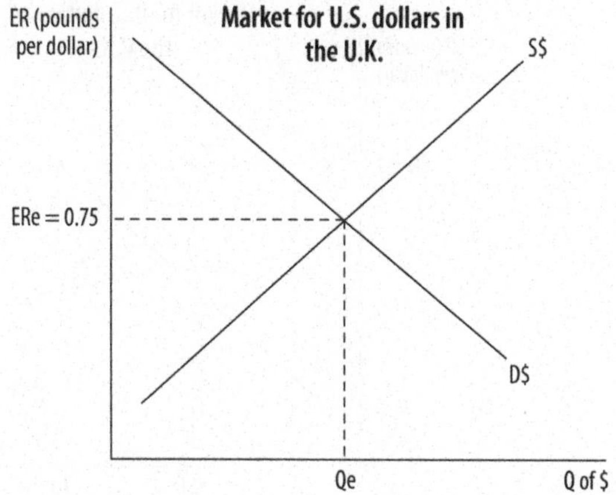


i. The equilibrium exchange rate (ERe) is the price at which the quantity of a currency demanded is equal to the quantity supplied.

ii. In the forex market for U.S. dollars in the U.K., the equilibrium is 0.75 pounds.

iii. At this price, British consumers and investors demand the same quantity of dollars for imports from, and investments in, the U.S. as Americans are willing to supply for the purchase of British goods and investments in the U.K.

C. Disequilibrium. Disequilibrium exchange rates create surpluses and shortages in the forex market.

1. Assume American forex traders offered U.S. dollars to British import firms and investors at a rate of 1 pound per dollar. The graph below shows what happens when the rate is set higher than equilibrium.

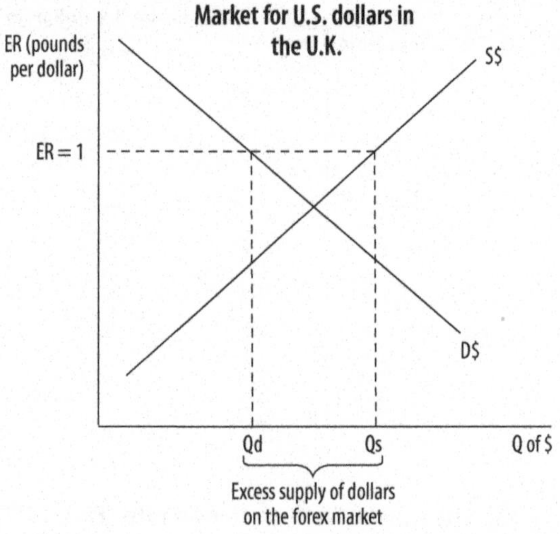


i. An exchange rate of 1 pound per dollar is a disequilibrium because the quantities supplied and demanded are not the same.

ii. Americans, who find British goods and investments more attractive when the dollar is worth 1 pound instead of 0.75 pounds, are willing to supply more dollars to the forex market.

iii. British consumers and investors, however, now find American goods and investments costlier at the higher exchange rate, so the quantity of dollars demanded has fallen.

iv. There is a surplus (excess supply) of dollars on the forex market.

2. An exchange rate set below equilibrium will cause a shortage in the forex market. Assume, for example, that British investors and consumers are willing to pay only 0.5 pounds per dollar. In our forex market we can see the outcome when the price is set at a rate below equilibrium.

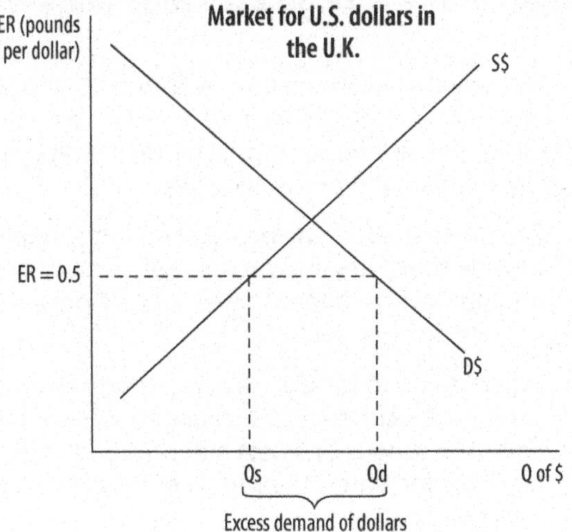


i. At 0.5 pounds per dollar, Americans who now find British goods and investment costlier and thus less attractive, are willing to supply fewer dollars (remember that each pound now costs $2).

ii. Meanwhile, British consumers and investors are more attracted to the now cheaper investments and imports from the U.S., so the quantity of dollars demanded has increased.

iii. Since the quantity demanded exceeds the quantity supplied, there is a shortage of dollars on the forex market.

3. When shortages or surpluses exist in a forex market, market forces tend to drive the exchange rate back to equilibrium.

4. The equilibrium exchange rate can only change when there is a shift in either the demand for, or the supply of, the currency, which will lead to either appreciation or depreciation of the currency.

***Labels in foreign exchange market diagrams are tricky and should be given particular attention when you're drawing these graphs. The vertical price axis should always make clear that the price of a currency is expressed in terms of another currency. The dollar market in Europe, for example, should be labeled, "the price of dollars in terms of euros." Alternatively, it could be labeled €/$, indicating that the axis shows the number of euros per dollar. If you use a fraction like this, the currency the graph is illustrating should always be in the denominator (below the line in the fraction).***

## Changes in the Foreign Exchange Market

A. Exchange Rate Determination. A currency will appreciate (increase in value) or depreciate (decrease in value) when one of the factors affecting demand for, or supply of, the currency changes causing a shift of the demand or supply curve.

1. Factors that affect the demand for, and supply of, a currency include the tastes and preferences of consumers at home and abroad, relative interest rates, relative price levels, speculation, and relative income levels.

2. When demand for Country A's exports changes, demand for Country A's currency also changes. When demand for other countries' goods or assets among Country A's consumers and investors increases, the supply of Country A's currency will shift on the forex market.

   i. For example, assume Japanese products are becoming increasingly fashionable in China.

   ii. In order to buy Japanese cars, clothes, and electronic goods, Chinese consumers need more Japanese yen (JPY).

   iii. Demand for yen increases on the forex market.

   iv. At the same time, Chinese consumers must exchange Chinese yuan (CNY) in order to buy yen, so the supply of yuan increases.

   v. The effect of the changing tastes of Chinese consumers is illustrated in the following graphs showing forex markets for the Japanese yen in China and the Chinese yuan in Japan.

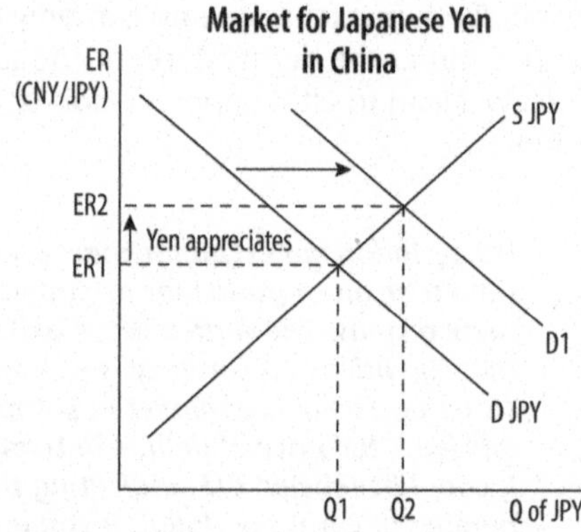

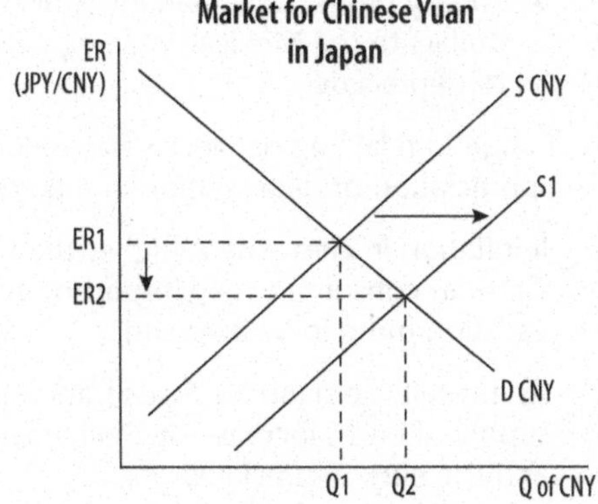


- In the first graph above, the increased demand for Japanese yen causes it to appreciate in the forex market for yen in China.
- In the second graph above, the increased supply of Chinese yuan causes it to depreciate in the forex market for yuan in Japan.
- The demand for yen and the supply of yuan are basically the same thing. Chinese households demand yen and supply yuan, so when demand for one increases, by definition the supply of the other also increases.
- Each currency's value is the reciprocal of the other, so when one currency depreciates, the other must appreciate.

3. A change in relative interest rates between two countries can cause shifts in the forex market due to inflows and outflows in the financial account of the balance of payments.
   i. Interest determines the rate of return on investments; when a country's interest rates increase, its bonds become cheaper and, therefore, demand for financial assets in that country will increase among foreign investors, causing the currency to appreciate.
   ii. For example, assume interest rates in Mexico increase.
      - Foreign investors, including Canadians, will demand more Mexican financial assets, for which Mexican pesos are needed.
      - The demand for pesos will increase in Canada, causing the price of the peso in Canadian dollars to increase.

- To buy pesos, Canadian investors must supply Canadian dollars to the Mexican market, causing the Canadian dollar to depreciate.

4. A change in relative price levels between countries can also cause an appreciation or depreciation of a currency on the forex market.
   i. If inflation in Germany is higher than inflation in Switzerland, German consumers may import more Swiss goods and vacation more in Switzerland.
   ii. As a result, demand for Swiss francs increases in Germany and supply of euros increases in Switzerland. The franc appreciates, and the euro depreciates.
   iii. A higher price level in a country relative to its trading partners will cause the currency in the country with higher inflation to depreciate and the currency of the country with lower inflation to appreciate. So, demand shifts to goods from the country with the lower inflation rate.
5. Fluctuations in relative income levels can also cause a change in equilibrium exchange rates.
   i. If Malaysian household incomes rise at a faster rate than Singaporean incomes, then Malaysians' demand for imports from Singapore will increase, causing demand for the Singapore dollar to rise and supply of Malaysian ringgit to increase.
   ii. The Singapore dollar will appreciate while the ringgit depreciates.
   iii. A rise in one country's national income relative to a trading partner will cause the country with rising incomes' currency to depreciate and the slower-growth country's currency to appreciate.
6. Speculation over future exchange rates can cause a shift in demand or supply of a currency today. The very expectation that a currency will appreciate (or depreciate) in the future can lead investors to demand more (or less) of that currency today.
   i. For example, assume there is widespread speculation that the government of Thailand will default on its debt in the next year. If this were to happen, the international investors in Thai government bonds would be holding worthless assets.

ii. In anticipation of the default, investors sell their Thai assets today and the demand for those assets simultaneously decreases.

iii. The fall in demand for Thai baht causes it to depreciate today, even though nothing fundamentally changed besides the speculation among investors of a future default.

iv. In this way, the expectation of a future change in the forex market acts as a self-fulfilling prophecy. If enough investors expect a currency to fall in value, it will likely happen, and if they expect it to appreciate, the currency will likely meet their expectations.

**B.** Fiscal Policy. A government's fiscal policies can also influence exchange rates because of their impact on aggregate demand, real output, the price level, and exchange rates.

1. An expansionary fiscal policy can cause a country's currency to depreciate as follows:

   i. Increasing AD from tax cuts or more government spending will cause domestic incomes and the domestic price level to rise, increasing demand for imported goods.

   ii. Higher demand for imports will cause foreign currencies to appreciate and the domestic currency to depreciate on the forex markets.

   iii. However, an expansionary fiscal policy could cause the domestic currency to appreciate.

   - If the fiscal stimulus is financed by a budget deficit, then the resulting increase in bond yields and domestic interest rates may lead to an inflow of foreign investment as foreigners seek to hold more of the country's financial assets (government bonds, savings accounts, etc.).
   - As a result of higher domestic interest rates, the currency could appreciate, causing a form of crowding out that reduces the expansionary effects of the fiscal stimulus.
   - Recall from Chapter 7, Part V that crowding out occurs when fiscal stimulus drives up interest rates and causes private investment to decrease; a similar effect could occur to net exports if higher domestic interest rates cause the currency to appreciate and make exports less attractive to foreign consumers.

2. Contractionary fiscal policies will have the opposite effect on the exchange rate, causing the currency to appreciate.
   i. Reduced AD will cause domestic incomes and the price level to decrease, reducing demand for imports.
   ii. Less import demand causes foreign currencies to depreciate and the domestic currency to appreciate on the forex market.
   iii. On the other hand, if a contractionary fiscal policy causes bond prices to rise and bond yields to fall, then foreign capital inflows will decrease and the domestic currency could depreciate, causing demand for the country's exports to rise and offsetting the contractionary effect of the government's fiscal policy.
3. Whether a particular fiscal policy causes a country's currency to appreciate or depreciate depends on the extent to which domestic interest rates are impacted by the change in the government's budget position relative to the impact of changes in domestic income and the price level.

C. Monetary Policy. A change in monetary policy affects a country's exchange rate in a more straightforward way than a change in fiscal policy.

1. An expansionary monetary policy will have the following effect on the exchange rate:
   i. Increased money supply causes the nominal interest rate to decrease.
   ii. The resulting increase in AD will cause domestic incomes and the price level to rise, increasing demand for imports.
   iii. Lower domestic interest rates cause foreign demand for the currency to fall and higher domestic incomes cause demand for foreign currencies to rise, so the domestic currency will depreciate on the forex markets.
2. A contractionary monetary policy will have the opposite effect on the exchange rate:
   i. A reduced money supply will result in a rise in the nominal interest rate.

ii. The resulting decrease in AD will cause domestic incomes and the price level to fall, reducing demand for imports.

iii. Higher domestic interest rates will cause foreign demand for the currency to increase and lower domestic incomes lessen demand for foreign currencies. Thus, the domestic currency will appreciate on the forex markets.

3. Unlike fiscal policy, the effect on the exchange rate of a change in monetary policy will reinforce the desired effect of the policy itself.

   i. An expansionary monetary policy meant to increase AD will cause the currency to depreciate, which will result in the rise of net exports, further contributing to the expansionary effect of the policy itself.

   ii. A contractionary monetary policy meant to reduce AD will cause the currency to appreciate, which will result in the fall of net exports, further contributing to the contractionary effect of the policy itself.

***Both the multiple-choice and free-response sections often ask you to identify the effect a change in government or central bank policy will have on the country's exchange rate in foreign exchange markets. Answering requires you to "connect the dots" and determine how the fiscal or monetary policy in question will affect domestic inflation, incomes, or interest rates, and then determine how that change will affect demand for, or supply of, the country's currency on foreign exchange markets.***

## IV. Changes in the Foreign Exchange Market and Net Exports

A. Exchange Rates and Trade Flows. The market for a country's currency and the markets for its goods and services are closely linked. As described in Part III above, a change in demand for a country's goods will cause a change in demand for its currency. A change in demand for foreign goods will affect the currency's supply as consumers trade their local currency for foreign currency in order to buy imports.

1. Factors that cause a currency to appreciate also cause the value of that country's exports to rise and the value of its imports to fall. Consequently, net exports will decrease. Consider the market for Canadian dollars in the U.S.:

   i. Increased demand for Canadian goods among Americans will move Canada's current account toward surplus and cause the Canadian dollar to appreciate.

   ii. Other factors may also cause the Canadian dollar to appreciate besides increased demand for its goods. For example, assume American investors' demand for shares in Canadian companies increases, leading to more foreign investment in the Canadian stock market.

      ➤ Demand for Canadian dollars will increase, and the dollar will appreciate.

      ➤ The stronger Canadian dollar causes the value of Canada's exports to increase and the value of its imports to decrease.

      ➤ Canadian households will now buy more American goods and American households will buy fewer Canadian goods.

      ➤ Canada's financial account has moved toward surplus due to increased foreign investment, while its current account moves toward deficit due to a stronger currency and falling net exports.

2. Factors that cause a currency to depreciate have the opposite effect on net exports.

   i. An outflow of foreign investment in Canadian stocks will cause the Canadian dollar to depreciate, making Canadian goods cheaper to foreigners and foreign goods more expensive to Canadians.

   ii. In this case, the financial account will move toward deficit while the current account moves toward surplus due to a weaker Canadian dollar.

3. The link between international financial and goods markets becomes clear based on our analysis of net exports, capital flows, and the real interest rates outlined above. Persistent imbalances in a country's current account can have implications for domestic stakeholders as well as the country's importers and exporters.

   i. Persistent current account deficits result in lower domestic employment and lower interest rates, as consumers buy more imports and capital inflows increase the supply of loanable funds in the deficit country's economy.

   ii. Persistent current account surpluses result in greater domestic employment and higher interest rates, as foreign demand boosts employment in the export sector and capital outflows deplete the domestic supply of loanable funds and drive interest rates up.

4. Under free market exchange rate systems, in which currencies are allowed to float freely based on flows in the current and financial accounts, persistent imbalances in the current account should be minimized.

   i. Trade deficits would decrease as falling demand for a currency leads to depreciation and an increase in the country's net exports.

   ii. Trade surpluses would decrease as strong demand for the currency leads to appreciation and a decrease in net exports.

## V. Real Interest Rates and International Capital Flows

**A.** Capital Flows. This term refers to movements of financial capital (money) between economies. Capital inflows occur when money flows into a country's economy as a result of foreign investment at home and capital outflows are when money flows out of an economy as a result of domestic investment abroad.

1. As outlined in Part I of this chapter, the flow of financial capital for investment is measured in the financial account of a country's balance of payments and corresponds inversely with the flow of goods and services in the current account. A move toward deficit in the current account would move a country's financial account toward surplus, as foreigners increase their ownership of a country's assets when it has a trade surplus with that country.

2. In an open economy, differences in real interest rates across countries change the relative values of domestic and foreign assets. Capital will flow toward the country with the relatively higher

interest rates, due to the higher return on investments made in that country's assets.

**B.** Central banks can influence the domestic interest rate in the short run, which, in turn, will affect net capital inflows.

1. A contractionary monetary policy will result in an increase in domestic interest rates and a net capital inflow, causing the currency to appreciate. The result will be a move toward surplus in the financial account of the balance of payments and a move toward deficit in the current account.
2. Expansionary monetary policies result in a lower interest rate and a capital outflow, causing the currency to depreciate. The outcome will be a move toward deficit in the financial account and a move toward surplus in the current account.

# PART III

## TEST-TAKING STRATEGIES AND PRACTICE QUESTIONS

Chapter 9

# Strategies for the Multiple-Choice Questions

The AP® Macroeconomics exam starts with a 60-question multiple-choice section which accounts for two-thirds (66.7 percent) of your final AP® grade. Each question is worth one point, for a total of 60 points. There is **no penalty** for incorrect answers, so there is no reason *not* to guess if you are running out of time and have not finished all 60 questions or encounter a question that you cannot figure out.

Every year the multiple-choice questions (MCQs) tend to follow a similar pattern in the order of questions. About ten questions are on topics from Unit 1: Basic Economic Concepts. The topics covered include opportunity cost, production possibilities, scarcity, the basic economic problem and economic resources, and basic supply and demand questions. The other 50 multiple-choice questions venture into the realm of macro-specific material.

Typically, questions on open economy and international trade appear late in the exam, just as they appear late in the syllabus. Don't let the order of the questions concern you too much, however. What is most important is the number of questions that are likely to appear on each topic from the syllabus. The College Board publishes the approximate percentage of the multiple-choice questions covering each unit. This information can also be found in Chapter 1 of this *Crash Course*.

## USE OF TIME ON THE MULTIPLE-CHOICE SECTION

You will have 70 minutes to answer the 60 multiple-choice questions, meaning that on average, you have 76 seconds per question. Don't interpret this to mean that you should *take* 76 seconds to answer each question. Some questions can be answered in far less than 76 seconds, while others will require more time to answer. Pacing yourself is important. If 35 minutes in the multiple-choice section have elapsed and you have not answered 30 questions, you are moving too slowly and may need to pick up the pace.

How do you know how much time to spend on certain questions? The trick is to identify what *knowledge* and which *skills* the question is assessing. Some questions test only basic knowledge from one section of the syllabus. Others test basic *skills*, while requiring only one piece of knowledge. On the other hand, some questions require knowledge of several sections of the syllabus and one or two skills to answer correctly. The relative complexity of the question should determine how much time you spend on a question. Less complex questions require less time, while those requiring more skills and knowledge should consume the most time.

## LEVEL 1 QUESTIONS—DEFINITIONAL

Expect about 10 to 20 of the multiple-choice questions to be what can be described as Level 1 questions. These are the easiest and the quickest to answer, because they require only one piece of knowledge or one skill.

**Example 1:** The unemployment rate measures the percentage of

(A) people in the labor force who do not have jobs

(B) people in the labor force who have a part-time job but are looking for a full-time job

(C) people who do not have jobs and have given up looking for work

(D) people in the adult population who do not have jobs

(E) people in the adult population who have temporary jobs

Most Level 1 questions are *definitional* in nature, which means they are basically testing to see if you know the definition of one of the terms from the syllabus. In the example above, the definition of "unemployment rate" is being tested. If you are familiar with this definition, answering this question should take almost no time at all. The unemployment rate measures the percentage of people in the labor force who do not have jobs. Therefore, (A) is the correct answer.

## OTHER EXAMPLES OF LEVEL 1 QUESTIONS

In each of the examples that follow, one basic piece of knowledge or one basic skill is being tested. These questions should be the quickest and easiest to answer in the multiple-choice section. Therefore, no more than 20 to 30 seconds should be required.

**Example 2:** The sum of which of the following expenditures is equal to the value of the gross domestic product?

(A) Consumer purchases, investment for capital goods, exports, and imports

(B) Consumer purchases, investment for capital goods, net exports, and inventories

(C) Consumer purchases, investment for capital goods, government purchases, and net exports

(D) Consumer purchases, government purchases, exports, and national income

(E) Investment for capital goods, government purchases, net exports, and inventories

**Example 3:** A worker is cyclically unemployed if

(A) he has lost his job at a factory that has moved overseas

(B) he is unable to find work because of a decrease in overall demand in the economy for goods and services

(C) he is out of work because the hotel that employed him closed for the off-season

(D) his skills are no longer needed in the economy

(E) foreigners now do his job more efficiently than he does

## LEVEL 2 QUESTIONS—ANALYTICAL

The next level of difficulty on the multiple-choice section requires you to apply more than one skill or piece of knowledge to come to a correct answer. Analytical questions are the most common in the multiple-choice section and will likely make up more than half of the 60 questions. These questions usually require a two-step process to solve for the correct answer. In addition to knowing a definition or a piece of knowledge, you may also be required to complete a calculation.

**Example 1:** Assume that the reserve requirement is 20 percent. If a bank initially has no excess reserves and $10,000 cash is deposited in the bank, the maximum amount by which this bank may increase its loans is

(A) $2,000

(B) $8,000

(C) $10,000

(D) $20,000

(E) $50,000

The above question tests whether or not you know what is meant by "reserve requirement" and also whether or not you know how to measure the change in a bank's excess reserves following a change in checkable deposits. If you know that 80 percent of the $10,000 can be loaned out (since 20 percent must be kept on reserve), then you should be able to determine that the correct answer is (B).

## OTHER EXAMPLES OF LEVEL 2 QUESTIONS

The questions below both require more than one thought process to solve. In each, a calculation or application of a skill learned in the course must be combined with one or more pieces of knowledge to come to a correct answer.

**Example 2:** Which of the following will necessarily result in a decrease in output:

I. A rightward shift of the aggregate demand curve

II. A leftward shift of the aggregate demand curve

III. A rightward shift of the aggregate supply curve

IV. A leftward shift of the aggregate supply curve

(A) I only

(B) III only

(C) I and III only

(D) II and III only

(E) II and IV only

**Example 3:** Answer the following question on the basis of this information about a hypothetical economy:

Full-time employed = 750

Part-time employed = 200

Unemployed = 50

Discouraged workers = 50

Based on the information, the official unemployment rate is approximately

(A) 10 percent

(B) 30 percent

(C) 5 percent

(D) 7 percent

(E) 25 percent

## LEVEL 3 QUESTIONS—SYNTHESIS

To synthesize means to pull your knowledge of several different topics together in order to answer a question. The most difficult and time-consuming questions in the multiple-choice section require this skill. You can expect between 10 and 20 questions to require synthesis. These questions will take the most time to answer—in some cases more than two minutes if multiple calculations or thought processes are needed. For synthesis questions, sketching quick graphs or solving simple math equations by taking scratch notes in the margin is highly advised.

**Example 1:** Under which of the following circumstances would increasing the money supply be most effective in increasing real gross domestic product?

| | Interest Rates | Employment | Business Optimism |
|---|---|---|---|
| (A) | High | Full | High |
| (B) | High | Less than full | High |
| (C) | High | Less than full | Low |
| (D) | Low | Full | Low |
| (E) | Low | Less than full | Low |

On the surface, this question appears to be simply about monetary policy. But when looked at closely, it is not asking a simple question such as, "*Which open market operation would a central bank use to lower interest rates*?" Rather, it is asking about the macroeconomic conditions under which expansionary monetary policy would be most effective.

This question requires that you pull together your knowledge from several parts of the syllabus. For example, you need to know that when interest rates are already low, expansionary monetary policy will do little to stimulate aggregate demand, because if firms were going to invest they would be doing it at the already low interest rates. Just this knowledge helps you eliminate options (D) and (E).

Next you would need to consider the level of employment at the time the monetary policy is implemented. Consider option (A); if an economy is already producing at its full-employment level and business optimism is high, an increase in the money supply may increase investment and aggregate demand. However, due to the tight labor markets and the lack of available resources, real gross domestic product will not increase by very much (remember, SRAS curve is nearly vertical beyond full employment), while inflation will increase rapidly. For this reason we can eliminate option (A).

Option (C) can be eliminated since whenever there is low business confidence, monetary policies will likely be ineffective, since lower interest rates will not be enough to encourage firms to invest.

Now consider option (B). If interest rates are high, then increasing the money supply should bring them down. If business optimism is high, the lower rates should stimulate new investment. Finally, if the economy is already producing at a level of output that is less than its full-employment level, then the economy has room to grow. The lower interest rates and high business optimism will encourage firms to invest in new capital equipment and hire unemployed workers, increasing the level of real gross domestic product while the price level remains fairly stable or increases only slightly. The correct answer, therefore, is option (B).

Clearly, the number of processes required to arrive at the correct answer of (B) is far greater than that required to answer a Level 1 or a Level 2 question because greater evaluation of various pieces of knowledge is involved. Therefore, Level 3 questions should take more time to answer than the other two types.

## OTHER EXAMPLES OF LEVEL 3 QUESTIONS

The questions below require the synthesis or evaluation of various pieces of knowledge and skills from different parts of the syllabus to answer. Therefore, they can both be considered Level 3 questions.

**Example 2:** Suppose that from 1985 to 1986, unemployment fell from nine percent to five percent and inflation (the change in the price level) fell from 4% to 1.5%. An explanation of these changes might be that the

(A) aggregate demand curve shifted to the left

(B) aggregate demand curve shifted to the right

(C) aggregate supply curve shifted to the left

(D) aggregate supply curve shifted to the right

(E) both aggregate demand and aggregate supply curves shifted to the left

**Example 3:** In a flexible system of exchange rates, an open-market sale of bonds by the Federal Reserve will most likely change the money supply, the interest rate, and the value of the United States dollar in which of the following ways?

| | Money Supply | Interest Rate | Value of the Dollar |
|---|---|---|---|
| (A) | Increase | Decrease | Decrease |
| (B) | Increase | Decrease | Increase |
| (C) | Decrease | Decrease | Decrease |
| (D) | Decrease | Increase | Increase |
| (E) | Decrease | Increase | Decrease |

**Tips from AP® Macro students:** The following are some other rules of thumb to keep in mind when approaching the multiple-choice section. Not all the suggestions below are true in every case, but many will be helpful in guiding you to the correct answer.

- If you are sure that two answers are saying basically the same thing in different ways, neither one is probably the right answer, since they both can't be right.
- If two responses are opposites, it is likely but not definite that one of these is the correct choice. Look especially for situations in which you can find the one choice distinct from the other four.
- Answers may be clumped by similarity, three that are similar and two that are obviously different. Much of the time, the correct answer is one of the three that are similar. It would be unusual for the correct answer to be one of two that are similar, since the AP® Macro exam tends to give you more options that *sound like they could be correct* and then make you choose from one of those.
- You need to know definitions. Even though there won't be many questions that are strictly definitional, knowing definitions is necessary to answer more of the complicated questions. Plus, the definitional questions are supposed to be the easiest ones, so you might as well aim to get those right.
- Use practice tests to study. Study the AP®-style practice questions in this book and take our online practice exam at *www.rea.com/studycenter*. You can also find additional practice exams at the College Board's AP® Central website.

- When taking practice tests, identify the answers you got wrong, look for trends, and go back and study those topics specifically. Focusing your time studying the concepts you are weakest in is better than trying to study every concept in the course equally.
- Never choose a multiple-choice answer without reading all the other options first. You may think you've read the right answer, but may discover that another option is even better.
- Cross off answers that you *know* are wrong. This will help you narrow down the possibilities to the best answer, and prevent you from re-reading answers you have already read and discounted as a possibility.
- Some of the hardest multiple-choice questions ask about relatively simple concepts but by using new or seemingly confusing phrasing. Look for ways to simplify the text in the questions or consider alternate meanings of words so you can make a better guess.

# Practice Multiple-Choice Questions

**Practice with the following AP®-style questions. Then go online to access REA's timed, full-length practice exam at *www.rea.com/studycenter*.**

*Unit 1: Basic Economic Concepts*
*2 questions (5%–10%)*

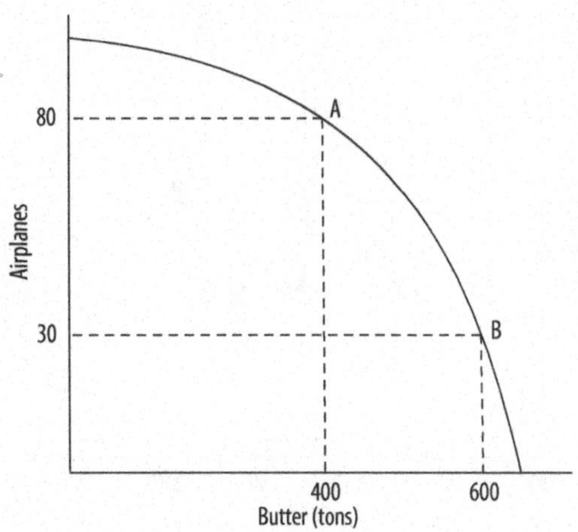


1. The diagram above shows an economy's current production possibilities curve for airplanes and butter.

   The opportunity cost of moving from point A to point B is

   (A) 80 airplanes

   (B) 30 airplanes

   (C) 600 tons of butter

   (D) 50 airplanes

   (E) 400 tons of butter

2. Which of the following events will cause the demand curve for tacos to shift to the right?

   (A) An increase in the price of hamburgers, a substitute for tacos

   (B) An increase in the price of tortilla chips, a complement to tacos

   (C) An increase in the price of tacos

   (D) A decrease in the price of tacos

   (E) A decrease in the cost of producing tacos

***Unit 2: Economic Indicators and the Business Cycle***
***3 questions (12%–17%)***

3. The graph below represents a country's business cycle.

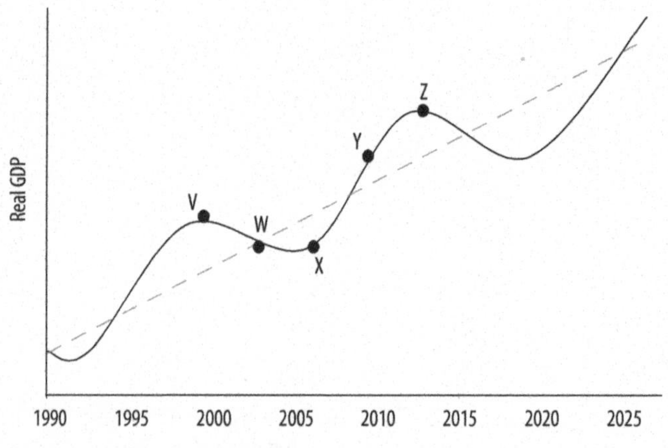


At which points on the graph is the country producing at its full employment level of output?

   (A) V, W, Y, and Z

   (B) V, Y, and Z

   (C) V and Z only

   (D) W only

   (E) X only

**4.** If in a specified year, nominal gross domestic product grew by 7% and real gross domestic product grew by 3%, inflation for this year would be

(A) –10%

(B) 10%

(C) –4%

(D) 4%

(E) 7%

**5.** Structural unemployment is most likely to be experienced when

(A) technological change makes certain kinds of skills redundant

(B) there is a fall in exports to other countries

(C) people choose to retire early

(D) more people are entering the labor force for the first time

(E) low business confidence leads firms to reduce output and employment

***Unit 3: National Income and Price Determination***
***6 questions (17%–27%)***

**6.** If an increase in household income from $40,000 to $45,000 causes an increase in consumption from $30,000 to $33,000, then the marginal propensity to consume is equal to

(A) 3

(B) 3,000

(C) 1.6

(D) 0.6

(E) 0.4

7. Which of the following will result in the greatest increase in aggregate demand?

   (A) A $100 increase in taxes

   (B) A $100 decrease in taxes

   (C) A $100 increase in government expenditures

   (D) A $100 increase in government expenditures, coupled with a $100 increase in taxes

   (E) A $100 increase in government expenditures, coupled with a $100 decrease in taxes

8. Which of the following observations about the short run and the long run are accurate?

| | **Short run** | **Long run** |
|---|---|---|
| (A) | Real GDP is fixed | Real GDP is flexible |
| (B) | There is only cyclical unemployment | There is only frictional and structural unemployment |
| (C) | Wages and other resource prices are fixed | Wages and other resource prices are flexible |
| (D) | There is only demand-pull inflation | There can be cost-push or demand-pull inflation |
| (E) | Real GDP is at full employment | Real GDP can be above or below full employment |

9. How will an increase in taxes on imported capital equipment intended to protect domestic producers of machinery most likely affect aggregate demand and aggregate supply?

| | **Aggregate demand** | **Aggregate supply** |
|---|---|---|
| (A) | Increases | Increases |
| (B) | Increases | No change |
| (C) | Decreases | Decreases |
| (D) | Decreases | No change |
| (E) | Increases | Decreases |

**10.** Cost-push inflation is caused by

(A) a decrease in aggregate demand

(B) an increase in aggregate demand

(C) a decrease in short-run aggregate supply

(D) an increase in short-run aggregate supply

(E) an increase in long-run aggregate supply

**11.** Assume that a country currently has a negative output gap. If policymakers make no effort to close the gap, which of the following will happen in the long run?

(A) A decrease in nominal wages and an increase in output

(B) Inflation and a decrease in output

(C) A rise in unemployment and recession

(D) An inflationary gap

(E) An increase in the wage rate and an increase in structural unemployment

## *Unit 4: Financial Sector*
## *5 questions (18%–23%)*

**12.** Which of the following best describes the relationship between interest rates and the prices of previously issued bonds?

(A) An increase in interest rates causes bond prices to rise.

(B) A change in interest rates does not affect bond prices.

(C) A decrease in bond prices causes a decrease in interest rates.

(D) An increase in interest rates causes bond prices to fall.

(E) Any change in bond prices causes interest rates to fall to 0%.

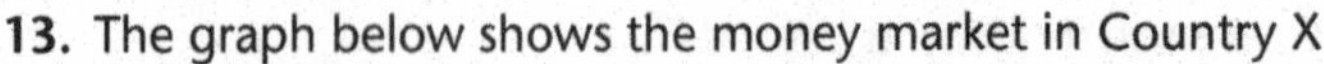

**13.** The graph below shows the money market in Country X

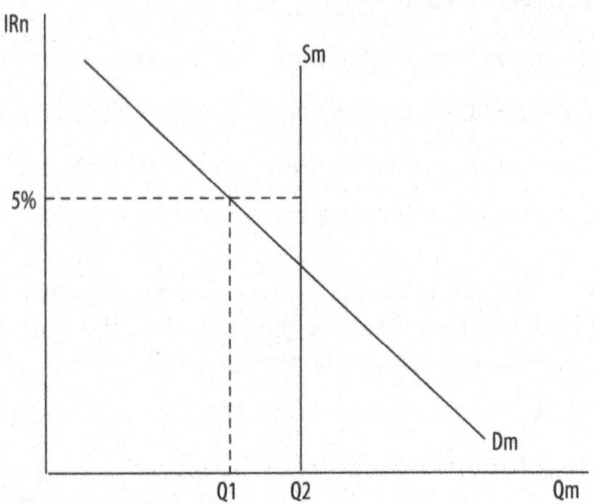


What is likely to happen to the interest rate which is currently at 5%, and the quantity of money demanded in Country X in the long-run?

(A) The interest rate will increase and the quantity of money demanded will increase.

(B) The interest rate will stay the same and the quantity of money demanded will decrease.

(C) The interest rate will decrease and the quantity of money demanded will increase.

(D) The interest rate will decrease and the quantity of money demanded will decrease.

(E) The interest rate will stay the same and the supply of money will decrease.

**14.** In Libertyville banks are required to keep 20% of their total deposits in reserve. Assume an individual makes a $1,000 cash deposit into the United Bank of Libertyville. What is the maximum increase in the money supply that could result from the individual's deposit?

(A) $5,000

(B) $800

(C) $4,000

(D) $200

(E) There will be no change in the money supply

**15.** Which of the following central bank actions would result in a decrease in private sector borrowing?

(A) An increase in the discount rate

(B) An increase in the money supply

(C) An increase in the purchase of government bonds on the open market

(D) A decrease in the reserve requirement

(E) A decrease in government spending

## *Unit 5: Long-Run Consequences of Stabilization Policies*
## *6 questions (20%–30%)*

**16.** Assume that the economy is in long-run equilibrium and the real growth potential for the economy is 3%. If the central bank increases the money supply by 3% and velocity remains constant, the most likely result will be:

(A) an increase in real GDP but not nominal GDP

(B) an increase in nominal GDP but a decrease in real GDP

(C) a decrease in real GDP and an increase in nominal GDP

(D) a decrease in nominal GDP and an increase in real GDP

(E) an increase in both real and nominal GDP

**17.** Which of the following policies would most likely stimulate private sector investment?

(A) A decrease in personal income taxes

(B) An increase in environmental regulations

(C) A revaluation of the currency on the forex market

(D) An open market purchase of government bonds by the central bank

(E) A decrease in the minimum wage

**18.** In Verminville the marginal propensity to consume (MPC) is 0.75. Assuming Verminville's current equilibrium national output is $600 billion below full employment, which of the following discretionary fiscal policies would be most likely to increase real GDP to its full employment level?

(A) A tax cut of $300 billion or an increase in government spending of $200 billion

(B) A tax cut of $600 billion or an increase in government spending of $400 billion

(C) A tax increase of $200 billion or a government spending decrease of $150 billion

(D) A tax cut of $1,800 billion or a government spending increase of $2,400 billion

(E) A tax cut of $200 billion or an increase in government spending of $150 billion

**19.** When will government deficits NOT lead to the crowding-out effect?

(A) When the government deficit spending forces private investment to contract

(B) When the government deficit spending is not accompanied by the purchase of government bonds by the Federal Reserve

(C) When the government deficit spending leads to an increase in real GDP and that induces private investment to increase

(D) When the government deficit spending leads to a decrease in real GDP and real interest rates drop

(E) When the government deficit spending leads to a decrease in foreign capital flows into the country

**20.** If the federal government increases its expenditures on goods and services by $10 billion and increases taxes on personal incomes by $10 billion, which of the following will occur in the short run?

(A) The federal budget deficit will increase by $10 billion

(B) The federal budget deficit will decrease by $10 billion

(C) Aggregate income will remain the same

(D) Aggregate income will decrease by up to $10 billion

(E) Aggregate income will increase by up to $10 billion

**21.** In order to increase its rate of long-run economic growth a government should undertake policies that

(A) encourage consumption over savings

(B) increase labor productivity

(C) encourage exports over imports

(D) increase government transfer payments

(E) ensure workers a fair, living wage

**22.** Use the Phillips curve graph below to answer the following question.

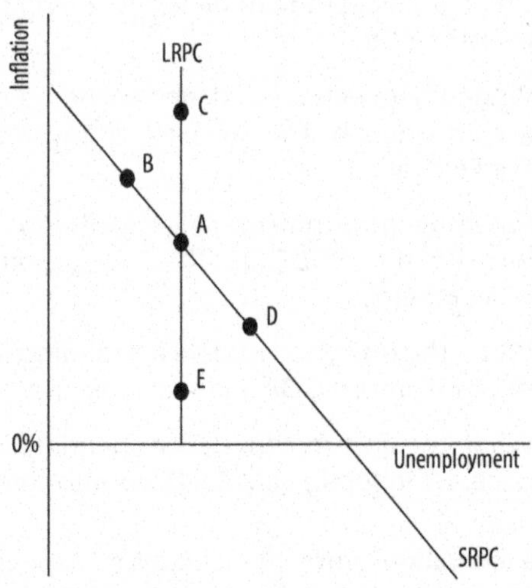


Assume the economy begins at point A. The central bank undertakes an expansionary monetary policy that increases the money supply at a rate faster than the real GDP growth rate. Which movements will occur in the short run and in the long run as a result of the central bank's policy?

| | **Short run** | **Long run** |
|---|---|---|
| (A) | A-B | B-C |
| (B) | A-D | D-E |
| (C) | A-C | No change |
| (D) | A-D | D-A |
| (E) | A-B | B-A |

***Unit 6: Open Economy—International Trade and Finance***
***3 questions (10%–13%)***

**23.** A decrease in Japan's demand for American goods would cause the value of the U.S. dollar to

(A) depreciate because of higher prices in the United States

(B) depreciate because Japan's demand for U.S. dollars decreases

(C) depreciate because the United States would be selling more dollars to Japan

(D) appreciate because Japan's demand for U.S. dollars increases

(E) appreciate because Japan would be selling more U.S. dollars

**24.** A net capital inflow will cause the real interest rate and the quantity of private sector investment to change in which of the following ways?

(A) Real interest rate decreases; quantity of private investment increases

(B) Real interest rate decreases; quantity of private investment decreases

(C) Real interest rate increases; quantity of private investment decreases

(D) No change in the real interest rate; quantity of private investment increases

(E) Real interest rate increases; no change in the quantity of private investment

25. A Taiwanese solar panel manufacturer acquires an ownership stake in a Canadian silicon mine to secure raw materials for its manufacturing plant. This transaction is recorded in the balance of payments as

(A) a credit to Canada's financial account and a debit to Taiwan's financial account

(B) a credit to Canada's current account and a debit to Taiwan's current account

(C) a credit to Canada's financial account and a debit to Taiwan's current account

(D) a debit to Canada's capital account and a credit to Taiwan's capital account

(E) a debit to Canada's financial account and a credit to Taiwan's financial account

## ANSWERS AND EXPLANATIONS

**Note:** Each answer explanation is labeled with the unit number and topic that you'll find in the College Board's AP® Macroeconomics Course and Exam Description. If you answer any of our practice questions incorrectly, restudy the corresponding topic until you're confident you've mastered the material.

1. (D) At point A the country is producing 80 airplanes. When it moves to point B, it must give up 50 airplanes. Opportunity cost is what is given up when making an economic decision; in this case that is the 50 additional airplanes it could have produced if it remained at point A, so (D) is the correct answer. **(1.2 Choice, Opportunity Cost, and the Production Possibilities Curve)**

2. (A) The price of substitute goods is a "demand shifter" or a determinant of demand. As hamburger prices rise, consumers will substitute more tacos into their diet at every price, shifting demand for tacos rightward, so (A) is correct. Tortilla chips are a complement for tacos, so as their prices rise consumers will demand fewer tortilla chips and tacos, shifting demand to the left, so (B) is incorrect. A change in the price of tacos does not shift the demand curve, rather it causes a movement along the demand curve, so (C) and (D) are incorrect. A decrease in

the cost of production will affect the supply of tacos, not the demand, so (E) is incorrect. **(1.4 Demand)**

3. (D) The long-run trend line (the dashed line) represents a country's full employment level of output. Points above this line represent positive output gaps and points below this line are negative output gaps. Only point W is on the dashed line, so (D) must be correct. **(2.7 Business Cycles)**

4. (D) The change in real GDP is the change in nominal GDP minus the inflation rate. With nominal GDP growth of 7% and real GDP growth of 3%, there must have been 4% inflation, so (D) is correct. **(2.6 Real vs. Nominal GDP)**

5. (A) Structural unemployment results from a change in the types of skills employers look for in workers, usually due to changing technologies, so (A) is correct. (B) describes cyclical unemployment, or that arising from a fall in demand for the country's output. Retiring early does not result in people becoming unemployed because they will not be actively seeking work, so (C) is incorrect. If more people are entering the labor force, it is likely that frictional unemployment will increase as they search for their first jobs, so (D) is incorrect. Unemployment resulting from a fall in output is cyclical, so (E) is incorrect. **(2.3 Unemployment)**

6. (D) The marginal propensity to consume is the ratio of the change in consumption resulting from a change in income. In this case the $3,000 increase in consumption represents 60% of the $5,000 increase in income, meaning the MPC = 0.6, so (D) is the correct answer. **(3.2 Multipliers)**

7. (E) is correct because it describes two changes to fiscal policy, both of which provide stimulus to spending in the economy. Increased government spending causes AD to increase, while a tax cut causes private sector spending to increase. (A) describes a contractionary fiscal policy, which would cause AD to decrease. (B) and (C) describe individual expansionary fiscal policies, both of which would cause AD to increase, but by less than the combined effect of a spending increase and a tax cut. (D) describes one change that would increase AD combined with one that would contract AD, the combined effect of which would be a limited increase in AD. **(3.1 Aggregate Demand)**

**8.** (C) In macroeconomics the short run is defined as the "fixed wage period" and the long run as the "flexible wage period," so (C) is correct. (A) is incorrect because the level of real GDP can change in both the short run and in the long run as a result of shifts in AD and/or AS. (B) is incorrect because any type of unemployment can exist in the short run, while in the long run a country will experience its natural rate of unemployment, which includes only structural and frictional unemployment. (D) is incorrect because shocks to demand or supply can cause either demand-pull or cost-push inflation in the short run. (E) is incorrect because it is backwards; in the short run real GDP can be above or below full employment, while in the long run real GDP will return to full employment once wages and other input costs have fully adjusted to the price level. **(3.4 Long-Run Aggregate Supply)**

**9.** (E) Protectionist measures like import tariffs will shift demand toward domestically produced goods, while at the same time raising the price of the goods being taxed. In this case, the taxed goods are capital equipment, so the cost of producing output would increase and SRAS would decrease, even as there is increased demand for domestically produced capital, so (E) is correct. The other answers describe shifts that would be less likely to result from the described change. **(3.1 Aggregate Demand and 3.3 Short-Run Aggregate Supply)**

**10.** (C) Cost-push inflation results from an increase in the costs of production in an economy, which causes a negative supply shock and a decrease in SRAS, so (C) is correct. A decrease in AD would cause a lower price level, not inflation, so (A) is incorrect. An increase in AD causes demand-pull inflation, not cost-push inflation, so (B) is incorrect. An increase in SRAS or in LRAS are both likely to cause lower inflation, not higher inflation, so (D) and (E) are incorrect. **(3.6 Changes in the AD-AS Model in the Short Run)**

**11.** (A) An economy experiencing a recession and a negative output gap will "self-correct" in the long run as nominal wages adjust to the lower price level and firms hire the now cheaper workers, leading to an increase in output, so (A) is correct. Inflation is unlikely to occur when there is a negative output gap, since there is excess capacity in the economy, which causes downward pressure on the price level. Unemployment is already high in a country with a negative output gap, and the country is already in recession; in the long run these problems will begin to resolve themselves as nominal wages fall, so (C) is incorrect. (D) and (E) are incorrect because inflation and rising wages are characteristics of a country with an inflationary gap, not a negative output gap. **(3.7 Long-Run Self-Adjustment)**

12. (D) is correct because interest rates and bond prices are inversely related. When interest rates rise, bond prices fall; when interest rates fall, bond prices rise. The other answer choices describe an incorrect relationship between interest rates and bond prices. **(4.1 Financial Assets)**

13. (C) The market seen here is in disequilibrium. There is an excess supply of money in the economy. To restore equilibrium, the interest rate must decrease and the quantity of money demanded must increase to Q2, so (C) is correct. If the interest rate increased, the disequilibrium would be worsened, so (A) is incorrect. If the interest rate stayed the same, the disequilibrium will persist, so (B) and (E) are incorrect. When the interest rate decreases the quantity of money demanded will increase, not decrease, so (D) is incorrect. **(4.5 The Money Market)**

14. (C) The initial deposit causes the bank's required reserves to increase by $200 and its excess reserves to increase by $800. Assuming the bank loans out all of its excess reserves, this $800 in new loans will be deposited in another bank, which will in turn loan out all of its new excess reserves. The ultimate size of the expansion in the money supply depends on the money multiplier. The $800 of new excess reserves must be multiplied by the multiplier to determine the impact on the money supply. Put another way, the $1,000 of cash could become $5,000 for an increase of $4,000. **(4.4 Banking and the Expansion of the Money Supply)**

15. (A) Private sector borrowing will fall when there is a contractionary monetary policy; only (A) describes such a change. (B), (C), and (D) describe expansionary monetary policies, and (E) describes a contractionary fiscal policy. **(4.6 Monetary Policy)**

16. (E) A real growth rate of 3% indicates that real output (GDP) will increase over time. However, if the money supply grows at

the same rate then prices should remain stable. Higher output at the same price level means that both real and nominal GDP increase, so (E) is correct. **(5.3 Money Growth and Inflation)**

**17.** (D) Private sector investment is responsive to changes in the interest rate. A policy that lowers the interest rate is thus needed. When a central bank purchases government bonds on the open market, the money supply increases and the interest rate falls, stimulating investment; so (D) is correct. Lower personal income taxes will stimulate consumption, but not investment, so (A) is incorrect. Increased government regulation will likely reduce investment as firms find it more costly to adhere to tighter regulations, so (B) is incorrect. Revaluation of the currency could lead to falling net exports, but not increased investment, so (C) is incorrect. (E) is incorrect because while a decrease in the minimum wage may lead firms to hire more workers, they may substitute labor for capital and actually invest less in new capital, which is now less attractive than hiring additional workers to increase output. **(5.1 Fiscal and Monetary Policy Actions in the Short Run)**

**18.** (E) The tax multiplier and the spending multiplier must first be calculated to determine the size of a discretionary fiscal policy that would increase output by $600 billion:

tax multiplier = $\frac{-0.75}{0.25} = -3$. Spending multiplier = $\frac{1}{0.25} = 4$.

The required change in taxes or spending can be determined by dividing the desired change in GDP by the tax and spending multipliers. The result is a decrease in taxes of $200 billion or an increase in government spending of $150 billion. **(5.1 Fiscal and Monetary Policy Actions in the Short Run)**

**19.** (C) Crowding out is the negative impact that government budget deficits can have on private investment as the result of the higher interest rates required to attract lenders to invest in government bonds. (C) describes a situation in which private investment increases as a result of the increase in GDP caused by the government's deficit, which is the opposite of crowding out, so (C) is correct. (A) describes a situation in which crowding out is happening. (B) describes a situation in which the government must borrow from the public, so crowding out could occur as the supply of loanable funds is negatively impacted by government borrowing. (D) describes an unlikely scenario in which government borrowing causes interest rates to fall, but the fall in GDP would likely induce private borrowers to reduce their own spending. (E) describes a situation in which there is a net capital outflow, reducing the supply of loanable funds and driving real interest rates up, which would in turn cause private investment spending to decrease; in other words, the crowding out of private investment. **(5.5 Crowding Out)**

**20.** (E) Since the spending multiplier is greater than the tax multiplier, there will be a net increase in aggregate income as a result of the changes in government spending and taxation described here. The increase in incomes resulting from the $10 billion increase in spending will be greater than the decrease in income resulting from the $10 billion increase in taxes. (A) and (B) are incorrect because the tax increase pays for the spending increase so there will be no effect on the budget. Aggregate income will increase because the spending increase will have a greater multiplier effect than the tax increase, so (C) and (D) are incorrect. **(5.1 Fiscal and Monetary Policy Actions in the Short Run)**

**21.** (B) Increased productivity is a primary driver of economic growth, as the output achievable by each worker increases with productivity; therefore, (B) is correct. (A) is incorrect because higher current consumption reduces the supply of funds available for investment in capital and technology, thus reducing the capital stock of the economy. While encouraging exports over imports may stimulate output in the short run, it will not produce new capital or increase the productivity of labor, thus (C) is incorrect. (D) is incorrect because increasing transfer payments may reduce the incentive of businesses and individuals to produce or to work efficiently; thus over time productivity and output could decline. (E) is incorrect because while ensuring a fair, living wage is a noble objective, it does not necessarily increase the country's potential output. **(5.7 Public Policy and Economic Growth)**

**22.** (A) is correct because in the short run when wages are sticky, the increased money supply will lead households and firms to spend more, increasing demand for labor and reducing the unemployment rate, causing demand-pull inflation. This increases output, leading to lower unemployment and increases the price level, causing more inflation. But in the long run, wages will adjust to the higher price level and unemployment will return to its natural rate along the LRPC at a higher inflation rate. (B) describes what would happen if AD decreased. (C) describes the long-run change as occurring in the short run. (D) describes a fall in AD followed by an increase in AD, while (E) describes what would happen if AD increased and then decreased. **(5.2 The Phillips Curve)**

**23.** (B) is correct because demand for dollars is tied to demand for American goods. Less demand for U.S. goods means less demand for, and a depreciation of, the dollar on the forex markets. While higher prices could cause the dollar to deprecate, (A) is incorrect because it is not the cause of depreciation described by the question. (C) is incorrect because to the contrary, the U.S. would be selling more dollars to Japan, who demands more dollars to buy American goods. (D) is incorrect because Japan would demand fewer, not more dollars, as demand for U.S. goods falls. (E) is incorrect because it is not Japan that sells U.S. dollars, but the U.S.; the dollar will depreciate, not appreciate, when demand for U.S. goods falls. **(6.2 Exchange Rates and the Foreign Exchange Market)**

**24.** (A) is correct because when more money flows into the country for investments in capital the supply of loanable funds increases, driving down the real interest rate and increasing the quantity of funds demanded for investment. (B), (C), (D), and (E) are incorrect because they describe changes that would not occur as a result of net capital inflows. **(6.5 Real Interest Rates and International Capital Flows)**

**25.** (A) is correct because the question describes a financial account transaction that would bring capital into Canada (a credit) from Taiwan (a debit). (B), (C), and (D) are incorrect because they describe current and capital account transactions which deal with purchase of goods or services, income transfers, current transfers, and capital transfers. (E) is incorrect because it reverses the debits and credit; money flows into Canada, not out, so Canada's financial account sees a credit, not a debit. **(6.1 Balance of Payments Accounts)**

Chapter 11

# Strategies for the Free-Response Questions

After completing the 60-question multiple-choice section, you will have a short break before you begin the FRQ section. FRQ stands for free-response questions. Don't be fooled, though, because the responses you provide in this section are hardly expected to be "free." In fact, there are some pretty clear rules of thumb you can follow to ensure that your answers to these questions fulfill the graders' expectations as well as present your responses in a way that demonstrates a clear understanding of the concepts, thereby ensuring that you earn a top score.

The FRQ section of the exam is 60 minutes long and the first 10 minutes is a mandatory reading period. The remaining 50 minutes may be spent writing your responses to three questions. The three FRQs are always in the following format:

- Question 1—the long FRQ: This question is always the longest of the three FRQs and usually includes more "parts" than questions 2 and 3. This question counts for half the FRQ score, so 5 of your 10 reading minutes and 25 of the 50 minutes you have to write in the FRQ section should be devoted to answering question 1.
- Questions 2 and 3—the short FRQs. The second and third questions on the FRQ section are always shorter and include fewer "parts" than question 1. Each of these questions is equally weighted and worth 25 percent of your FRQ score, so these should be given approximately 12.5 minutes each, or a total of 25 minutes between them, in addition to half of your planning and reading time.

The FRQ section can be your worst enemy or your best friend, depending on how well-prepared you are. The best way to be prepared is to have a good idea of what is most likely to appear in each of three FRQs, and to have completed as many practice FRQs as you can get your hands on. Fortunately for you, the College Board releases all of its past FRQs to students, *with scoring guides*. Take advantage of this free resource, bookmark the site in your browser and visit it before every unit test your teacher gives you: *https://apstudents.collegeboard.org/courses/ap-macroeconomics/assessment.*

## WHICH TOPICS WILL THE FRQs COVER?

While technically the topics covered in each FRQ can come from any section of the syllabus, there are topics that seem to be tested more commonly in each of the three questions, lending some predictability to the makeup of the FRQ section.

The table below shows the topics tested over several years in the FRQ section.

| FRQ #1 | FRQ #2 | FRQ #3 |
|---|---|---|
| Phillips curve (SR and LR), AD/AS, fiscal policy, OMO, money market, SR to LR in AD/AS | Loanable funds market, investment demand and real interest rates, forex market, determinant of exchange rates | RRR, OMO, money multiplier, bond market |
| AD/AS, determinants of AD, Phillips curve (SR and LR), automatic fiscal policy, loanable funds market with crowding-out SR to LR in the AD/AS model | Forex markets, impact of exchange rates on AD/AS, monetary policy's effects on exchange rates | Calculating GDP, nominal and real, price indices, nominal and real wages, nominal and real interest rates |
| AD/AS, fiscal policy, SR to LR in AD/AS, loanable funds market with crowding out, investment demand | Money market, money demand, bond market, OMO | Forex markets, impact of exchange rates on AD/AS, determinants of exchange rates |
| AD/AS, fiscal policy, SR Phillips curve, crowding out, PPC | OMO, money market, effect of monetary policy on exchange rates | Determinants of AD/AS, impact of various supply and demand shocks |
| Phillips curve (SR/LR), OMO, money market, AD/AS | Forex market, loanable funds market, determinants of exchange rates | RRR, money multiplier, OMO |
| AD/AS, short-run Phillips curve, fiscal policy, SR to LR in AD/AS | RRR, OMO, money multiplier, money market, effects of inflation | Forex market, determinants of exchange rates, loanable funds market |

From the table above, you can see that FRQ #1 always requires students to draw an AD/AS diagram. Other topics and graphs that commonly appear in FRQ #1 are:

- Short-run and long-run effects of changes to AD or AS;
- Movements along and shifts in the Phillips curve, both short run and long run;
- A money market diagram illustrating the effect of a monetary policy action;
- A loanable funds diagram illustrating the crowding-out effect of a fiscal policy action;
- On rare occasions, a forex market showing an appreciation or depreciation of a country's currency.

FRQs #2 and #3 generally cover a range of topics from the syllabus, some of the most common of which include:

- exchange rates, forex markets, and determinants of exchange rates;
- the effect of a change in deposits in the banking system, using the money multiplier;
- causes and effects of changes to the nominal and real interest rates illustrated in the money market and the loanable funds market;
- money market showing the effect of a monetary policy action;
- occasionally a Phillips curve diagram showing the trade-off between inflation and unemployment.

***Actual FRQs from the AP® exam can be found on the College Board's AP® Central website. Be sure to review these questions for added practice.***

## STRUCTURE OF AN FRQ

Free-response questions follow a fairly standard structure. They always include multiple "parts" (a, b, c, etc.) and almost always require you to draw a graph. The standard prompts on an FRQ are the following:

### SHOW:

FRQ #1 always requires at least one, but usually more than one, diagram *showing* some macroeconomic effect. Questions that ask you to *show* something are usually accompanied by the words *"Using a _______ diagram,"* in which the blank would tell you which diagram to use. Sometimes, however, it will say, *"Using an appropriate diagram, show . . ."* In such a case, it is up to you to decide which diagram to use.

A question asking you to show something will be worth at least two points. One point for showing the correct effect, another for drawing a correctly labeled diagram. Depending on the complexity of the diagram required, such a question may be worth as many as three or four points. Even if you are confused about how to show an effect, you can often earn some or most of the points by labeling an appropriate diagram.

### IDENTIFY:

Identification questions should be the easiest to answer. They may not actually use the word "identify," but may ask you to identify indirectly by asking how something will change. For example: *"How will the higher real interest rate affect aggregate demand?"* or *"Indicate what will happen to the unemployment rate in the short run as output declines."* In such a question, all that is expected of you is to identify the result of something happening. In this case, *AD would decrease* or *the unemployment rate would rise.* Such a response would earn you one point, which is all such a question would be worth.

Unless the question explicitly asks for an explanation, it is not necessary for you to provide one. Having a good explanation in mind when you form your answer, however, is advisable since it increases the odds that you will have the right response.

## CALCULATE:

Calculations require you to apply one of the formulas you learned in class. Some of the things you may be called upon to calculate are:

- nominal GDP from a set of data;
- a price index from a set of data;
- the inflation rate from a set of data;
- the change in GDP that will result from a particular fiscal policy (using the spending multiplier), or the size of a change in spending needed to bring about a particular change in GDP;
- a change in the money supply following a change in checkable deposits or following an open-market operation by the Fed;
- a change in a bank's required or excess reserves following a change in checkable deposits or an open-market operation by the Fed;
- the real interest rate using nominal interest rate and inflation data;
- the opportunity cost of one good in terms of another.

Calculation problems are generally only worth one point each. If you get the calculation right, you score the point. If you get it wrong, the point is subtracted from your final score. Sometimes you will be asked to show the work you used in the calculation.

Correctly solving calculation problems is a skill that can be perfected through practice. To prepare for these questions, you should become familiar with all of the calculations identified above and complete as many past FRQs as possible to become familiar with the type of calculation that appears in the FRQ section.

Remember, calculators are not allowed on the AP® Macro exam, so all calculations must be done from scratch with pen and paper. Fortunately for you, this also means that the test creators cannot expect you to handle really nasty numbers. So, if you get a calculation that seems messy, it may indicate that you made an error in setting up the problem.

## EXPLAIN:

Explanations are not always required to earn the points on one part of an FRQ. But sometimes they are, and if they are, the question will make it perfectly clear that an explanation is expected. Study the following two examples and determine the difference between them:

- Example 1: "How will the change in the interest rate you identified in part (b) affect aggregate demand?"
- Example 2: "Explain how the change in the interest rate you identified in part (b) will affect aggregate demand."

At first glance, there may appear to be no difference between these two questions. However, example 1 is only a one-point question, while example 2 is worth at least two points. Here's why:

- The first example is an *identify* question. It is basically asking you to identify how a change in interest rates affects aggregate demand. A correct answer would be that AD either increased, decreased, or stayed the same. No explanation is needed for example 1.
- Example 2 asks you to *explain* how a change in the interest rate affects aggregate demand. To earn the two (or more) points this question is worth, you would need to not only indicate how AD changes, but also offer an explanation. Assume in part (b) you indicated that interest rates increased. A suitable answer to this question would then be:

  "The increase in interest rates will increase borrowing costs for firms, which will lead to less investment, reducing the level of aggregate demand in the economy."

This response clearly explains *why* AD decreases, whereas for example 1 a simple *"AD decreases"* would have been suitable.

## TIPS FROM AP® MACRO STUDENTS

This chapter has attempted to demystify the free-response section of the AP® Macroeconomics exam. While this section may be intimidating at first, it is actually the easiest to prepare for and to succeed in if you know what you're getting into. Below are some final student tips for how to succeed on the FRQ section:

- If a question does not say "explain," don't attempt an explanation.
- Look for the key words "identify," "show," and "explain," and do exactly what the question asks.

- Study past FRQs on the College Board's AP® Macro student resource page. Use the scoring guidelines and become familiar with how they are graded.
- Master the graphs. Much of your FRQ grade depends on the quality and accuracy of the diagrams you draw. Correctly labeling graphs and drawing them large and with great detail is the best way to ensure you will earn easy points on the FRQs.
- Practice calculations. Almost every FRQ exam requires at least one calculation. Chapter 2 of this book includes a list of the formulas you need to know for the AP® Macro course and exam. Familiarize yourself with them and know how to use them.
- Sometimes less is more. Keep in mind that AP® exams are graded by real teachers, who will read thousands of FRQs in a week. Being wordy may harm you. Be concise and to the point, and express your thoughts in as few words as necessary.
- Plan more to write less. The 10 minutes of reading time is not enough to ingest all that is going on in all three questions. On the other hand, it takes far less than 50 minutes to craft neatly in the answer book the responses necessary to earn all the credit on all the questions. Some students use as much as 20 or even 30 minutes of the 60-minute period reading, analyzing, and recording rough responses to all three questions in the question folder and only half or a bit more of their time copying these graphs and explanations into the pink response book. Practice will help you correctly allocate your time.
- No tricks. FRQs tend to be straightforward and not subject to nuanced differences of interpretation. It is far more common that a single multiple-choice question will be a "trick question."
- Use context. Sometimes a part in the middle of an FRQ item will challenge you. Usually there is a logical flow of all the parts to a question, and you can use this to your advantage. Consider what was asked before and what is asked after the item troubling you; you may now understand the middle part more clearly.

# Economics Glossary

**Aggregate demand**—shows the total quantity of goods and services consumed at different price and output levels.

**Aggregate demand-aggregate supply (AD-AS) model**—uses aggregate demand and aggregate supply to determine and explain price level, real domestic output, disposable income, and employment.

**Aggregate expenditure**—all spending for final goods and services in an economy: $C + I_g + G + Xn = AE$.

**Allocative efficiency**—distribution of resources among firms and industries to obtain production quantities of the products most wanted by society (consumers); where marginal cost equals marginal benefit.

**Appreciation** (of the dollar)—an increase in the value of the dollar relative to the currency of another nation, so that a dollar buys more of the foreign currency and thus foreign goods become cheaper; critical to long-run trade equilibrium.

**Asset**—items of monetary value owned by a firm or individual; opposite is *liability*.

**Average fixed cost** (AFC)—firm's total fixed cost divided by output.

**Average product**—total output produced per unit of a resource employed (total product divided by the quantity of input).

**Average total cost** (ATC)—firm's total cost divided by output, equal to average fixed cost plus average variable cost (AFC + AVC = ATC).

**Average variable cost** (AVC)—firm's total variable cost divided by output.

**Balance of payments account**—summary of a nation's current account and its financial account.

**Balance of trade**—a nation's current account balance; net exports.

**Balance sheet**—statement of the assets and liabilities that determines a firm's net (solvency).

**Barrier to entry**—artificial prevention of the entry of firms into an industry.

**Bond**—financial instrument through which a borrower (corporate or government) is contracted to pay the principal at a specified interest rate at a specific date (maturity) in the future; promissory note.

**Breakeven point**—output at which a (competitive) firm's total cost and total revenue are equal (TR = TC); an output at which a firm has neither an economic profit nor a loss, at which it earns only a normal profit.

**Budget deficit**—amount by which the spending of the (federal) government exceeds its tax revenues in any year.

**Budget surplus**—amount by which the tax revenues of the (federal) government exceed its spending in any year.

**Capital**—resources (buildings, machinery, and equipment) used to produce goods and services; also called *investment goods.*

**Capital account**—section of a nation's international balance-of-payments balance sheet that records foreign purchases of U.S. assets (money in) and U.S. purchases of foreign assets (money out).

**Capital account inflow (outflow)**—reflects the net difference between foreign funds invested in the home country minus the domestic funds invested in the foreign country; component of the balance of payments account.

**Capitalism**—free market economic system in which property is privately owned and the invisible forces of supply and demand set price and quantity.

**Cartel**—overt agreement among firms (or countries) in an industry to fix the price of a product and establish output quotas.

**Change in demand**—change in the quantity demanded of a good or service at all prices; a shift of the demand curve to the left (decrease) or right (increase).

**Change in supply**—change in the quantity supplied of a good or service at all prices; a shift of the supply curve to the left (decrease) or right (increase).

**Circular flow model**—flow of resource inputs from households to businesses and of goods and services (g/s) from businesses to households. A flow in the opposite direction of money—businesses to households for inputs and from households to businesses for g/s—occurs simultaneously.

**Comparative advantage**—determines specialization and exchange rate for trade between nations; based on the nation with the lower relative or comparative cost of production.

**Competition**—Adam Smith's requirement for success of a free market, a market of independent buyers and sellers competing with one another; includes ease of access to and exit from the marketplace.

**Complementary goods**—goods that are used together, so if the price of one falls, the demand for the other decreases as well (and vice versa).

**Consumer price index (CPI)**—index that measures the prices of a set "basket" of some 300 goods and services bought by a "typical" consumer; used by government as a main indicator of the rate of inflation.

**Consumer surplus**—that portion of the demand curve that lies above the equilibrium price level and denotes those consumers that would be willing to buy the goods and services at higher price levels.

**Contractionary fiscal policy**—combination of government reduction in spending and a net increase in taxes, for the purpose of decreasing aggregate demand, lowering price levels, and thus controlling inflation.

**Corporation**—legal entity ("like a person") chartered by a state or the federal government; limits liability for business debt to the assets of the firm.

**Cost-push inflation**—when an increase in resource costs shifts the aggregate supply curve inward, resulting in an increase in the price level and unemployment; also termed *stagflation.*

**Cross elasticity of demand**—ratio of the percentage change in quantity demanded of one good to the percentage change in the price of another good. If the coefficient is positive, the two goods are substitutes. If the coefficient is negative, they are considered complementary.

**Crowding-out effect**—caused by the federal government's increased borrowing in the money market that results in a rise in interest rates. The rise in interest rates results in a decrease in gross business domestic investment ($I_g$), which reduces the effectiveness of expansionary fiscal policy.

**Current account**—section in a nation's international balance of payments that records its exports and imports of goods and services, its net investment income, and its net transfers; component of the balance of payments account.

**Cyclical deficit**—government budget deficit caused by a recession and the resultant decline in tax revenues.

**Cyclical unemployment**—type of unemployment caused by recession; less than full employment aggregate demand.

**Deadweight loss (efficiency loss)**—the foregone total societal surplus associated with the levy of a tax that discourages what had heretofore been a mutually advantageous market transaction.

**Deflation**—decline in the economy's price level; indicates contraction in business cycle or may signal expansion of total output (aggregate supply moves to the right).

**Demand**—the quantity of a good or service that buyers wish to buy at various prices.

**Depreciation** (of the dollar)—decrease in the value of the dollar relative to another currency, so that the dollar buys a smaller amount of the foreign currency and therefore the price of foreign goods increases; tends to reduce imports and increase exports.

**Determinants of demand**—factors other than price that alter (shift) the quantities demanded of a good or service.

**Determinants of supply**—factors other than price that alter (shift) the quantities supplied of a good or service.

**Discount rate**—interest rate that the Federal Reserve Banks charge on the loans they make to commercial banks (different from the federal funds rate).

**Disposable income**—personal income minus personal taxes; income available for consumption expenditures and saving.

**Durable good**—consumer good with an expected life (use) of three or more years; decrease in sales indicates recession, as contraction affects these goods before nondurables.

**Economic efficiency**—use of the minimum necessary inputs to obtain the most societally beneficial quantity of goods and services; employs both productive and allocative efficiency.

**Economic profit**—total revenue of a firm minus its economic costs (both explicit and implicit costs); also termed *pure profit* and *above-normal profit.*

**Economies of scale**—savings in the average total cost of production as the firm expands the size of a plant (its output) in the long run.

**Elastic demand**—product or resource demand whose price elasticity is greater than 1. This means that the resulting percentage change in quantity demanded is greater than the percentage change in price.

**Elastic supply**—product or resource supply whose price elasticity is greater than 1. This means that the resulting percentage change in quantity supplied is greater than the percentage change in price.

**Equilibrium price**—price at which the quantity demanded and the quantity supplied are equal (intersect), shelves clear, and price stability occurs.

**Equilibrium quantity**—quantity demanded and supplied at the equilibrium price.

**Excess capacity**—plant resources underused when imperfectly competitive firms produce less output than that associated with achieving minimum average total cost.

**Expansionary fiscal policy**—combination of government increases in spending and a net decrease in taxes for the purpose of increasing aggregate demand, increasing output and disposable income, and lowering unemployment.

**Expected rate of return**—profit a firm anticipates it will obtain by purchasing capital goods; influences investment demand for money.

**Factors of production**—resources: land, capital, and entrepreneurial ability.

**Federal funds rate**—the interest rate banks and other depository institutions charge one another on overnight loans made out of their excess reserves; targeted by monetary policy.

**Financial account (capital account)**—the difference between a country's sale of assets to foreigners and its purchase of foreign assets; component of the balance of payments account.

**Fixed cost**—any cost that remains constant when the firm changes its output.

**Fixed exchange rate**—rate of currency exchange that is set, prevented from rising or falling with changes in currency supply and demand; opposite of floating exchange rate.

**Frictional unemployment**—unemployment caused by workers' voluntarily changing jobs or workers' being between jobs.

**Full employment unemployment rate**—natural rate of unemployment when there is no cyclical unemployment. In the United States it equals between 4% and 5% because some frictional and structural unemployment is unavoidable.

**Gross domestic product (GDP)**—total market value of all final goods and services produced annually within the boundaries of the United States, whether by U.S. or foreign-supplied resources.

**Horizontal merger**—merger into a single firm of two firms that produce the same product and sell it in the same geographic market.

**Hyperinflation**—a very rapid rise in the price level; an extremely high rate of inflation.

**Imperfect competition**—all market structures except pure competition; includes monopoly, monopolistic competition, and oligopoly.

**Implicit cost**—the monetary income a firm sacrifices when it uses a resource it owns rather than supplying the resource in the market; equal to what the resource could have earned in the best-paying alternative employment; includes a normal profit.

**Indifference curve**—curve showing the different combinations of two products that yield the same satisfaction or utility to a consumer.

**Inelastic demand**—product or resource demand for which the elasticity coefficient for price is less than 1. This means the resulting percentage change in quantity demanded is less than the percentage change in price.

**Inelastic supply**—product or resource supply for which the price elasticity coefficient is less than 1. The percentage change in quantity supplied is less than the percentage change in price.

**Inferior good**—a good or service the consumption of which declines as income rises (and vice versa), with price remaining constant.

**Inflation**—rise in the general level of prices.

**Inflation (rational) expectation**—a key determinant that impacts the loanable funds market for both borrowers and lenders.

**Inflationary gap**—amount by which the aggregate expenditure and schedule must shift downward to decrease the nominal gross domestic product (GDP) to its full employment noninflationary level.

**Interest**—payment for the use of borrowed money.

**Inventories**—goods that have been produced but remain unsold.

**Inverse relationship**—the relationship between two variables that change in opposite directions; for example, product price and quantity demanded.

**Kinked demand curve**—demand curve for a noncollusive oligopolist, which is based on the assumption that rivals will follow a price decrease and ignore a price increase.

**Law of demand**—the principle that, other things being equal, an increase in the price of a product will reduce the quantity of that product demanded, and conversely for a decrease in price.

**Law of diminishing marginal utility**—the principle that as a consumer increases the consumption of a good or service (g/s), the marginal utility obtained from each additional unit of the g/s decreases.

**Law of diminishing returns**—the principle that as successive increments of a variable resource are added to a fixed resource, the marginal product of the variable resource will eventually decrease.

**Law of increasing opportunity costs**—the principle that as the production of a good increases, the opportunity cost of producing an additional unit rises.

**Law of supply**—the principle that, other things being equal, an increase in the price of a product will increase the quantity of that product supplied, and conversely for a price decrease.

**Liability**—a debt with a monetary value; an amount owed by a firm or an individual.

**Liquidity**—the ease with which an asset can be converted—quickly—into cash with little or no loss of purchasing power. Money is said to be perfectly liquid, whereas other assets have a lesser degree of liquidity.

**Loanable funds market**—a conceptual market wherein the demand for money is determined by borrowers and the supply is determined by lenders. Market equilibrium prices the interest rate.

**Long run**—time frame necessary for producers to alter resource inputs and increase or decrease output; time frame necessary for adjustments to be made as a result of shifts in aggregate demand and supply.

**Lorenz curve**—a model that demonstrates the cumulative percentage of population and their cumulative share of income; used to show shifts in income distribution across population over time.

**$M_1$, $M_2$, $M_3$**—money supply measurements that increasingly broaden the definition of money measured; critical to monetarism and interest rates.

**Macroeconomics**—the portion of economics concerned with the overall performance of the economy; focused on aggregate demand–aggregate supply relationship, and the resultant output, income, employment, and price levels.

**Marginal benefit**—change in total benefit that results from the consumption of one more unit of output.

**Marginal cost**—change in total cost that results from the sale of one more unit of output.

**Marginal product**—change in total output relative to the change in resource input.

**Marginal propensity to consume**—change in consumption spending relative to a change in income.

**Marginal propensity to save**—change in saving relative to a change in income.

**Marginal revenue**—change in total revenue that results from the sale of one more unit of product.

**Marginal revenue cost (MRC)**—change in total cost with the addition of one more unit of resource input for production.

**Marginal revenue product (MRP)**—change in total revenue with the addition of one more unit of resource input for production.

**Marginal utility**—the use a consumer gains from the addition of one more unit of a good or service.

**Market failure**—the inability of the free market to provide public goods; over- or underallocation of goods or services that have negative/positive externalities; used to justify government intervention.

**Microeconomics**—portion of economics concerned with the individual elements that make up the economy: households, firms, government, and resource input prices.

**Monetary policy**—policy basis on which the Federal Reserve influences interest rates through manipulation of the money supply to promote price stability, full employment, and productivity growth.

**Money**—any article (paper note, metal coin) generally accepted as having value in exchange for a good or service.

**Money supply**—defined, measured, and reported as $M_1$, $M_2$, $M_3$.

**Monopsony**—a market structure in which there is only one buyer of a resource input or good or service.

**MR = MC principle**—law stating that to maximize profit and minimize loss, a firm will produce at the output level where the marginal revenue is equal to the marginal cost.

**MRP = MRC formula**—equation showing that to maximize profit and minimize loss, a firm will employ a resource input quantity when the marginal revenue product is equal to the marginal resource cost of the resource input.

**Multiplier**—the effect that a change in one of the four components of aggregate expenditure has on gross domestic product (GDP).

**Natural monopoly**—an industry in which the economy of scale is so large that one producer is the most efficient least-cost producer; usually regulated by government.

**Natural rate of unemployment (NRU)**—frictional and structural unemployment, the full employment rate, zero cyclical unemployment.

**Net export effect**—any monetary or fiscal policy action is magnified (+ or –) by the effect that the change in U.S. dollar value (interest rates effect exchange rates) has on import and export prices.

**Nominal**—any economic measurement that is not adjusted for inflation. (e.g. nominal wages vs. actual wages that account for inflation.)

**Nominal interest rate**—the interest rate that is not adjusted for inflation.

**Normal good**—a good or service (g/s) the consumption of which increases as income increases (opposite of inferior g/s).

**Normal profit**—where price equals average total cost, and cost includes the implicit cost of entrepreneurial value.

**Oligopoly**—a market structure in which a few firms have a large market share and sell differentiated products. In oligopolies, firms tend to have large economies of scale, pricing is mutually dependent, and price wars can occur; there is a kinked demand curve.

**Perfectly elastic demand**—infinite quantity demanded at a particular price; graphed as a straight horizontal line.

**Perfectly elastic supply**—infinite quantity supplied at a particular price; graphed as a straight horizontal line.

**Perfectly inelastic demand**—quantity demanded does not change in response to a change in price; graphed as a vertical straight line.

**Perfectly inelastic supply**—quantity supplied does not change in response to a change in price; graphed as a horizontal straight line.

**Phillips curve (short run)**—a model that demonstrates the inverse relationship between unemployment (horizontal) and inflation (vertical axis).

**Phillips curve (long run)**—a model demonstrating that after inflation expectations have been adjusted for, there is no trade-off between inflation and unemployment because it is vertical and equal to the natural rate of unemployment.

**Price**—the sum of money necessary to purchase a good or service.

**Price = MC**—in a purely competitive market model, the principle that a firm's demand is perfectly elastic and equal to price, so that a firm will maximize profit when price equals marginal cost if price is equal to or greater than average total cost (ATC) and minimize loss if price is greater than average variable cost (AVC).

**Price ceiling**—a price set below equilibrium by government.

**Price elasticity of demand**—percentage of change in quantity demanded divided by percentage of change in price; measures responsiveness to price changes.

**Price elasticity of supply**—percentage of change in quantity supplied divided by percentage of change in price; measures responsiveness to price changes.

**Price fixing**—illegal collusion between producers to set an above-equilibrium price.

**Price floor**—a price set above equilibrium by government.

**Producer surplus**—that portion of the supply curve that lies below equilibrium price and denotes producers that would bring the goods or services to market at even lower prices.

**Progressive tax**—a marginal tax rate system in which the percentage of tax increases as income increases and vice versa (such as U.S. federal income tax brackets).

**Proportional tax**—a flat tax system in which the percentage of tax remains fixed as income changes.

**Pure competition**—market structure in which so many firms produce a very similar good or service that no firm has significant control over market price; a "price taker."

**Pure monopoly**—market structure in which one firm is the sole producer of a distinct good or service and thus has significant control over market price; a "price maker."

**Quantity demanded**—various amounts along a consumer demand curve showing the quantity consumers will buy at various prices.

**Quantity supplied**—various amounts along a producer supply curve showing the quantity producers will sell at various prices.

**Recession**—two consecutive business quarters of negative real gross domestic product (GDP).

**Regressive tax**—a set tax percentage the average rate of which decreases as the taxpayer's income increases, and vice versa; an example is sales tax.

**Shortage**—difference between the quantity demanded for a good or service and the quantity supplied at a below-equilibrium price ($Q_d > Q_s$).

**Short run**—the length of time during which a producer is unable to alter all the inputs of production.

**Sole proprietorship**—an unincorporated business owned by an individual.

**Specialization**—concentration of resource(s) in the production of a good or service that results in increased efficiency of production.

**Stock**—an ownership share in a company held by an investor.

**Structural unemployment**—unemployment resulting from a mismatch of worker skill to demand or location.

**Substitute**—goods or services that are interchangeable. When the price of one increases, the demand for the other increases.

**Supply-side economics**—macroeconomic perspective that emphasizes fiscal policies aimed at altering the state of the economy through $I_g$ (short run) and the aggregate supply (long run).

**Surplus**—difference between the quantity demanded of a good or service and the quantity supplied at an above-equilibrium price ($Q_d < Q_s$).

**Tariff**—a tax on imports/exports.

**Tax**—a required payment of money to government, for which the payer receives no direct goods or services.

**Trade deficit**—amount by which a nation's imports exceed its exports.

**Trade-off**—forgone alternative use of a resource in the production of a good or service.

**Trade surplus**—amount by which a nation's exports exceed its imports.

**Variable cost**—cost of inputs that fluctuates as a firm increases or decreases its output.